Intellectual
Property

Intellectual Property

THE TOUGH NEW REALITIES
THAT COULD MAKE OR BREAK
YOUR BUSINESS

Paul Goldstein

PORTFOLIO

PORTFOLIO
Published by the Penguin Group
Penguin Group (USA) Inc., 375 Hudson Street,
New York, New York 10014, U.S.A.
Penguin Group (Canada), 90 Eglinton Avenue East, Suite 700,
Toronto, Ontario, Canada M4P 2Y3 (a division of Pearson Penguin Canada Inc.)
Penguin Books Ltd, 80 Strand, London WC2R 0RL, England
Penguin Ireland, 25 St. Stephen's Green, Dublin 2, Ireland (a division of Penguin Books Ltd)
Penguin Books Australia Ltd, 250 Camberwell Road, Camberwell, Victoria 3124, Australia
(a division of Pearson Australia Group Pty Ltd)
Penguin Books India Pvt Ltd, 11 Community Centre, Panchsheel Park, New Delhi–110 017, India
Penguin Group (NZ), 67 Apollo Drive, Rosedale, North Shore 0745, Auckland, New Zealand
(a division of Pearson New Zealand Ltd.)
Penguin Books (South Africa) (Pty) Ltd, 24 Sturdee Avenue, Rosebank, Johannesburg 2196,
South Africa

Penguin Books Ltd, Registered Offices:
80 Strand, London WC2R 0RL, England

First published in 2007 by Portfolio,
a member of Penguin Group (USA) Inc.

1 3 5 7 9 10 8 6 4 2

Publisher's Note
This publication is designed to provide accurate and authoritative information in regard to the subject matter covered. It is sold with the understanding that the publisher is not engaged in rendering legal, accounting or other professional services. If you require legal advice or other expert assistance, you should seek the services of a competent professional.

Library of Congress Cataloging-in-Publication Data

Goldstein, Paul, 1943–
Intellectual property : the tough new realities that could make or break your business /
Paul Goldstein.
p. cm.
Includes bibliographical references and index.
ISBN 978-1-59184-177-7
1. Intellectual property—United States.   2. Intellectual property—Economic aspects—
United States.   I. Title.
KF2979.G64 2007
346.7304'8—dc22   2007014193

Printed in the United States of America
Set in New Caledonia
Designed by Helene Berinsky

*To my colleagues at Stanford Law School
and Morrison & Foerster LLP*

CONTENTS

Intellectual Property

Introduction

Intellectual property. The term itself suggests the nature of the challenge. How can a product of the mind—an invention, a song, a brand, a business secret—become the subject of precise, bounded property rights? No idea is entirely original; every innovative business borrows, sometimes extensively, from its competitors and others. How can lawmakers draw a line that crisply states, This is yours and that is mine?

Companies spend millions, sometimes billions, of dollars researching and developing new products, knowing that they will have to write off the investment if a court should hold that the invention trespasses on another company's patent. Book publishers, film studios, and record labels invest in creating and marketing copyrighted works that inevitably build on themes, incidents, and other elements taken from earlier works. Which of these elements are in the public domain, free for the taking, and which are not? Many of the best-known and most valuable brand names—Burger King, McDonald's—are little more than descriptive words and common names. How can a company appropriate such names to its own exclusive use? When a departing employee takes a company's trade secrets and know-how with him, what part of this information belongs to the company and what part, derived from his own skill and training, belongs to him? Marking off the boundaries of intellectual assets is like drawing lines in water.

Elusive as intellectual property boundaries are, the business value they secure is enormous. Commentators cite breathtaking figures to indicate the scale of intellectual assets in the modern economy: "76 percent of the Fortune 100's total market capitalization is represented by intangible assets, such as patents, copyrights, and trademarks," and "an estimated 80 percent of the value of the Standard & Poor's 500 is made up of intangible assets of all kinds." By one recent estimate, the nation's copyright and patent industries alone contributed almost 20 percent of private industry's share of U.S. gross domestic product and were responsible for close to 40 percent of all private industry growth.

Impressive as these numbers are, the profits generated by intellectual assets can be even more striking. In 1986 media entrepreneur Ted Turner paid $1.6 billion for the MGM film studio, quickly selling off the studio's tangible assets—production and distribution operations, film laboratory, and real estate—in a deal that left him with $1.2 billion invested in the copyrights to MGM's film library, including such classics as *Casablanca, Gone With the Wind,* and *The Wizard of Oz.* In 2004, when MGM was again on the block, analysts estimated that its James Bond franchise alone was worth $1 billion, encompassing not only DVD revenues from the twenty Bond films already in the MGM library, but also the revenues to be earned from new releases, for which they estimated profits at no less than $125 million for each film, not counting product placements. (In one Bond film, *Die Another Day,* automaker Ford arranged for the placement of tie-in advertising for three of its brands—Aston Martin, Thunderbird, and Jaguar—and cameo appearances for another three. Estimates of the placement deal's value ranged in the tens of millions.) In 1999, Salton Inc. paid George Foreman and his partners $137.5 million to use the former heavyweight champion's name and image to market the Lean Mean Grilling Machine and other kitchen products, a payday for which the boxer did not have to land—or suffer—a single blow.

Intellectual property, this most profitable of all business assets, is also the least stable. One reason is that, far more than any other business asset, patents, copyrights, trademarks, and trade secrets are constructed of legal rules. Equally important is that, far more than other legal doctrines, the rules that define intellectual property are the subject of constant change. Intellectual property's boundary lines are inherently uncertain and can shift from one judicial decision to the next. When in 2000 a federal court declared the patent on Prozac invalid, the value of Eli Lilly shares plummeted more than 30 percent. In 2002 a judge ruled that rival suppliers had not infringed Gemstar's patents on an on-screen program guide, and the company's stock dropped 39 percent in value. The stock of Visx, a leading vision-correction laser company, fell 41 percent after a similar ruling. Smart business practice requires an understanding of the forces that produce uncertainty and change in intellectual property law, and if not always the insight to predict their outcomes, then at least the ability to plan for them.

Like so many companies before and since, Eastman Kodak learned about uncertainty and change in intellectual property law the hard way. On April 20, 1976, after seven years and hundreds of millions of dollars spent on research and development, Kodak introduced its first instant camera and film. One complication was that the Polaroid Corporation had beat it to market by twenty-nine years; another was that Polaroid had surrounded its inventions with hundreds of U.S. and foreign patents. Six days following Kodak's product announcement, Polaroid filed a patent infringement lawsuit against the company in federal district court in Boston, Massachusetts, Polaroid's home turf. On September 13, 1985, after years of pretrial discovery and a two-and-a-half-month trial, District Judge Rya Zobel handed down her decision: Kodak had infringed seven Polaroid patents. A month later, Judge Zobel ordered an injunction against Kodak, which, subject to appeal, would effectively take the company out of the instant photography business.

Even putting aside the $600 million that Kodak had already lost in instant photography the usual way—costs exceeding revenues—the loss from the Polaroid lawsuit was staggering: $494 million, according to the company, to shut down plants, dispose of inventory, and compensate the millions of customers whose instant cameras were now worthless because the company could not produce film to be used in them; tens of millions of dollars in lawyers' fees; and, after a separate damages trial, a total judgment of $873 million—which continues to stand as the largest patent award ever made.

A favorite sport of stock analysts is to handicap intellectual property infringement cases, and the differences among their estimates can offer a graphic index of the range of legal risk. The first predictions of Polaroid's ultimate recovery in *Polaroid v. Kodak,* made shortly after Judge Zobel handed down her liability decision, ranged from $30 million to $100 million. The estimates grew over the next three years, ranging from $300 million to $1 billion. After the damages trial, but before announcement of the damage award, the upper end of the range rose to $2 billion. When Judge A. David Mazzone, who oversaw the damages trial, finally awarded Polaroid $873 million, Polaroid stock dropped 23 percent and Kodak's rose over 10 percent, to adjust for the analysts' earlier wrong estimates. And these estimates failed to account for the largest legal shift of all: between the time Kodak introduced its products and Judge Zobel announced her decision, the legal standard for determining patentability had markedly changed in favor of patent owners like Polaroid.

Why are intellectual property rules so much more mercurial than other property rules? (If real property rules were similarly unstable, the Empire State Building, fully rented one day, would be open to squatters the next.) The answer stems from the fact that intellectual assets—inventions, entertainment, brand names, collections of data, trade secrets—are information and, as such, are inexhaustible; unlike the Empire State Building, information can be used by unlimited numbers of people without impairing the ability of still other unlimited numbers to use it too. Lawmakers recognize that without property rights to protect innovations from freeloading competitors, businesses will hesitate to invest in innovation—which is why legislatures enact intellectual property laws. But lawmakers also understand that to impose intellectual property rights necessarily means turning away prospective users who are unable or unwilling to pay the price for access to the protected information, even though their use of the information will deprive no one else of it—which is why they impose limitations on intellectual property rights that would be unimaginable in the case of other forms of property rights. Schools cannot photocopy instructional materials for their students without first paying for copy machines, paper, and ink. But copyright law's fair use doctrine regularly gives teachers a free ticket to copy the very content of the material itself.

Judges, legislators, and lawyers commonly speak of "balance" in intellectual property law, and this is certainly a desirable goal. But balance—at least if it implies stability—is an illusion. No law that seeks to encourage both the production *and* use of information can possibly achieve more than a momentary equilibrium. Because support for investment incentives inevitably undermines support for free access—this is the paradox of property rights in information, and the subject of chapter 1—all balances are temporary; the slightest current of public or political sentiment can shift the balance by extending property rights one day and restricting them the next.

Intellectual assets have long lives—patents last for twenty years from the date of application, copyrights can last ninety-five years or longer, and trademarks and trade secrets are potentially perpetual—and there is no more important intellectual property management objective than to anticipate an intellectual asset's legal future over its lifetime. Kodak's intellectual property lawyers could not have anticipated the specific legal changes that tipped the judicial scales in Polaroid's favor over the long course of that lawsuit. However, history shows that the forces producing change in intellectual property law are themselves predictable and can offer a rough index of the directions that change will take.

Each form of intellectual property expands and shrinks at its own pace. American patent law has experienced sharp peaks and valleys of protection over its history; as will be seen in chapter 2, the generous patent standards applied in *Polaroid v. Kodak* were part of an ascent toward a peak that lasted through the 1990s and into the new century, but is now poised for a judicial and legislative backlash. Copyright's ups and downs have been less dramatic, and, as shown in chapter 3, lawmakers concerned that a too-robust copyright will stifle the growth of new technologies have been carving new inroads into the law. Trademark law is for the first time flowering into a full-fledged intellectual property right, an evolution traced in chapter 4, but in time we can expect that it too will encounter a cyclical reversal. Trade secret law, viewed as a property right in the nineteenth century, became a more limited doctrine in the twentieth century, but, as will be seen in chapter 5, is today on a trajectory that will lead to expansive property rights once again, albeit in dramatically different forms, such as protection for databases. The impact of the Internet, the subject of chapter 6, has been to exaggerate these current trends in patent, copyright, trademark, and trade secret laws, and the impact of globalization, the subject of chapter 7, has been to disperse these trends rapidly through foreign markets, including some, particularly in Asia, that at one time rejected intellectual property altogether.

In this book I will examine the most important forms of intellectual property, using legal case studies to illustrate routes to success and failure in managing legal risk and extracting value from these assets. I will also shine a light on the underlying forces of change that make intellectual property so challenging as a business asset. As you will see, the risks and rewards of intellectual assets are no less manageable than those of other business activities. However, the management tools differ, and the experience of the most successful intellectual asset companies reveals not only a healthy respect for the margins and mishaps that these assets can produce, but also the need to merge legal and business perspectives in managing them. The central lesson of this book is that every business decision involving intellectual assets is ultimately a legal decision, and that every legal decision is at bottom a business decision. If intellectual property is economically too important to be left to lawyers, it is also too legally charged to be left to managers.

Intellectual property, though it may seem to some to be an esoteric or even exotic topic, is in fact an intensely practical matter, and I have in this book drawn on forty years' experience not only teaching and writing in the field, but also practicing in it. My faculty position at Stanford Law School has given me the time to write and maintain two treatises and two standard texts on domestic and international intellectual property law, as well as articles exploring the law's encounters with new technologies. My association as counsel with one of the country's largest law firms has given me the opportunity to provide intellectual property advice to clients ranging from two-person start-ups to Fortune 500 companies (including one company that made the jump from the first category to the second). These parallel careers have also enabled me to observe intellectual property lawmaking close-up, working on law reform with congressional committees and international governmental organizations. I hope that the insights drawn from these experiences will help to guide companies large and small as they navigate the tricky passages where the law and business of intellectual assets converge.

1

The Intellectual
Property Paradox

The name Polaroid is synonymous with instant photography, but
without patents Polaroid could not have dominated the market as it
did for the entire history of this once popular medium. In the course
of the *Polaroid v. Kodak* trial, in which Polaroid sued Kodak for infringing twelve patents on its instant photography films and cameras,
one Polaroid official described the company's founder, chairman, and
chief inventor, Edwin Land, as "fierce" about patents. At the company's
annual meeting, the day after it filed its lawsuit, Land told shareholders, "This is our very soul we're all involved in. This is our whole
life. . . . The only thing that is keeping us alive is our brilliance. The
only way to protect our brilliance is patents."

Kodak understood this fervor because it too was a company founded
on patents. More than sixty years before Edwin Land applied for his
first patent, George Eastman applied in the United States and Europe
for patents on his own pathbreaking photographic inventions, ultimately erecting an intellectual property fortress as impregnable in its
domain as was Polaroid's. By 1976, when Kodak announced its entry
into the instant photography market, the Rochester company controlled
an estimated 85 percent of the conventional, amateur film market in the
United States and 53 percent of the camera market.

The views of innovators like Land and Eastman rarely change: more patents are preferable to fewer, and the broader the reach of these patents, the better. But views of lawmakers do change. Patent standards and remedies can shift even over the span of a single trial, particularly when, as in the case of *Polaroid v. Kodak*, the trial stretches over fifteen years. Pretrial discovery alone consumed close to five years, with Polaroid requiring Kodak to turn over 268,000 pages of documents; in turn, Polaroid produced 40,000 documents. Kodak took 298 days of depositions and Polaroid 164. Kodak's deposition of Dr. Land lasted twelve days; the depositions of other Polaroid inventors and project leaders took longer. The trial before Judge Zobel went on for two and a half months, with Dr. Land testifying for a total of thirteen days—six days of direct examination by Polaroid's lawyers and seven days of cross-examination by Kodak's. By Polaroid's estimate—Kodak did not dispute the figure—the company's attorneys' fees for the litigation added up to $48 million.

The Risks—and Rewards—of Legal Uncertainty and Change

One legal standard that changed over the course of the Polaroid trial was the statutory requirement that, in order for the U.S. Patent and Trademark Office to grant a patent, the applicant must show not only that the invention was new at the time he invented it, but also that it was "nonobvious"—not readily apparent—to workers reasonably skilled in the art. Even if the applicant convinces a patent examiner of the invention's novelty and nonobviousness, and the PTO issues a patent, another company, if sued by the patent owner, can ask the court to invalidate the patent on the ground that the PTO erred in its findings of novelty or nonobviousness. The company can also ask the court to find that, even if the patent is valid, its own product did not infringe it.

In venturing into Polaroid's minefield, Kodak clearly understood that the legal boundaries of a patent are far less defined than the boundaries of a parcel of real property, and the company used due diligence in determining which, if any, of Polaroid's issued patents would hold up on judicial review. (Judge Mazzone expressly declined to find that Kodak's infringement was willful—a finding that could have led to a trebling of the $873 million damage award.) As Kodak's research and development effort got under way, the company retained a prominent intellectual property lawyer, Francis T. Carr, to compare Kodak's planned products and processes to the subject matter encompassed by Polaroid's patents and to opine on whether any of the Kodak inventions infringed on valid Polaroid patents. Carr, a partner in the New York intellectual property boutique Kenyon & Kenyon, later estimated that he and his legal team looked at 200 to 250 known Polaroid patents (he used the term "known" because "it was not clear at any point in time that all Polaroid patents had been located"). He then delivered written opinions to his client that sixty-seven key Polaroid patents were invalid or, if valid, would not be infringed by Kodak's products and processes.

When Kodak relied on Frank Carr's legal opinion that Polaroid's relevant patents were either invalid or not infringed, it was betting that a judge would agree—and, if not a federal district judge like Rya Zobel, then the federal appellate judges who review district court patent decisions. Neither bet was high-risk, for few patents are bulletproof. Despite surviving examination in the PTO, an issued patent, once it becomes the subject of litigation, has an almost fifty-fifty chance of being ruled invalid by a trial court. Indeed, Judge Zobel found three of Polaroid's patents to be invalid, one of them without even the necessity of a trial. And, despite the rigors of trial, appellate courts have in some years overturned as many as half of district court patent decisions, although the average is lower.

If, as seems likely, Frank Carr had been meticulous in parsing the Polaroid patents to ensure that Kodak infringed none that was valid, what went wrong? One problem was simply that no legal rule—and no lawyer's opinion—could have drawn a bright boundary line indicating which elements of the inventions belonged to Polaroid under its patents and which elements were free for others, including Kodak, to manufacture. The second problem, characteristic of all intellectual property laws, is that they change. Legal opinions are no better than the legal rules they are based on, and in this case the legal standard for invention—crucial to determining the validity and scope of Polaroid's patents—had changed between the time Frank Carr wrote his opinions and when Judge Zobel rendered her decision.

At the time Carr wrote his opinions for Kodak, jurisdiction over patent appeals in the United States was in the several regional courts of appeals, and although the standards of invention applied by these courts differed, all more or less followed the rigorous standard for patentability adopted by the U.S. Supreme Court, requiring that, to receive a patent, a combination of old elements must demonstrate a "synergistic effect," the whole being demonstrably greater than its constituent parts. What Carr did not anticipate was that in 1982 Congress would consolidate jurisdiction over patent appeals from the district courts in a single new court, the Court of Appeals for the Federal Circuit, nor that in 1983 this new Court of Appeals would effectively reject the Supreme Court standard (not a common thing for a lower court to do!). Consequently, by the time District Judge Zobel rendered her decision in 1985, it was the new, more relaxed standard that adherence to Federal Circuit authority required her to apply.

The change in the standard of patentability was only one of the unhappy surprises that awaited Kodak in its litigation with Polaroid. At the time Kodak started developing its instant photography products, the company expected that even if it lost at trial the court would under then-prevailing practice automatically postpone an injunction until the appeal could be decided. Kodak could then continue in business— uninterrupted if the appeal was decided in its favor, and possibly subject to a negotiated license with Polaroid if it was not. But in 1983 the Court of Appeals for the Federal Circuit changed the rule on injunctive relief—a development that Polaroid lawyer Herbert Schwartz, from another leading intellectual property firm, Fish & Neave, called "a monumental change in the law"—and subsequently Judge Zobel refused to postpone Polaroid's injunction pending Kodak's appeal. The decision exposed Kodak for the first time to a real risk that its instant photography business would be closed down. As a law student at the University of Pennsylvania, Schwartz had published an article on patent injunctions in the student-run law journal, and so "had very well in mind" the Federal Circuit's change in the rule on stays. "I thought we ought to take a run at trying to persuade the court not to stay the injunction. When we got to the part, which was conventional, to stay the injunction, and the judge asked for briefs on it, Kodak was stunned to hear it."

Cecil Quillen, the in-house Kodak lawyer who oversaw the *Polaroid* litigation and subsequently became the company's general counsel, recalls that when they were assembling the affidavits and other papers to oppose Polaroid's request for an injunction, CEO Colby Chandler declared in his affidavit that if Kodak were enjoined pending the appeal, the company would not return to the instant photography business, regardless of how the appellate court decided. Quillen asked Chandler, "'Do you really want to say that?' It was possible that we could be enjoined and then in fact Judge Zobel's decision would be reversed and we'd be able to get back into business. And he said, 'Yes, I want to say that. If we're shot down, we're not coming back.'"

Kodak argued in court that if its production and sale of film were enjoined its cameras would become useless since neither Polaroid nor any other manufacturer had film on the market that could substitute for Kodak's; this, Kodak insisted, would be particularly damaging to a company whose "reputation and goodwill are based in part on the fact that Kodak does not desert its customers." Further, if required to shut down, "800 full-time and 3700 part-time employees would lose their jobs." Acknowledging that Kodak's claims of irreparable harm from an injunction were "seductive," Judge Zobel nonetheless declined to stay the injunction. "It is worth noting," she wrote, "that the harm Kodak will suffer simply mirrors the success it has enjoyed in the field of instant photography. To the extent Kodak has purchased that success at Polaroid's expense, it has taken a 'calculated risk' that it might infringe existing patents."

Facts and personalities are as important in trial practice as are legal rules, and there is no question but that Edwin Land's thirteen days of testimony dominated the *Polaroid v. Kodak* trial. According to a biographer, Land spent months before the trial working with colleagues, "teaching himself the ways he would explain to an unfamiliar audience the intricacies of the art he had practiced in his laboratory over the past thirty-seven years." Walter Hanley, a member of Kodak's trial team, remembered that Land gave the impression that all of these inventions—he held 533 patents, second only to Thomas Edison—were his personal achievements. "What he brought with him was the fact that he had basically created this field, this market. That was what was impressive, not the patents that were involved in the case."

For Judge Zobel, Land's presence underscored the differences in corporate culture between Polaroid and Kodak. Land, she recalled, was "fabulous" as a witness because he was fighting for his intellectual children, "protecting what was his." He painted a picture of Polaroid as a small company that used its brainpower to reach elegant solutions. Kodak, by contrast, had assigned thousands of researchers and spent tens of millions of dollars to arrive at what he believed was a copycat solution. Land's success on the witness stand was no accident, and stemmed from his intensely personal perspective on the case. "In Land's view," according to a biographer, "to lose this battle would be to reward the results of committee effort, group think, legal cheese-paring, the cynical assumption that no individual can stand in the way of a large, powerful, well-equipped phalanx."

Just as courts may weigh the moral value of creativity in favor of intellectual property owners, they will sometimes weigh the opprobrium of piracy against alleged infringers. Noting that it was "by no means decisive on the question of infringement of any particular patent," Judge Zobel's opinion nonetheless observed that in September 1973 Kodak's Development Committee suggested to researchers that "development should not be constrained by what an individual feels is potential patent infringement." But in a talk he later gave to a patent lawyers group, Kodak lawyer Frank Carr pointed out a telling omission in Judge Zobel's reference: following the suggestion that researchers should not be constrained by concerns for patent infringement, the Development Committee added the admonition, "The patent office should be consulted"—presumably meaning that researchers should in all questionable cases obtain review of their work by Kodak's patent department. Kodak was following smart R&D practice—research and develop freely, and leave legal judgments to the experts. But the litigation lesson to be drawn from Judge Zobel's opinion is clear. If you engage in competitive research, you should never leave a paper trail that might later be construed to suggest that you were heedless of the intellectual property rights of your competitor.

For U.S. companies that exploit their intellectual assets in foreign markets—and few intellectual asset companies today lack a global outlook—the uncertainties in U.S. law are compounded by those in foreign law. Intellectual property rules vary from country to country.

Having had its patents upheld in the United States, Polaroid might have hoped to enjoy the same success in every other country where it had obtained patents on the same inventions. But the reality was very different. Even before Polaroid filed its lawsuit in the United States, Kodak initiated actions for revocation of key Polaroid patents in several countries, including Austria, Germany, and the United Kingdom. It succeeded in getting one or more of the Polaroid patents revoked in all. In Britain's High Court, Polaroid initially won a preliminary injunction against Kodak's distribution of its products, but the injunction was later reversed by the Court of Appeal.

As central as they may be, legal uncertainty and legal change are but two of the risks of intellectual assets. As with all innovations, there is also the risk of technological failure; the more substantial or nonobvious the technological leap, the less predictable its success will be. When, following a picture-taking expedition in pre-Polaroid days, Land's impatient three-year-old daughter Jennifer asked her father why she couldn't immediately see the photographs he had just taken, there was no guarantee that his incredible will would in fact produce a solution. Intellectual assets also suffer ordinary market risk. By the time Judge Mazzone rendered his $873 million damage award against Kodak in 1990, the arrival of new, easy-to-use 35mm cameras from Japan, their popularity enhanced by the sudden widespread availability of one-hour photo finishers, had substantially eroded the market for instant photography. Even Polaroid's vice president for manufacturing at the time, I. McAllister Booth, conceded in the damages trial that the quality, convenience, and economy of 35mm prints exceeded that of instant ones. From this, Judge Mazzone concluded that Polaroid's main competition was conventional photography, not Kodak's instant camera. Preoccupied with their dazzling technology and their patent lawsuit, the two companies had been jousting on the rear deck of the *Titanic*.

Why IP Law Is So Uncertain and Changeable—or, the Paradox of Public Goods

A single fact defines the business opportunities and legal challenges of intellectual assets: their use by one person will not limit their use by anyone else. (Compare a loaf of bread whose consumption by one person will preclude its consumption by another.) The instant photographic processes invented by Dr. Land and his team at Polaroid fit this definition because they could be used by millions of consumers without diminishing the ability of untold millions more to use them too. Bruce Springsteen's "Born to Run" can be listened to by two or two million listeners without diminishing its simultaneous or subsequent enjoyment by twenty million more. Thomas Jefferson, a grudging supporter of intellectual property rights, eloquently captured this essential characteristic of information: "He who receives an idea from me, receives instruction himself without lessening mine; as he who lights his taper at mine, receives light without darkening me."

It is the inexhaustibility of intellectual assets that makes healthy, and sometimes extraordinary, margins possible. Because the value of a patent, copyright, trademark, or trade secret is economically distinct from the tangible good in which it is embodied—camera, CD, label, or soft drink—an intellectual asset company can center its calculation of risk and reward on intellectual property elements alone. Polaroid understood the difference between intellectual goods and commodity goods when in the early years of its instant photography business it focused capital investment on research and development, while subcontracting the manufacture of film and cameras to others, including Kodak, and leasing rather than purchasing plants and equipment.

Healthy margins characterize many intellectual assets. Lenovo understood the financial lure of intellectual assets when as part of its 2004 deal to buy IBM's PC business it acquired a five-year license to apply the IBM brand to its PCs. (Lenovo also understood the importance of building its own brand, and moved quickly to substitute the Lenovo name for IBM's on its products and advertising.) Kodak trademarks, such as the Kodak name and distinctive yellow box, have contributed significantly to gross margins on photographic film that have reached as high as 80 percent. Once its patent on a product expires, a company can rely on trade secrets to ensure continued profitability by protecting the often complex processes used in manufacturing the product.

Intellectual assets will only produce healthy margins—indeed, in most cases, will only produce *any* margins—if and to the extent that property rights protect them. The few artfully drawn lines that, together with the oversized ears, nose, and shoes, make up the Mickey Mouse character, have earned hundreds of millions of dollars for the Walt Disney Company, but only because the company's copyrights and trademarks in the character have protected it from knockoffs ranging from T-shirts and wristwatches to lunch pails and theme park mannequins. Even after the Mickey Mouse copyright expires in 2023, trademark law will continue to provide a measure of protection for the character, for Mickey Mouse is as much a brand as he is an entertainment product.

But inexhaustibility creates a dilemma for the creation of property rights in intellectual assets. Economists classify goods whose use by one person will not diminish use by others as "public goods"—the classic examples in addition to information are lighthouses, public education, and national defense—and observe that to grant property rights in information will necessarily violate a basic tenet of contemporary economic policy by decreasing the welfare of one class of users—those unable or unwilling to pay for access to information—without increasing the welfare of another class of users—those who are willing and able to pay the intellectual property owner's asking price. The problem of intellectual assets is that without property rights they will be underproduced, but with property rights they will be underused. Hence the paradox, or riddle, of intellectual property: What is always too little and too much?

A standard solution to the problem of public goods is for government to pay for the production and maintenance of these goods out of the public treasury and to make their benefits available "free" to everyone. This is the rationale behind public expenditures for education, lighthouses, and defense. It is also the reason for substantial government grants to scientific research. In 2005, total federal obligations for research and development were roughly $107 billion (broken down roughly into $27 billion for basic research, $28 billion for applied research, and $52 billion for development), compared to about $73 billion (spread among basic and applied research, and development) five years earlier.

A problem with government subsidy—one that is particularly severe in the case of information products like inventions, entertainment, and brands—is that it is largely divorced from consumer preference. Voters can more or less be expected to express at the ballot box their preferences for investment in education, coastal safety, and defense. But few Americans, at least, would be willing to trade private for public choice over the selection of products available on the supermarket shelf or hardware counter any more than they would want government to choose the films they watch or the books they read. Brands will almost always win out over government-specified Grades A, B, and C.

The framers of the U.S. Constitution acknowledged the superiority of private property rights over government subsidy in stimulating investment in invention and literary and artistic production when, in Article 1, Section 8, Clause 8, they empowered Congress "to promote the progress of science and useful arts, by securing for limited times to authors and inventors the exclusive right to their respective writings and discoveries." (A separate provision, Article 1's Commerce Clause, gave Congress the necessary authority to enact a trademark law.) The copyright-patent clause contains not only a grant of power, but a limit on its exercise, and reflects the framers' judgment that a utilitarian calculus offers the most appropriate resolution of the intellectual property paradox: Congress may grant exclusive rights to "authors" and "inventors," but only so far as is necessary to encourage them to produce "writings" and "discoveries"; legal inducements beyond that should be avoided as unnecessary to the law's central object. If a fourteen-year patent term was all that was required at the time to attract the right level of investment to invention, Congress should not make the term one day longer. The restriction to "limited times" is only the most explicit of these limitations, and, in theory at least, no exclusive right should be extended any further than is necessary to ensure the optimum level of investment in writings and discoveries.

As Congress has gone about the task of enacting patent and copyright laws, it has been less than vigilant in observing this constitutional principle, and for good reason: no one has ever seriously attempted to measure, even crudely, the economically correct level of inventive and artistic production in the United States, much less calibrate the amount of investment that would lead to that level of production, or the legal rights that would be required to induce that investment. In 1985, Congressman Robert W. Kastenmeier, who was at the time chairman of the House Judiciary Committee's subcommittee dealing with copyright, patent, and trademark, startled the intellectual asset community, particularly its Washington representatives, when he announced that henceforth any industry that petitioned Congress for change in intellectual property law would do well to demonstrate that, as a result of the change, "the aggregate public benefit should outweigh the proprietary gains which result from protection. Congress can safely move forward if the cost to the public of the monopoly is deemed to be less than the value to the public of the total benefits caused by the law." No intellectual property legislator had ever made such a demand for empirical evidence before, and—after one frail attempt at proof made by the record industry in the next bill to come before Kastenmeier's subcommittee—none has been made since.

Technological advance, far more than cool utilitarian assessments, is the main trigger for change in intellectual property law, often, but not always, in the direction of expanding the subject matter protected and the rights granted. Technological disruptions produce new markets, and new markets trigger scrambles for intellectual asset advantage, forcing lawmakers to decide whether and to what extent intellectual property rules should regulate the new market. The biotechnology revolution made it politically inevitable that Congress and the courts would extend patent protection to these new inventions, and that the United States, the center of research in the field, would lead the drive for protection. No one doubted that, once computer software became commercially important, intellectual property protection would extend to it, too; the only question was whether the chosen vehicle would be copyright, patent, or a custom-crafted software statute. Because the dominant software companies at the time preferred copyright, Congress amended the Copyright Act in 1980 to encompass computer programs, and over the next decade or more, the rest of the world followed.

Like new types of intellectual assets, new technologies for distributing these assets also presage legal change, although the precise direction and extent of change will be harder to predict. In the late 1960s

and early 1970s, when community antenna and cable television services first emerged in rural areas across the United States, the question
arose as to whether their operators should be required to pay for the
copyrighted content they carried. The Supreme Court twice ruled that
they should not, but in 1976 Congress changed the law and said that they
should be made to pay. But new technologies do not always produce extensions of rights, and particularly not when the use at issue directly
touches the consumer pocketbook. When in 1980 the motion picture
studios sought legislation that would give them a royalty every time a
videocassette was rented, a broad-based lobbying campaign by rental
stores and their customers brought the initiative to a dead halt.

The Unique Scalability of Intellectual Assets

Where economists view intellectual assets as inexhaustible, businesses
view them as scalable. A motion picture that successfully opens on a
hundred screens can be quickly released to many hundreds more and,
through broadcasts and cable, satellite, and Internet transmissions, can
be delivered to hundreds of millions of people around the world with
little added expenditure other than for marketing. A pharmaceutical
can move from clinical trials to worldwide distribution with no increased investment in the research and development that created it. A
cost-accounting technique for bidding on government contracts can,
within the limits of secrecy, be applied to thousands of contracts.

Scalability is cumulative. A patent on a pharmaceutical can give its
owner control not only over that drug, but over all the drugs that improve on it. If Able Co. holds the patent on aspirin, Baker Inc., the inventor of buffered aspirin, must obtain a license from Able before it
can sell its improved product. By 2004, twenty films had been spun
out of Ian Fleming's popular James Bond novels, each building on the
consumer value created in the original and each requiring the assent
of the copyright owner of the underlying rights. Frito-Lay first acquired trademark rights in "Fritos," then in "Cheetos," "Doritos," and
"Tostitos," acquiring a virtual lock on *"tos"* as a brand-name suffix for
snack foods and effectively creating a platform for marketing the
brand.

Intellectual property platforms can be as treacherous for those who do business on them as they are profitable for their owners. Kodak discovered the perils of trying to do business on a platform owned by another when in 1970 it began work on developing an instant color film that would be compatible with the Polaroid instant cameras then on the market. After spending close to $100 million on the project, Kodak abandoned it two years later, at least in part because of technical difficulties in producing the film. But it may also have been no coincidence that abandonment of the project came shortly after Polaroid introduced the entirely new SX-70 system. According to internal Kodak memoranda, the new film, because it was incompatible with the SX-70, would be obsolete even before it was released.

Few companies have the resources themselves to reach every potential market. This is where intellectual property licenses come in. Through license agreements with well-placed licensees, a company can exploit its intellectual assets in product, service, and geographic markets that it lacks the resources to enter itself; it can also delegate enforcement of rights to licensees. Marshall Phelps and Dan McCurdy, respectively the former heads of licensing at IBM and Lucent Technologies (Phelps later moved to Microsoft), have observed two particular rewards from licensing a patent or other intellectual property to a competitor: licensing can diversify a firm's revenue stream by capturing royalties from the competitor's products; and, "if Company A's licensing revenues enable it to increase its research and development, while Company B opts to license Company A's innovation rather than developing its own, Company A is likely to extend its technological edge over its rivals."

Polaroid's arrangement with Kodak for the development of instant film illustrates the point made by Phelps and McCurdy. From the beginning of Polaroid's venture into color photography, Kodak was its key partner in producing the new film. Not only did Kodak manufacture the negative "peel-apart" films for the first Polaroid color cameras, it also contributed its own experience with color chemistry to Polaroid's development efforts. According to Elkan Blount, who had served as general manager of research at Polaroid, it "was a splendid collaboration—all the participants enjoyed the effort and learned a great deal. Many patents were issued as a result of this collaboration; almost all of the primary ones were assigned to Polaroid, including forty or so in my own name."

It was Polaroid's move to the SX-70 system, employing an integrated film product that did not require the user to peel the negative from the positive, that ultimately doomed the collaborative relationship between the two companies and precipitated *Polaroid v. Kodak*. When in April 1968 Polaroid told Kodak of the new film it had invented, and Land showed photographs made with the new method to Kodak's vice president of research, the two at first discussed a new licensing arrangement under which Kodak would invest in further developing and manufacturing the film for Polaroid. But Kodak's president, William S. Vaughn, had reached Kodak's mandatory retirement age at about this time and his successor, Dr. Louis K. Eilers, "didn't understand why we should commit our production resources to someone else's business." According to Cecil Quillen, when Eilers told Land that Kodak would be willing to produce the new film, "but only on the understanding that we'll be able to put the product under our own label at some agreed-upon date," Land resisted. As Polaroid chairman William J. McCune later testified at the damages trial, "A stumbling block was always that we couldn't see how giving Kodak a license to make products competitive with ours would allow us to stay in business."

Copyright and trademark owners, because their rights are less robust than those enjoyed by patent owners and consequently offer fewer opportunities for market dominance, regularly use intricate licensing and price discrimination schemes to increase revenues. Motion picture companies first release their films to movie theaters, where the admission price is highest; several months later they sell DVDs to video stores and Internet services where viewers can rent the film for less; then comes home television pay-per-view, followed a year later by pay television; and as many as three years later the film may appear "free" on network television. Licensing of merchandise rights in such valuable assets as celebrity names and likenesses and sports team logos has also become a major global business.

Licenses achieve more than scalability. Business also uses them to reduce the risk of legal uncertainty. An Internet company, uncertain about whether its distribution of copyrighted music will infringe the music owners' rights, must choose between defending its position in court and taking a license from the copyright owner. The copyright owner, similarly uncertain about the reach of its rights, and fearful that an adverse judicial decision will become a precedent applicable to other Internet users as well, will often be motivated to grant a license on terms the Internet user can accept.

The uncertainty of litigation is why most intellectual property lawsuits end in settlement, with the alleged infringer taking a license from the patent owner. Before the *Polaroid v. Kodak* trial, Judge Zobel encouraged executives from the two companies to meet, without their outside counsel present, to try to settle the case between them. Cecil Quillen, who presented Kodak's position at the meeting, said, "We didn't persuade them, and they didn't persuade us, and no offer came directly out of the meeting." However, "on the eve of the trial, Polaroid told the judge that they would be willing to settle the case for 5 percent of film and camera sales, past and future." Kodak studied the proposal, but finally rejected it. Kodak chairman Walter A. Fallon said, "We can't afford that kind of settlement. We're not making any money on the product now and our most optimistic projections are such that we're not going to make that kind of money on the product." Quillen added, "Now, with hindsight, we wish like hell we'd taken the 5 percent."

But even license agreements cannot promise ironclad protection against legal change. Courts will decline to enforce an otherwise valid agreement that extends the term or scope of protection beyond what the patent law allows. In a landmark 1969 decision, *Lear v. Adkins,* the U.S. Supreme Court gave patent licensees the right to challenge the licensed patent's validity and to stop paying royalties at any time during the patent term. (Courts had long held that licensees are privileged to stop paying royalties if a third party obtained a ruling that the patent was invalid. But when the licensee itself sought to challenge validity, courts thought that it would be unfair to let the licensee attack the very patent it had bargained for.) The Court in *Lear* acknowledged that there was a conflict of principle: "On the one hand, the law of contracts forbids a purchaser to repudiate his promises simply because he later becomes dissatisfied with the bargain he has made." But "on the other hand, federal law requires that all ideas in general circulation be dedicated to the common good unless they are protected by a valid patent."

The paradox of intellectual assets—that without property rights, too little information will be produced, but with property rights, too little will be used—requires lawmakers in every case to strike a compromise between private rights and public use. At least in theory, and at least in the United States, free use is the default principle; private rights, it is said, are no more than a necessary evil, calculated to stimulate investment in inventions, entertainment, and brands. In fact, the history of intellectual property reveals no such constant principle, but instead an uneven expansion of subject matter and rights, albeit one that is different for each form of intellectual property.

In the case of patents, Congress and the courts strike the balance between private property and free use with an eye to markets and the specific conditions of technological innovation, for patents may stifle competitive research more in some industries, such as electronics, than in others, such as pharmaceuticals. In the case of copyright, constitutional concerns for free speech constrain the scope of private rights, leaving far more leeway for competitive entry than does patent law. In trademark law, consumer expectations are at least as much a touchstone for lawmakers as are the interests of competing brand-name users. Trade secret law embodies a trade-off between business incentives to innovate and employee interests in mobility.

PATENTS. Two objectives define the balance that lawmakers strike for patent law: to promote investment in worthwhile technological innovation, and to make the products of this innovation available to consumers at the lowest possible price. Reconciling these objectives can be complicated, for too great an emphasis on exclusive rights may in fact impede rather than advance innovation. A single semiconductor chip may embody hundreds, even thousands, of patented inventions, few of them owned by the chip's producer. Such dense "patent thickets" can stifle a company's development of new products unless it first obtains licenses from the dozens of other companies that own the patents surrounding its invention. One privately engineered solution is for two or more patent-owning companies to enter into cross-licenses, obtaining for each company the freedom it needs to produce its goods. This strategy will not work, however, when one of the patent owners— often a so-called patent troll—is not itself engaged in manufacturing and so cannot be bought off with a cross-license.

Patents confer more robust rights, and consequently offer greater opportunities for market control, than any other form of intellectual property. A single patent, such as Robert Kearns's patent on the intermittent automobile windshield wiper, can dominate a market. (The patent won Kearns $30 million in damages from Ford and Chrysler.) When Amazon.com prevailed against BarnesandNoble.com for infringing its 1-Click online shopping patent, it won more than a lawsuit; the trial court shut down BarnesandNoble.com's use of the popular feature for two successive Christmas seasons. Early in the 1990s, Honeywell prevailed against the Minolta Camera Company for infringing its patents on the technology for autofocus cameras—the patents had slumbered unused in Honeywell's patent portfolio before it was brought to the company's attention by a Minneapolis law firm—and Honeywell subsequently settled with Minolta for $127.5 million. Settlements with thirteen other camera manufacturers in Asia and the United States quickly followed, netting Honeywell a total of $314.5 million.

The control conferred by patents is a periodic source of worry to lawmakers, as is the countervailing concern that firms need stronger protection to support their investment in socially valuable research and development. The historical cycles of low and high protection that result from these competing concerns date back two centuries. A half century after adopting their first patent laws in the early 1800s, many European nations had second thoughts. The Netherlands repealed its patent law in 1869, and Switzerland, which had so far failed to adopt a patent system, repeatedly rejected proposals to enact one. In Britain, speakers in both houses of Parliament argued for the abolition of patents, and a bill passed by the House of Lords proposed to cut back the patent term. Only by the last quarter of the nineteenth century did patent systems right themselves across Europe. Similar antipatent rumblings surfaced in the United States in the late 1930s, and by 1942 U.S. courts were upholding only 10 percent of litigated patents. Modest reforms followed. Decades later, complaints about a patent system again out of control triggered major reports from the Federal Trade Commission and the National Academy of Sciences proposing reforms to increase the quality of issued patents; substantial legislative proposals followed.

Shifts in antitrust attitudes also have an impact on patent planning. Industry observers have faulted Xerox for its failure to secure intellectual property protection for several important computer-related inventions developed at its Palo Alto Research Center (PARC) in the 1970s, among them the graphical user interface that Apple later appropriated for the Macintosh, and that eventually Microsoft appropriated for Windows. But Xerox's earlier experience with its photocopying patents may at least partly explain the company's ambivalence toward intellectual property. In 1975, even as scientists and engineers at PARC were inventing new computer-related tools, Xerox was settling a six-year antitrust proceeding involving its pathbreaking photocopying technologies on terms that compelled it to give patent licenses—some of them free—to its competitors. The result doubtless darkened the company's thoughts about assembling a robust patent portfolio in the computer field, particularly since federal courts at the time were not overly hospitable to the idea of software patents. But antitrust and intellectual property currents shift, and just a few years later, as copyright emerged as a potent doctrine for protecting software and the antitrust climate for intellectual property turned markedly more temperate, Xerox might have approached its innovations more aggressively.

Contemporary pressures for patent reform reveal a major fault line dividing intellectual asset companies. Electronics companies, the principal victims of weak patents and aggressive patent trolls, are pressing for higher patent standards and less draconian remedies, while pharmaceutical companies, which must often rely on a small handful of patents to protect their billion-dollar R&D investments, are lobbying for stronger patents. Other industry divisions are more complicated. On any given day, a single company may want a patent system that lets patents be easily obtained and broadly construed, as well as one that makes patents hard to obtain and construes them narrowly. In the *Polaroid* litigation, Kodak had a natural interest in stringent standards that would invalidate, or at least narrowly confine, Polaroid's patents. But as a major patent owner itself, the company was also interested in more generous patent standards. Fifteen years after *Polaroid,* Kodak was aggressively pressing its portfolio of patents in the field of digital imaging, filing lawsuits against Sony, the leading producer of digital cameras, and settling an earlier action against Sanyo with a license agreement.

COPYRIGHT. Copyright protects virtually all forms of expression, from novels, motion pictures, music, and dance to instruction manuals, maps, bookkeeping forms, and computer programs. The overriding object of copyright law is to make the greatest variety of entertainment and information products available to consumers at the lowest possible price. Technology, more than any other single force, has driven copyright's expansion. The first U.S. copyright act protected only books, maps, and charts. But as new technologies created new media for disseminating information and entertainment, record companies and film studios arrived at the copyright table, followed by, among others, software and semiconductor companies, each pressing Congress to protect their works. Nor does copyright expand only to encompass new forms of creativity. Copyright owners also go to Congress whenever a new technology emerges for exploiting copyrighted works—radio, television, cable, photocopying, satellite, the Internet—each time seeking an extension of their exclusive rights to embrace the markets opened by these technologies.

No copyrighted book, song, or movie can control a market the way Polaroid's patents controlled the market for instant photography or Robert Kearns's patent controlled the windshield wiper market. Because copyright protects only expression, not ideas, competitors are free to copy and exploit another's ideas, no matter how novel and valuable the ideas may be. A college textbook publisher, observing the success of another publisher's introductory economics text, will hire a team of editors and economics instructors to extract the uncopyrightable concepts that make the first text so popular, typically the book's style and conceptualization of materials (neither of which is protected by copyright), taking care to stay clear of the precise manner in which the earlier text organizes and expresses its ideas (which is protected by copyright). Just as Kodak did in retaining Frank Carr to examine Polaroid's patents, the textbook publisher will hire lawyers to write infringement opinions, meticulously parsing legal precedents to determine what elements the publisher can safely lift from the copyrighted text and what appropriations would lead to legal liability.

Political and cultural concerns over free speech have from the beginning kept copyright in check, and explain not only the law's prohibition against protection for ideas, but also the many safety valves that in compelling circumstances allow for free educational, scholarly, and other nonprofit uses of copyrighted works. Political pressures for free use—and a correspondingly less robust copyright—wax and wane. They have been on the rise since the turn of the present century, with the widely held (and mistaken) perception that copyright is improperly constraining creativity on the Internet; and they can be expected to persist until orderly, compensated licensing arrangements for the use of copyrighted content on the Internet replace the current free-for-all.

TRADEMARKS. Two forces, one historical, the other contemporary, today shape American trademark law—and consequently the business risk and reward from such assets as brand names and product packaging. Historically, trademark law's concern was to protect consumers from confusion as to the source of goods. (Trademark law evolved out of the old English law of fraud and passing off; when a customer orders Coca-Cola at a lunch counter and is served Brand X Cola instead, the Coca-Cola Company can—and does—sue for passing off.)

The contemporary trend in trademark law is to give legal force to the practice of brand extension, giving trademark owners rights not only in the markets where their brands first acquired fame, but in other markets as well. (When the Coca-Cola Company licenses "Coca-Cola" T-shirts, few purchasers believe the garments were produced by the company.) Under this so-called dilution doctrine, companies today enjoy plenary control not only over renowned brands like Kodak and Coca-Cola, but less famous brands as well, effectively creating a platform from which they can exploit the value of their brands through sales or third-party licensing across a range of goods and services. This is protection of information for its own sake, as a public good, much as patent law protects inventions and copyright law protects entertainment. However, while dilution is an ascendant theme in contemporary trademark law, the historical concern to prevent consumer confusion continues to figure prominently in legislative and judicial decisions.

Just as in the case of patents and copyrights, Congress and the courts have limited the scope of trademark protection to leave elbow room for competitors. A small but profitable niche exists for competitors to make collateral uses of well-known trademarks. An independent auto repair shop is free to call itself "Otto's Mercedes, Porsche, and BMW Repair," and the purveyor of cut-rate fragrances can advertise its products as being identical to the gilt-edged brands. In one case, where a company trumpeted its perfume to be an exact duplicate of Chanel No. 5, but at a fraction of the price, the trial court enjoined the company from using the Chanel name to promote its product, but the court of appeals reversed the decision. "By taking his 'free ride,'" the appellate court observed, "the copyist, albeit unintentionally, serves an important public interest by offering comparable goods at lower prices." As long as there was no patent on the formula for Chanel No. 5, and as long as the competing perfume was identical, the competitor was free to identify its product by referring to the Chanel trademark.

At the same time that dilution doctrine was revolutionizing trademark law by giving exclusive rights to brand names in yet untapped markets, another branch of trademark law, dealing with celebrity endorsements, was transforming itself into an entirely new body of law, the right of publicity. Starting in the 1970s, lawyers succeeded in convincing courts, and eventually state legislatures, to fashion a new intellectual property right to sustain investment in exploiting the names of celebrities such as sports figures and rock stars. The right of publicity today extends not only to exploitation of a celebrity's name, but to his or her likeness and voice as well. (Singer Tom Waits recovered over $2 million when Frito-Lay used a voice that sounded like his to advertise its Doritos corn chips.) In the United States and Canada alone, retail sales of products licensed by celebrities and their estates is today a $3 billion business.

Although intellectual asset companies are a force for change in all fields of intellectual property law, brand asset companies have a unique way of accomplishing legal change. The Coca-Cola Company enjoys trademark rights not only in the name "Coca-Cola," but also in its voluptuously configured glass bottle. The bottle became a valuable, legally protected trademark not because Congress or the courts first declared that product packages could be trademarks, but because the Coca-Cola Company first marketed the bottle *as if* it were a trademark; the Patent Office only later agreed to register it as one. Other companies followed the same route, treating sounds, shapes, colors, even fragrances as their proprietary trademarks before Congress, the courts, or the Patent Office expressly brought these new forms of brand identity under legal protection. Similarly, when companies extended their brand names into markets far from those in which they originally won their fame, such as automaker Porsche AG licensing its name for the manufacture of sunglasses, it was the courts that followed, holding that dilution doctrine gave them rights in those markets. The clear message to a company seeking to expand the scope of its rights in a brand name is to go to market first—and in a way that will ensure the desired legal response—and go to Congress or the courts only later.

TRADE SECRETS. As a rule, intellectual property law withholds protection from ideas. Because ideas are the building blocks for innovation, it is thought that to subject them to legal control would seriously curb the flow of new products and services. (Business method patents are the main exception to the rule that intellectual property does not protect ideas, but they are also a central target of contemporary attacks on excessive patent protection.) How, then, can a company profit from such pioneering ideas as the routing scheme behind the Federal Express overnight delivery service, eBay's online auction, or Bill James's advice to the Boston Red Sox on how to acquire players? The answer is secrecy.

Although secrecy will rarely last long enough for a company to reap the full value of its idea, it remains the principal means by which a company can secure the value of ideas for new products and services. When business writers cite outsized numbers to suggest the scale of intellectual assets in the modern economy—the claim, for example, that an estimated 80 percent of the value of the Standard & Poor's 500 companies consists of intangible assets—it is trade secrets that make up a substantial, if not dominating, portion of that number. Trade secrets encompass not only secret processes and formulas, but also the vast reserve of human capital that resides in such assets as customer lists, executive salary structure, competitive bids, inventory management systems, and the incalculable know-how that it takes to run a business.

Trade secret law serves the same societal interest in promoting private investment in technological innovation as does patent law. But, more so than with patents, trade secrets and associated know-how are where a company's intellectual property policy intersects its human resources policy. Decisions affecting one policy usually implicate decisions on the other. According to a 2000 study of start-ups in the Inc. 500 list of companies, over 70 percent of them were founded by people using ideas they had acquired at earlier jobs. Although case law and legislation have historically limited companies' attempts to hold their employees hostage through contract restrictions and trade secret injunctions, cracks have begun to appear in legal doctrine. In one case, a court adopted a rule of "inevitable disclosure" to bar a high-level PepsiCo beverage employee from joining Quaker Oats' Gatorade division, since PepsiCo was able to demonstrate a strong probability that the departing employee would disclose PepsiCo secrets to its competitor.

Among other objects, trade secret law will protect an invention while it is being readied for application to the Patent Office. But, with increasing frequency, trade secrets also offer an alternative to patent protection. Even with its massive patent portfolio, Eastman Kodak well understands the virtues of trade secrecy. According to company general counsel Gary Van Graafeiland, "Kodak happens to be a company that relies to a pretty fair degree on trade secrets." Otherwise, he said, "you create a road map for your competition by the patent applications you file."

One reason trade secrets have a lower legal profile than other intellectual assets is that trade secret law depends heavily on industry norms, the accumulated patterns of personnel and security practices in a particular industry or region. Another reason is that trade secret litigation is so often a last resort. Companies worry that competitors

will use the pretrial discovery process to pry out still more proprietary information. Even with court-enforced secrecy orders in place,
it is hard to keep information secret once it has become the subject
of litigation.

Companies that do venture into trade secret litigation often have
competitive objectives other than protecting the particular secret in issue. In 1997 Kodak sued a former company executive, charging that he
had leaked to Minnesota Mining and Manufacturing Company proprietary information about Kodak's process for making the plastic base
used in consumer film. Kodak also sued 3M and its film-making spin-
off, Imation Corp., under federal racketeering laws for stealing its secret processes and the blueprints for a film-making machine. The suit
alleged that 3M and its subsidiaries went so far as to provide the former Kodak executive with a wish list targeting specific Kodak technologies. But, several months later, Kodak purchased Imation's medical
imaging business, settling its trade secret lawsuit against Imation and 3M
as part of the deal.

INTERNET. Far more than any earlier technology for distributing information, the Internet emblemizes the nature of intellectual assets as
an inexhaustible public good. Like Thomas Jefferson's taper, the Internet
enables the simultaneous use of inventions, entertainment, and information by millions of users without hampering their use by millions of others. This, and the fact that the Internet has brought consumers
face-to-face with intellectual property owners as never before, has created popular pressure to reduce existing legal protections for intellectual
assets. At the same time, the Internet has given intellectual property
owners an unprecedented opportunity to carve out new distribution
channels and to target the marketing of their goods and services to individual consumer preference. By dramatically lowering entry barriers to
the distribution of intellectual goods, and shrinking lead time to Internet
time, the Internet has unleashed competitive and political pressures that
have in turn increased the instability of intellectual property rules. For
years to come, it will be the site not only of continuing clashes between
intellectual asset owners and users, but also of public and private ex-

perimentation with new ways to strike the intellectual property balance.

Internet patents have proved particularly problematic. Patents on such questionable inventions as Amazon.com's 1-Click purchasing tool and Priceline's reverse-auction method for Internet purchase of airline tickets have been used to control whole segments of the Internet's marketing infrastructure. Following a five-week trial, eBay suffered a $29.5 million judgment for infringing a patented method for using a credit card to lock in an online offer. In its 10-K report filed in March 2003, before the decision came down, eBay stated that "even if successful, our defense against this action will be costly and could divert our management's time. If the plaintiff were to prevail on any of its claims, we might be forced to pay significant damages and licensing fees, modify our business practices or even be enjoined from conducting a significant part of our U.S. business." These Internet forays have triggered a legal backlash that may eventually take the form of more rigorous patent standards, increased antitrust scrutiny, and possibly other antipatent measures.

For copyright owners, the Internet at once holds out a rich source of profit as digital rights management promises revenues from a vast new distribution channel, and at the same time presents the chilling prospect that free peer-to-peer sharing of entertainment products will wipe out paying markets, old and new, and turn this new arena into a free-for-all of unregulated copying by individual users. Record companies rejected overtures from Napster to convert its outlaw peer-to-peer service into a legitimate, licensed source of music, but, five years later, Warner Bros. Home Entertainment Group announced a deal with yet another peer-to-peer scofflaw, BitTorrent, to distribute Warner Bros. films legally over the Internet. For Internet service providers like Yahoo!, Google, and eBay, the Internet offers not only the opportunity to erect platforms for entertainment and shopping services but also the risk of copyright liability for facilitating unauthorized copying by users.

In the late 1990s, consumer product companies, accustomed to organizing their brand-name management around centuries-old principles of trademark law, were suddenly confronted by the new reality of Internet domain names. What does a trademark owner like Daimler-

Benz do when it discovers that a spoiler has adopted "Mercedes" as its global domain name, directing users interested in Mercedes automobiles to an unauthorized, and perhaps unflattering, site? Domain names so seriously disrupted the settled ways of conducting brand name business that the Internet Corporation for Assigned Names and Numbers hastily cobbled together a Uniform Domain Name Dispute Resolution Policy that contractually binds domain registrants to prescribed procedures for resolving trademark–domain name disputes.

GLOBAL MARKETS. For many companies, the revenues to be earned from exploiting an intellectual asset abroad will approach or exceed those to be earned at home. Foreign markets offer unique opportunities to price-discriminate in the sale of intellectual goods: selling high in some national markets, low in others, and employing legal importation restrictions to prevent arbitrage. However, because intellectual property rights and remedies are governed not by the law of the intellectual asset owner's home country but by the law of the country in which the asset is exploited, and because different countries strike the intellectual property balance differently, a company doing business abroad must attend to the details of local law as closely as it does to the law at home.

Kodak's attack on the validity of the Polaroid instant photography patents, which failed in the United States but succeeded in Germany, is just one example of the global dissonance of intellectual property rules. Johnson & Johnson's patent litigation with Boston Scientific over coronary stents is another. In December 2000, Johnson & Johnson won a $324.4 million patent infringement suit against Boston Scientific in Delaware; less than a year later, a German court ruled that Johnson & Johnson infringed on a patent licensed to Boston Scientific, while a Dutch court ruled that the same stents did not infringe. Microwave lamp producer Fusion Systems' frustrating encounters with the Japanese patent system in the late 1980s led to trade pressures from the United States, and ultimately to changes in Japanese practice. A warning from Fusion CEO Donald M. Spero, writing in the *Harvard Business Review* in 1990, remains pertinent to foreign intellectual property ventures today, and not only in Japan: "I believe that every CEO who does business in Japan must have a personal and complete understanding of the Japanese patent system, its hazards, the true costs of mistakes, and some guideposts for maneuvering through this perilous environment."

Intellectual asset owners interested in securing the value abroad of their patents, copyrights, trademarks, and trade secrets have regularly pressed for international harmonization of intellectual property standards, usually at the highest levels of protection. Countries like India that have historically been net importers of intellectual goods generally want little or no intellectual property protection for foreign goods within their borders. By contrast, countries like the United States that are net intellectual asset exporters want their goods to receive high levels of protection abroad, and lobby for international agreements that will ensure protection for their nationals comparable to what they receive at home.

Multilateral treaties aimed at intellectual property harmonization, first adopted in the late nineteenth century, attracted a widening membership over the course of the twentieth century. Because, however, these treaties lacked effective enforcement mechanisms, pressure mounted toward the end of the twentieth century for a multinational arrangement that would both heighten existing international standards and enforce them vigorously. The World Trade Organization's Agreement on Trade-Related Aspects of Intellectual Property Rights, with 150 members as of 2007, was the result.

U.S. trade officials may in the next several decades learn the wisdom of the maxim to be careful what one wishes for. A country's intellectual balance of trade can shift over time. The United States was a net intellectual property importer in the nineteenth century; it became a net exporter in the twentieth century; and it may, at least in some fields, become a net importer once again, as comparative advantage in research and development, as well as in the production of intellectual goods, moves to other regions, most prominently Asia. When this occurs, the strong treaty norms that the United States continues to fight for today will work against the new balance of intellectual trade deficits, as U.S. consumers pay increased amounts for innovations from abroad. But what may be bad for America is not necessarily bad for

American companies. Smart American companies like Cisco, Hewlett-Packard, and Microsoft have already observed the nascent shift in comparative intellectual asset advantage and established thriving research and development facilities in China and elsewhere in Asia.

Mapping Legal Change to Reduce Legal Uncertainty

Technological change and shifting social and economic currents regularly disrupt the patent, copyright, trademark, and trade secret rules that protect intellectual assets. When such disruptions occur, the paradox of intellectual assets—that without property rights these assets will be underproduced, but with property rights they will be underused—deprives legislators and judges of steady compass points to guide their lawmaking. The resulting instability and unpredictability of intellectual property law presents a special challenge to intellectual asset companies, large and small. But if lawmakers lack firm guideposts, markers do exist, as do best practices, to guide managers in anticipating the level and direction of change in intellectual property law. Precedent—how lawmakers have altered these rules in the past—is one guide; so, too, are developments in related fields and shifts in popular sentiment.

2

======

Patents

Companies in the business of invention not only own patents, they infringe them—a fact that invariably complicates decisions on how, and how much, to invest in producing new products. In theory, the investment guidelines are straightforward. The prospect of obtaining a patent and enforcing it against competitors will draw research and development toward inventions that fall within the scope of the Patent Act and are likely to meet the act's standards for protection, just as the risk of infringement will draw investment away from too closely emulating the patented inventions of others.

Neither goal is easily attained. The Patent Act's description of the five classes of protectible inventions is straightforward enough: "any new and useful process, machine, manufacture, or composition of matter, or any new and useful improvement thereof." (The first manufacturer of aspirin tablets could have sought a patent on the "process" by which it combined the product's chemical components; on the "machine" designed to produce the aspirin tablets; on the tin container—"manufacture"—in which it sold the aspirin; on the aspirin itself as a "composition of matter"; and on its subsequent addition of a buffering to the aspirin as an "improvement.") The standards that the act imposes on these five classes of invention are also unequivocal. (The aspirin producer would have to demonstrate to the U.S. Patent Office that each of the inventions was "novel" in the sense that it was not previously known or used by others; "nonobvious" in the sense that it would not have been obvious to an ordinarily skilled worker in the field to make the invention; and "useful" in the sense that the invention achieves some positive result.)

In practice, certainty is more elusive. For more than a decade, courts divided on whether computer programs came within one of the Patent Act's five classes of invention, the Supreme Court weighing in on the question no fewer than three times. The nonobviousness standard, as Kodak discovered in *Polaroid v. Kodak*, is even less predictable. In 2006, the Patent Office reviewed 332,000 applications, granting patents on 54 percent of them, often only after an initial rejection of the application and subsequent negotiation between the applicant and the Patent Office examiner. Nor is approval by the Patent Office an assurance of validity. A patent owner that sues for infringement of its patent in court will almost invariably meet the defense that the Patent Office erred in granting the patent, and that the patent is consequently invalid. Only 1.5 percent of issued patents become the subject of litigation; only 0.1 percent are litigated to trial; and courts hold about 45 percent of all litigated patents invalid.

As Kodak also discovered in the *Polaroid* litigation, it is no easy matter to avoid patent infringement, even after engaging experienced counsel to analyze a competitor's patents to determine whether a product falls within the scope of the competitor's patent claims. The multitude of patents that crowd at least some fields of invention make it impracticable to discover them all in order to avoid infringing any one. The best that a company in the business of invention can do is to try to predict whether patent law standards will rise or fall over the life of an invention and, in light of these changing standards, to estimate which side of the patent blade—protection or infringement—will cut more deeply into its investment decisions.

By most measures, the American patent system today is poised to cut back on protection. In March 2006 a lawyer for the Business Software Alliance, an electronics industry trade group, observed that "five or six years ago there wasn't a single CEO in the technology business who actually thought about patents," but that today "every CEO worries about patents." The worries are well founded. By 2005, the growth of patent litigation outpaced all other forms of federal litigation: from 1995 to 2005 the number of patent lawsuits grew by 78 percent as against a 12 percent rise in the total number of federal case filings over that period. (Copyright lawsuits rose by 24 percent during this period and trademark lawsuits by 29 percent; a decade earlier these cases far outnumbered patent cases, but by 2004 patent suits were close to the most litigated of the three.) A September 2005 survey by the Intellectual Property Owners Association showed that almost three-quarters of member respondents expected the resources required for patent litigation to grow over the next three years.

Increasing numbers of issued patents—from 113,834 in 1995 to 157,717 in 2005—and their decreasing quality are also part of the gathering storm. (The 2005 IPO survey found roughly half its company respondents dissatisfied with patent quality.) Yet another indication that patent protection is poised for a cyclical downswing is that, after more than twenty years in which it only occasionally reviewed decisions from the expansionist Court of Appeals for the Federal Circuit, the U.S. Supreme Court has in recent years intensified its review—and reversal—of decisions from the lower court.

There is no surer sign that change is coming than the emergence in policy discussions of a villain. The burden of popular criticism of the American patent system today has fallen on the shoulders of companies that acquire patents not to manufacture and distribute inventions, but to license the patents, under threat of litigation if necessary, to companies that have unwittingly crossed the patent's boundaries. These are the widely vilified "patent trolls"—a term coined by an Intel lawyer at the time his company was sued for $7 billion by a small Chicago patent company, because trolls live under bridges that they did not themselves build and demand payment of a toll to cross them. The demonization of these patent owners, particularly by companies like Intel that both generate and practice their own patents, is unsurprising. When one manufacturer sues another for patent infringement, each has a stranglehold on the other, and the not uncommon resolution is for the two companies to settle the lawsuit by cross-licensing patents between themselves, not only releasing the stranglehold but enabling each to improve its products by incorporating its competitor's technology. However, because a patent troll has no manufacturing business that is itself subject to patent lawsuits from others, it has no need for a cross license and can hold out for a sometimes extortionate amount of cash.

During the last major assault on the American patent system, in the 1930s, critics identified patents with the evils of industrial monopoly. However, patents are "monopolies" only in the sense that any property right confers exclusive rights on its owner. If the patent "monopoly" has few of the baleful effects of industrial monopoly, it does intrude more deeply into a nation's economy than do other forms of intellectual property. The dominating economic importance of patents stems in part from the scope of their subject matter. Not only can patents extend to "anything under the sun that is made by man," as a U.S. Senate report put it, but they protect the very functionalities—mechanical, chemical, biological, electronic—that lie at the heart of industrial growth and productivity. A patent entitles its owner to control virtually every economically valuable use of its invention over the life of the patent (twenty years from the date it is applied for). And these rights are absolute. Unlike the copyright owner who must show that an accused infringer actually copied his work, or the trademark owner who must prove consumer confusion, or the trade secret owner who must prove a breach of confidence or other form of improper appropriation, a patent owner need prove only that the alleged infringer made, sold, used, or imported the patented invention or offered to do any of these acts.

American patent law operates on a winner-take-all principle, and one effect of lowered patent standards is to magnify the principle's defects. As between two or more companies working toward the same inventive goal, it is the one that first conceives the invention—has some idea of a useful result to be achieved and some specific method for achieving that result—and reduces the invention to practice that in the United States will receive the patent. (In other countries the patent goes not to the first inventor but to the one who first files his application in the national patent office.) The result is that laggard rivals lose twice: not only will they be denied a patent on an invention for which they may have spent on research and development as much as or more than the company that won the patent race, but, should they attempt to recoup that investment by making, using, or selling the invention, they will also be subject to an injunction upon suit by the patent owner. The pioneering telephone patents were the object of such a race. Although Elisha Gray filed in the U.S. Patent Office on the same day as Alexander Graham Bell, Bell was able to prove that he was the first inventor, and was consequently entitled to a monopoly over his invention to the exclusion of everyone else, including Gray. In ideal circumstances a laggard company will drop out of the patent race once it learns what research and development projects its competitors have under way and how far along they are toward completion. But most companies cloak their research and development as well as the early stages of their patent application in secrecy, and a competitor's efforts to peek behind that cloak will be rewarded with civil—or even criminal—liability for trade secret theft.

At the threshold of the next great cycle in patent protection, the hard question is not whether, or even when, patent law will begin to scale back, but how. Following major reports from the Federal Trade Commission in 2003 and the National Research Council in 2004 on current difficulties with the American patent system, Congress drafted proposals that set patent policy on the path of reform. The path is elusive, not because of any lack of well-tried solutions, for lawmakers in the United States could easily draw on techniques long used in other countries to blunt the edge of patent law that cuts into competitive research. Many countries, for example, decline to give the winner of a patent race an injunction against the inventor who places second or further back in the field, and instead give the runners-up a compulsory license entitling them to practice the invention upon payment of a reasonable royalty to the patent owner. The reason reform in the United States is hard is that, while some important industries—most notably electronics—regularly feel the edge of the patent blade that cuts into competitive research, other no less important industries (the pharmaceutical industry is the most vocal) depend upon the other edge of that blade to secure the billion-dollar investments they require to develop and bring new drugs to market. As you will read later on in the chapter, the source of both concerns traces to legal developments, beginning in the 1980s, that transformed the impact of patents on American economic life.

Cycles of Protection: 1623–1952

The origins of contemporary patent law lie in the English Crown's grants of privileges to foreign tradesmen and craftsmen in the fourteenth and the fifteenth centuries to spur the adoption of modern manufacturing methods. For example, in 1331 Edward III issued letters patent (the term means open letters addressed to the public) to John Keyes of Flanders to introduce advanced weaving techniques into England. By the sixteenth century, these privileges had evolved into manufacturing monopolies given to subjects as well as to foreigners, such as the grant by Edward VI to one Henry Smythe of a twenty-year monopoly on the production of Normandy glass within the realm. To ensure that they served the purposes of the Crown, these later patents regularly included a revocation clause, entitling the sovereign to revoke the grant any time he found it to be "inconvenient or prejudicial to the realm," most typically because of the patentee's failure to continue practicing the invention.

Inevitably, the appetite for commercial monopolies expanded beyond the bounds of true invention, and by the late sixteenth century, monopoly grants to court favorites and royal factories for the production of such staples as vinegar and starch joined the earlier Crown grants and privileges for new forms of manufacture, an abuse that led in 1623 to the Statute of Monopolies. While outlawing nonproductive patents, such as those for vinegar and starch, the new law excepted monopolies for true inventions. And to ensure that only worthy inventions received protection, the statute imposed conditions that substantially anticipated those enforced by patent statutes today—among them that patents will be granted only to the first and true inventor, and only for products not already in use at the time of the grant. The statute limited the patent term to fourteen years or fewer so that, since apprentices at the time served for seven years, the patent would effectively protect the master inventor over the course of two generations of trainees.

The American colonies, and later the states, followed the English practice of awarding patents through private acts passed in response to individual petitions, while imposing conditions to ensure that the patents were practiced in the public interest. However, the first U.S. patent law was a general rather than a private act, and authorized patents for "any useful art, manufacture, engine, machine, or device, or any improvement therein not before known or used." A patent board composed of the secretary of state, the secretary of war, and the attorney general would examine the claimed invention and, if it was "sufficiently useful and important," would grant a patent for a term of up to fourteen years. The burden of examining patent applications soon proved too heavy, and in 1793 a new federal patent law substituted the simple act of registration for the previous examination system. Although the new registration system was less costly to administer than the old, it had its own deficiencies, and over time it became evident that the benefits of an examination system—a government-issued document on which inventors and competitors alike could rely to specify the precise scope of the patent's claims—outweighed its costs. In 1836, Congress reinstated the examination system and fixed the patent term at fourteen years with a seven-year renewal period. To the chagrin of many observers, the U.S. Patent Act in force today strays little from the structure and principles of the 1836 act.

The American patent system thrived across the nineteenth century, particularly in its last decades, with the U.S. Supreme Court regularly deciding several patent cases each year. (The decisions generally upheld the patent owner's claims.) The patents that came before American courts during this period—among them the barbed wire patent, the Morse telegraph patent, and the Bell telephone patent—helped to define the law as well as mark the period's extraordinary industrial growth.

From the 1850s through the 1860s, while patents flourished in America, they came under attack in Europe, where the Dutch repealed their patent law in 1969 and the Swiss rejected proposals to enact one. The debates in Europe broadly ventilated the arguments for and against a patent system. To the argument that a man has a natural right to his own ideas, one that should extend against their theft by others, came the answer that more than one person can create an idea, and that to give a patent to one person is to bar all the others from using what they themselves created. Inventions may be necessary to industrial progress and patents may be necessary to stimulate invention, but, the critics argued, once the administrative and institutional costs of a patent system are taken into account, cheaper ways exist to produce inventions. To the argument that without a patent the inventor will keep his invention secret, depriving society of valuable information, the critics offered two responses: few inventions can be kept secret for long, and even if one inventor managed to do so, another would soon invent it independently.

The Europeans were not alone in their reservations about patents—recall Thomas Jefferson's grudging acceptance of patents as a solution to the problem of public goods—and it required only the right historical moment for this skepticism to surface in America. That moment was the Great Depression. In 1938, Congress created the Temporary National Economic Committee in response to a message from President Franklin D. Roosevelt calling for an examination of the concentration of economic power in the United States and its negative impact on the American economy; among the topics to be considered was the possible "amendment of the patent laws to prevent their use to suppress inventions, and to create industrial monopolies." When the TNEC disbanded almost three years later, among its recommendations were the adoption of compulsory licenses to prevent the suppression of patents and also "to provide for their availability for use in an equitable manner in any industry where they are a major factor"; limitation of the patent term to twenty years from the date of filing; and consolidation of all patent appeals from the regional circuit courts of appeals to a single specialized patent court.

By 1952, when Congress enacted the first major revision of the Patent Act since 1870, the postwar economic boom had reduced Depression-era pressures for TNEC-style patent reform, and the 1952 act reflects no traces of the earlier concerns for industrial monopolies; indeed, over objections from the Justice Department's Antitrust Division, the act extended the patent owner's rights over unpatented subject matter used in connection with patented inventions. The revised law made no concessions at all to the TNEC proposal for compulsory

licenses, and the move to a single court for patent appeals did not occur until the creation of the Court of Appeals for the Federal Circuit in
1982. Alteration of the patent term to twenty years from the date of
application, rather than seventeen years from the date of issue, did not
occur until 1995 as part of U.S. implementation of the WTO TRIPs
Agreement.

The TNEC's deliberations and proposals had a greater impact on
the patent climate in the courts, particularly the Supreme Court, dramatically altering patent owners' expectations about both the validity
and infringement of their patents. The inventiveness standard required of patented subject matter was particularly responsive to popular currents. The number of patents held valid and infringed by U.S.
courts of appeal—43 percent in 1928, 35 percent in 1929—fell to 19
percent in 1938, shortly after the TNEC hearings, and dropped further, to 10 percent, following a 1941 Supreme Court decision, *Cuno
Engineering v. Automatic Devices*, requiring that, for a patent to be
valid, the invention must display a "flash of creative genius." (In the
Cuno case, the Court specifically cited a TNEC study to justify the new
standard as necessary to suppress "a class of speculative schemers who
make it their business to watch the advancing wave of improvement,
and gather its foam in the form of patent monopolies.") The proportion
of valid and infringed patents fell further, to 7 percent, in 1952, following another stiffening of patent standards by the Supreme Court. In
one 1949 case, Justice Robert Jackson, dissenting, complained that
"the only patent that is valid is one which this Court has not been able
to get its hands on." In response, the 1952 act relaxed the standard of
invention, and, starting in 1954, judicial validity findings began to rise
to their pre-TNEC levels.

The High Protectionists Take Charge: 1980–2005

Several events combined in the 1980s to enlarge the scope and power
of American patents. In 1982 Congress created the Court of Appeals
for the Federal Circuit to hear appeals from trial court patent infringement decisions across the country and to replace with a single national
standard the patchwork of patentability standards previously applied

by the regional courts of appeal. Whether intended by Congress or not, the newly harmonized standard turned out to be more favorable to patent owners than those previously applied by many if not most of the regional courts of appeal; indeed, the CAFC has tipped the patent scales in favor of patent owners generally. The great irony, of course, is that an institution proposed by the TNEC four decades earlier, presumably to stabilize rigorous patent standards, has had exactly the opposite effect.

Support for patent owners came from other quarters as well. In 1981, under the leadership of Assistant Attorney General William F. Baxter, the U.S. Justice Department overturned antitrust restrictions on research and development collaborations and rejected earlier rules constraining patent licenses—the so-called Nine No-Nos—such as prohibitions on license terms that required patent licensees to purchase unpatented materials from the licensor. Congress undertook major new initiatives to use patents to spur industrial growth, among them the 1980 Bayh-Dole Act, which fostered university-industry collaborations by making it possible for universities to patent the results of federally funded research. Congress also added tax deductions for R&D expenses. Finally, two U.S. Supreme Court decisions in the early 1980s, one opening the door to patents for computer programs, the other holding that a live, man-made organism could qualify for patent protection, established new high-water marks for an already ascendant patent system.

Software Patents

Until March 3, 1981, when the U.S. Supreme Court in *Diamond v. Diehr* for the first time upheld a patent on a computer program, the patent status of computer software had been in doubt. Two years earlier, when Dan Bricklin, the twenty-eight-year-old Harvard Business School student who created Visicalc, the first electronic spreadsheet, asked his lawyer about obtaining a patent on the invention, he was told that the prospect was too remote to justify the expense of an application. According to his collaborator, Robert Frankston, "We should have patented the spreadsheet idea. But at the time, our lawyer did not think it would be worth the few thousand dollars it would cost to try."

With the advantage of lead time, the two were able to sell half a million copies of the program, but after that, the appearance of competitive spreadsheets—any one of which might have infringed their patent had they obtained one—consumed Visicalc's market share.

If the aim of patent law is to protect new and useful products, and if the core of invention in computer programs lies in their utility, why did the Supreme Court take until 1981 to open the door to patent protection? The most likely answer is resources. Determinations of novelty—that no one previously knew or used the invention—and nonobviousness, the two central conditions of patentability, require expert examiners to analyze the relevant prior art, and the Patent Office had neither an organized database of prior art on software-related inventions nor a sufficient cadre of software-trained examiners to conduct these analyses. The Patent Office's solution was to sidestep these limitations by ruling, on increasingly questionable grounds, that a computer program simply did not qualify as a "process, machine, manufacture, or composition of matter, or any new and useful improvement thereof "—a determination that it could make without a single examiner having to assess the prior art. The Court of Customs and Patent Appeals, the predecessor to the Court of Appeals for the Federal Circuit, was more concerned about the integrity of patent law than about the Patent Office's information or personnel shortages, and regularly overturned these unpatentability decisions, sending the cases back to the Patent Office for determination of novelty and nonobviousness.

Appeals to the U.S. Supreme Court only stirred the confusion. In its first software case, in 1972, the Court ruled against the patentability of a process for converting numbers from one form to another in a general-purpose computer on the ground that a patent for the process would give the inventor a monopoly over the mathematical formula that underlay the process. But, the Court added cryptically, such a process might be patentable if it transformed a physical article "to a different state or thing." Six years later, the Court again rejected a software patent, this time for a method to be executed by a computer for calculating and updating alarm limits used to signal abnormalities in the catalytic conversion process. The Court acknowledged that the proposed patent presented no danger of preempting the algorithm involved, but concluded that the patent owner was seeking protection for a naked principle, not a practical result. As it did in the earlier case, the Court intimated how an astute patent applicant could redraft its software claims to bring them within the statutory subject matter: "An inventive *application* of the principle may be patented."

Finally, in a case that came before the Court three years later, the patent applicant got the nuances right, claiming not a bare algorithm, but rather "a process for molding raw, uncured synthetic rubber into cured precision products." To be sure, the process embodied an algorithm—the Arrhenius equation used in calculating the cure time in the rubber molding process—but subordinated the algorithm to the practical operation of the process, using a digital computer to solve the Arrhenius equation, including constant measurement of temperatures inside the rubber molding press. Form, not substance, prevailed, and in *Diamond v. Diehr* the Supreme Court read the patent claims to encompass no more than a process for molding rubber products and transforming an article "to a different state or thing." It was not, the Court concluded, "an attempt to patent a mathematical formula." So long as the invention produced concrete results—and, of course, passed the novelty and nonobviousness tests—a patent could protect it.

Once the Supreme Court opens the door to a new form of intellectual property subject matter, it is commonly only a matter of time before lower courts and the Patent Office loosen the standard for protection. Software patents were no exception. In 1994, the Court of Appeals for the Federal Circuit ruled that a patent applicant could effectively bring its software within the traditional category of "machine" simply by describing his invention to include the software running on a general-purpose computer. Finally, in 1995, the Patent Office retreated from its stern antisoftware position and announced that it would treat computer programs as patentable subject matter as long as they were embodied in a tangible medium, such as floppy diskettes. The development forced the office to confront the historical exclusion of protection for business methods, such as techniques for pricing stocks or evaluating new financial instruments: What if an applicant embedded its business method in a computer program?

In *State Street Bank & Trust Co. v. Signature Financial Group*, the

Federal Circuit in 1998 upheld the patentability of a claim for a data processing system that implemented a "hub and spoke" mutual fund pricing system, finding the required "useful, concrete, and tangible result" in the determination of a "final share price momentarily fixed for recording and reporting purposes" calculated by a computer. A flood of applications for financial product software followed, including Cantor Fitzgerald's applications for "Methods and Systems for Trading Futures Contracts for Intangible Assets," "Systems and Methods for Bid/Offer Spread Trading," and "System and Methods for Shifting Bids and Offers in a Trading Interface"; Chase Manhattan's "System and Method for Executing Deposit Transactions over the Internet" and "Supply Chain Financing System and Method"; and GE's "Method and System for Developing a Time Horizon Based Investment Strategy" and "System and Method for Automated Risk-Based Pricing of a Vehicle Warranty Insurance Policy." And if the Patent Office will grant patents to financial strategies, why not to legal strategies? By late 2006, it had granted forty-eight patents for tax-reduction techniques, with many more applications pending.

The problem is that while patents for business method "inventions" have sailed through the Patent Office, few are likely to meet the objective standards of novelty and nonobviousness set by the courts. Just as the Patent Office had limited resources to examine software applications through the 1970s and beyond, today it has neither the systematic and comprehensive collection of prior art against which to compare these putative inventions nor the trained examining corps needed to conduct the comparisons. When these patents reach the courts in infringement cases, the harsh and searching light of the adversary process can be expected to reveal their defects, resulting in their judicial invalidation. As law professor Richard Gruner, a former IBM patent lawyer, put it in the title of an important article on the subject, "Everything Old Is New Again."

Patenting Life

In 1980, the Supreme Court opened the door to patent protection for yet another controversial category of inventions: living organisms. The hurdles to protection were high. Congress and the courts had long excluded patent protection for products or phenomena of nature, and there was also a decades-old precedent from the antipatent era of the 1930s and 1940s that had rejected a patent on a mixture of bacteria used to inoculate legumes on the ground that "the qualities of these bacteria, like the heat of the sun, electricity, or the qualities of metals, are part of the storehouse of knowledge of all men."

The invention before the Court in 1980, from GE researcher Ananda Chakrabarty, was genetically engineered bacteria capable of breaking down crude oil. The Patent Office examiner had ruled the invention ineligible for a patent on the ground that it was a product of nature and also because it was a living organism. An appeals board inside the Patent Office set aside the first ground for rejection—as manipulated by Chakrabarty, the bacteria could hardly be considered a product of nature—but sustained the second: living organisms could not be patented. The appeal, when it reached the Supreme Court, was destined to produce a landmark. In laboratories across the country, recombinant DNA research was fueling a new biotechnology industry with the promise of innovative, lifesaving drugs, and major industry forces and research institutions—among them the Pharmaceutical Manufacturers Association, Genentech, and the University of California—filed amicus briefs with the Supreme Court in support of patents for life forms.

The Supreme Court's 5–4 decision in *Diamond v. Chakrabarty* endorsed patents for living organisms in the most ringing terms, underlining the importance of an openhanded patent system for business investment in new technologies. Rejecting the argument that resolution of the patentability of inventions such as Chakrabarty's should be left to Congress, the Court responded that the general terms of the Patent Act excluded any ambiguity on the point: "The subject matter provisions of the patent law have been cast in broad terms to fulfill the constitutional and statutory goal of promoting 'the Progress of Science and the useful Arts' with all that means for the social and economic benefits envisioned by Jefferson."

With *Chakrabarty* on the books, the progression from bacteria to higher life forms was all but inevitable. In 1985 the Patent Office Board of Appeals ruled that plant varieties were patentable, and in 1987 that a genetically engineered species of oyster was patentable subject matter. Religious and animal rights groups, which had voiced their objections in an amicus brief in *Chakrabarty*, continued to press their position, particularly when the Patent Office announced that it would consider patent applications for vertebrates, and issued its first such patent, in 1988, on the "Harvard Mouse," or Oncomouse, genetically engineered by a Harvard researcher for enhanced susceptibility to cancer, and consequently of particular use in cancer research. In other countries, religious and philosophical objections slowed Harvard's efforts to obtain a patent on the Oncomouse, and although the university eventually obtained patents in Europe and Japan, Canada's Supreme Court ruled, seventeen years after an application was filed there, that Parliament was better placed than the judiciary to decide the patent status of animals.

While the *Chakrabarty* case was still making its way through the courts, several other patent applications for biotechnology inventions awaited word from the Supreme Court on whether inventions in this new field were patentable. One, which named Stanford researcher Stanley N. Cohen and University of California–San Francisco researcher Herbert W. Boyer as coinventors, was for a method of joining and replicating DNA of different species developed by the two scientists in the early 1970s. The technique could convert bacteria into genetic factories for producing a wide range of otherwise elusive substances, such as insulin and hormones.

Although the head of Stanford's Office of Technology Licensing had to persuade Cohen and Boyer to apply for a patent, the investor community recognized the invention as a breakthrough with potential for wide commercial application long before the first Cohen-Boyer patent issued. In April 1976, three months after meeting with Boyer, venture capitalist Robert Swanson formed Genentech, Inc. to exploit the new technology. Less than two weeks later, with the patent still pending, Swanson sought a worldwide nonexclusive license from Stanford and UCSF to use the Cohen-Boyer technology, as well as an exclusive license to produce one class of hormones. Recognizing that the technology was foundational, the two universities agreed only to a nonexclusive license. When Genentech went public on October 14,

1980, the company's stock price immediately rose from $35 to $88. On December 2, 1980, less than six months after the *Chakrabarty* decision, the Patent Office issued the first of the Cohen-Boyer recombinant DNA patents.

At the time Stanley Cohen and Herbert Boyer developed their breakthrough method for combining DNA sequences in bacterial plasmids, the opportunities for universities and university-based inventors to license the results of federally funded research were problematic at best. Through the 1970s, federal policy in the area was a patchwork. In the case of some inventions, the federal agency that sponsored the underlying research would place the results in the public domain; in other cases, the university could obtain a patent on the results, but could offer only nonexclusive licenses. Denied exclusivity, few businesses had the incentive to make the further investment required to bring the product to market. Exceptions were sometimes made. A university that wanted to patent research results could petition the funding agency to have ownership transferred to it, and in some cases universities negotiated institutional patent agreements that streamlined the transfer process. It was such an institutional agreement between Stanford and the National Institutes of Health, which had partially funded the Cohen-Boyer research, that made it possible to grant commercial licenses for the patented method.

In 1980, spurred by concerns that potentially valuable results of federally sponsored research were not being commercially exploited, Congress passed the Bayh-Dole Act, making it possible for small businesses and nonprofit organizations such as universities to retain patent ownership of inventions produced under federally funded projects. (With much less fanfare, Congress expanded Bayh-Doyle's coverage in 1983 to include large companies.) In the case of universities and other nonprofit organizations, one of the conditions required for patent ownership was that the contractor share royalties with the inventor and devote any remaining royalties to scientific research or education. Twenty-five years later, in fiscal year 2004, technology licensing deals generated more than $1.03 billion for U.S. colleges and universities.

The convergence of government, university, and business interests added new drama to the licensing of biotechnology inventions. In the case of the Harvard Oncomouse, DuPont had in 1981 contributed $6 million to support Harvard researcher Philip Leder's use of the recombinant DNA techniques that produced the mouse. Although the National Institutes of Health also funded Leder over this period, DuPont had negotiated for an exclusive license to any patents resulting from the research, and when the patent issued, DuPont charged only modest license fees for use of the Oncomouse in basic research. In the mid-1990s, however, DuPont sought more substantial license fees from commercial users, and though its licenses to university researchers remained free, the company imposed burdensome reporting requirements. Continuing friction between DuPont and university researchers over these license terms required NIH to broker new, more liberal terms for NIH scientists or grantees so long as the research did not serve commercial interests.

The aims and methods of science and commerce do not always coincide, and critics both inside and outside the academy regularly attack university patent and licensing practices. One objection is that the public should not be required to pay twice for federally funded research—first in tax dollars, and later in the increased prices paid for patented goods. (This objection overlooks the fact that research subsidies often fail to support the considerable expense of product development.) Another objection is that commercial objects have displaced dispassionate scientific judgment in setting the agenda for university research. Scientific principles of openness and early publication will sometimes conflict with patent law's requirements of prefiling secrecy, and in clashes between the two, patents do not always win. U.S. patent law, which allows an inventor to publish his inventions for as long as a year before he or she applies for a patent, strikes a rough compromise between science and commerce. But foreign legal systems offer no such grace period and will bar a patent for any invention that has been published before the inventor applies for the patent. Although journal publication of the Cohen-Boyer results did not bar a patent in the United States—the publication came within the U.S. Patent Act's one-year grace period—it did forfeit the possibility of obtaining patents in other countries.

✸ ✸ ✸

The transformation of patent law that began in the 1980s was about more than just software and biotech. The Patent and Trademark Office came to view fee-paying patent applicants, not the American public, as its "customers," and granted an increasing proportion of patents on a growing number of applications. Where the period from 1930 to 1982 saw an increase in patent grants of less than 1 percent in each year, the period from 1983 to 2002 saw an average annual increase of 5.7 percent, far exceeding the grant rates in Europe and Japan. For each application, examiners spend on average eighteen hours over two to three years reading the application, searching and comparing prior art, and negotiating with the applicant. But the Patent Office's employee bonus system implicitly rewards examiners for allowing, not rejecting, applications.

The Court of Appeals for the Federal Circuit made it easier to enforce these patents and to obtain monetary and permanent injunctive relief against infringers, and also to obtain preliminary injunctive relief against alleged infringers. Books such as *Rembrandts in the Attic* and *Edison in the Boardroom* encouraged companies to search through their portfolios for patents that could be licensed and, if not licensed, litigated. Because patent owners can file infringement cases in any U.S. judicial district where the allegedly infringing products are sold, "rocket dockets"—most notably the U.S. district court in the small town of Marshall, Texas—sprang up, offering patent claimants speedy discovery, early trial dates, and fast trials.

Pharmaceuticals versus Electronics: The Battle for Patent Law's Next Frontier

In *Innovation and Its Discontents,* an incisive examination of the American patent system, economists Adam B. Jaffe and Josh Lerner trace the historical arc of patent protection in the United States and observe that "the 'pro-patent' policy changes of the 1980s and 1990s can be seen as the inevitable, perhaps even desirable, historical 'backswing' after a long period of weakening patents." But in their view, this "does not capture the totality of what has occurred." Rather, "what has happened is the combination of a strengthening of patent rights with a weakening of the standards for the granting of patents. There are no natural or historical roots for this particular combination of changes. There is no evidence that anyone considered the likely effects of combining stronger patents with easier-to-get patents. When we then add in a final factor—that the changes manifested themselves most dramatically in technologically and economically crucial sectors such as software and biotech—we have the unusual combination of circumstances necessary for a 'perfect storm,' a complex and intensifying policy mess rather than a gently swinging pendulum."

The great upsurge in patent scope and enforcement over the past quarter century has divided patent industries into two warring camps. On the one side are the high protectionists, led by the pharmaceutical companies, whose business model of investing hundreds of millions of dollars in risky research and development aimed at producing a few blockbuster drugs argues for high standards of patentability and vigorous enforcement. On the other side are the low protectionists, led by electronics and software companies, whose pattern is to invest modestly in developing large numbers of incremental advances, few of which present any risk of not working or require the twenty-year patent term or the robust array of rights that are a necessity for drug companies. Also, because software advances are typically incremental, and software patents are so much more numerous than pharmaceutical patents, they create hazards of innocent infringement for software producers overall, which is why electronics companies argue for lower, less vigorous patent enforcement, including relief from injunctions and curbs on litigation. This confrontation between two important American industries promises that patent reform will not only be halting, but subject to the vagaries of political life. So long as the present tensions remain unresolved, instability will continue as a salient feature of American patent law.

Some of the problems of overpatenting can be at least partly resolved through private agreements. One is the problem presented by "thickets" of mutually blocking patents. Carl Shapiro, one of the country's leading patent economists, has described these patent thickets as "a dense web of overlapping intellectual property rights that a company must hack its way through in order to actually commercialize new technology." They are a particular obstacle in the electronics industry, where the sheer numbers of patents will often make it impracticable if not impossible for a company to identify, much less analyze, all of the patents that may touch on its own inventive activity and to evaluate a patent's validity and the possibility of infringement.

The only thing new about patent thickets is their number and density. In the early twentieth century, research and development in commercial radio technologies produced hundreds of patents that enabled each patent-owning company to hold up development by the others. Nor is the business solution to patent thickets—cross-licensing among patent owners—particularly novel. During this same period, at the initiative of the U.S. Navy, which was concerned that the British Marconi firm would dominate international wireless communications, several leading patent owners formed the Radio Corporation of America to acquire rights under Marconi's U.S. patents and to cross-license rights under other patent portfolios, with each of the patent owners becoming an RCA shareholder. At one time, over two thousand patents filled the RCA pool.

Sometimes cross licenses are entered into ad hoc, with one company cross-licensing its portfolio to another; if one portfolio is more valuable than the other, money will change hands. Other times, as in the case of RCA almost a century ago, cross licenses will be structured as a patent pool. In 2005 about twenty companies pooled their patents in order to cross license rights to advances in radio frequency identification technology that would replace the use of bar codes to check the flow of goods through a supply chain; licenses would be available to interested companies on terms described as "fair, reasonable and nondiscriminatory." The consortium scaled its royalty payments to patent owners in proportion to their inventions' value to the pool.

Some problems with the patent system are so abusive and pervasive that reform has attracted little serious objection from any quarter. One such abuse involved manipulation of the Patent Act's requirement that the Patent Office keep patent applications secret until a patent issues (if a patent is ultimately denied, the invention remains the inventor's trade secret) and its provision for "continuations" under which an applicant could extend the pendency of his application—and expand the scope of the application—for as long as thirty years or even more. The abusive tactic was periodically to file for continuations that effectively expanded the secret application to encompass new systems or devices made by others so that, when the patent finally issued, the owner could sue an entirely unsuspecting manufacturer of goods claimed to be covered by the patent. Because these patents surfaced unnoticed from the deep, they got the name "submarine patents."

No one played the patent system's secrecy card better than Jerome Lemelson and his lawyer, Gerald Hosier. As one of Lemelson's former lawyers quipped, "in many cases, Lemelson didn't patent inventions. . . . He invented patents." His pursuit and licensing of patents, which by 2001 had reportedly netted him $1.5 billion in royalties, began modestly, with a $2 million settlement from Sony in 1974 and a $5 million license negotiated with IBM in 1981, but shifted into high gear in the early 1990s. That was when Lemelson retained Hosier on a contingent fee basis, giving him a share of all amounts recovered (common in personal injury cases but at the time unusual in patent litigation) to threaten suits on Lemelson's patents on machine vision and bar code technology against Japanese automakers ($100 million settlement); European automakers and Japanese electronics manufacturers ($350 million); and then Ford, GM, and Chrysler (for undisclosed settlements).

Part of Jerome Lemelson's litigation strategy for his machine vision and bar code patents was to sue not the equipment manufacturers, but hundreds of their customers—including giants like Wal-Mart—who would find it less costly to settle than to litigate, particularly if they could then proceed against their vendors for indemnity. Only when one vendor-manufacturer finally fought back, filing an action for a declaratory judgment that the Lemelson patents were invalid, did the offensive end. The aggrieved manufacturer prevailed in an argument that went to the very heart of complaints about long-pending submarine patents: that Lemelson's eighteen- to thirty-nine-year delay in prosecuting his applications in the Patent Office was unreasonable, and rendered the patents unenforceable. Although the trial court dismissed the argument, the Court of Appeals for the Federal Circuit upheld it, citing two Supreme Court decisions from the 1920s that a patent applicant must act diligently, and ultimately invalidated all of the patents in suit.

Congress acted too, amending the Patent Act to reduce the attractions of submarine patents. One reform converted the patent term from seventeen years from the date the patent issued to twenty years from the date the application was filed; few patent applicants will want to delay in the Patent Office if they know that the tactic will effectively shorten their period of protection. Although the change conforms U.S. practice to that in other countries, and was enacted as part of U.S. implementation of the WTO TRIPs Agreement, support from Ford Motor and other Lemelson targets left no doubt of its aims. Also, in 1999 Congress passed legislation establishing the default rule that patent applications will be published eighteen months from their filing date, again following practice in other countries. Although an applicant can elect not to have its application published after eighteen months, the change has made publication a new norm in U.S. patent practice, one that, like the new patent term, reduces the operation of the secrecy principle.

One solution to the standoff between the pharmaceutical and electronics industries is for Congress to tailor its reforms along industry lines. In an important article published in 2003, law professors Dan Burk and Mark Lemley proposed that courts adjust general patent doctrines to fit the needs of particular industries. Among the several "policy levers" they suggest are to adjust the patent statute's nonobviousness standard to fit the invention practices of individual industries, and to give truly major "pioneer" patents broader protection than merely incremental ones. Congress can do the same. For example, the Hatch-Waxman Act, passed in 1984, extends patent terms by up to five years for human drug products, medical devices, and food and drug additives subject to regulation under the Federal Food, Drug and Cosmetic Act in order to compensate, at least partially, for FDA regulatory delays that can effectively shorten these products' commercial life under patent.

Another targeted reform, presently limited in the Patent Act to business method patents, could be expanded, at least to other software and electronics inventions, without substantial opposition. The reform follows the so-called prior user right adopted in other countries. Japanese patent law, for example, provides that if B independently makes an invention and undertakes to exploit it before A files a patent application on the same invention, B will be entitled to a compulsory nonexclusive license to continue to exploit the invention after the patent issues to A. (Without this privilege, A could enjoin B from practicing its invention.) When Congress introduced a prior user right for business method patents in 1999, it did so in terms that gave the prior user an absolute defense to an infringement action and not just a compulsory license; however, the prior user must have reduced the invention to practice at least one year before the patent application was filed, and used it commercially prior to the patent application.

Probably the most consequential division between high and low protectionists centers on American patent law's all-or-nothing principle, which empowers a patent owner to shut down a later inventor's business even if the inventor offers to pay a reasonable license fee. The all-or-nothing principle is particularly punishing to infringers whose products contain valuable, noninfringing elements that cannot be separated from the infringing elements. Without the all-or-nothing injunction remedy, Jerome Lemelson could not have forced defendants to agree to licenses for sums vastly greater than any value his patented product added to their own product.

Although the prospect of an injunction will motivate a patent owner to demand—and a patent defendant to pay—more in settlement than if the defendant faced only the prospect of reasonable royalty damages, just how much more will vary with the infringer's circumstances and the nature of its goods or services. Electronics, software, and Internet companies, whose goods and services often embody several patented inventions—a single microprocessor may embody hundreds of different patented inventions—will suffer particularly from injunctive relief since settlements paid to owners of as few as four or five electronic patents embodied in a single piece of software could easily exceed the total revenues to be earned from the product.

Patent laws outside the United States depart from the all-or-nothing principle by providing compulsory licenses in prescribed categories of cases, effectively depriving patent owners of injunctive relief and remitting them instead to court-ordered reasonable royalties. (Courts rarely have to order these payments because patent owners, knowing that only such limited relief is in prospect, will negotiate for reasonable rates.) Although U.S. patent law allows few such compulsory licenses, its provision for injunctive relief states that courts "*may* grant injunctions in accordance with the principles of equity," implying that a court could withhold injunctive relief in cases where its effect would be harsh or unjust, and award instead only a reasonable royalty. Nonetheless, the Court of Appeals for the Federal Circuit consistently ruled that once infringement is shown, injunctive relief is virtually automatic, and this appeared to be settled law in the United States until in November 2005 the U.S. Supreme Court agreed to review the Federal Circuit's decision in *MercExchange v. eBay*, applying the automatic injunction standard.

In September 2001, MercExchange, a Great Falls, Virginia, company founded by a patent lawyer–engineer, filed suit in the federal district court for the Eastern District of Virginia, one of the "rocket dockets," alleging that eBay's "Buy it Now" feature, enabling prospective bidders to purchase an item immediately at a fixed price instead of waiting for the outcome of the auction, infringed on three electronic commerce patents owned by MercExchange's founder. In May 2003, the jury found that eBay and its subsidiary Half.com had willfully infringed two of the three patents, and in August the judge ordered eBay to pay $29.5 million in damages, but declined to order an injunction shutting down the online auction's use of the feature. One reason was the growing public concern over the quantity and quality of business method patents being issued by the Patent Office, a concern that the court concluded "lent significant weight against the imposition of an injunction, particularly in this case where the patentee does not practice its patents, nor has any intention of practicing its patents."

In March 2005, the Federal Circuit affirmed the trial court's findings of patent validity and infringement—the first time the appellate court upheld a business method patent following a trial. But the court reversed the trial court's decision denying injunctive relief. "A general concern regarding business-method patents," the court ruled, "is not the type of important public need that justifies the unusual step of denying injunctive relief." As to the bargaining leverage that the injunction gave to MercExchange in its threat to close down this aspect of eBay's business, the Federal Circuit observed that this "additional leverage in licensing" is "a natural consequence of the right to exclude and not an inappropriate reward" to a patentee like MercExchange.

When the Supreme Court agreed to review the case, it was no coincidence that Intel, Yahoo!, Google, and Cisco, among other electronics companies, lined up as amici curiae (friends of the court) behind eBay, arguing for discretion in decisions on injunctive relief, while large pharmaceutical and biotech companies and trade associations, as well as universities, sided with MercExchange, which argued for virtually automatic injunctions. At the arguments before the Court in late March 2006, Justice Antonin Scalia asked a question of eBay's counsel that he presumably thought went to the heart of the historic rationale for injunctions in patent cases: "We're talking about a property right here. . . . That's what the patent right is. And all he's asking for is, 'Give me my property back.' " (In fact, courts have long withheld injunctions in real property cases if granting the remedy would injure the public interest. In one leading case, New York's high court withheld injunctive relief, but granted damages, against a nuisance-producing cement plant because the plant's economic benefits to the community exceeded its pollution costs to its neighbors.)

If Justice Scalia's question sent chills through eBay and its amici, they could at least take heart that another headline-grabbing patent infringement suit, this one involving the BlackBerry wireless e-mail service, had also recently been in the news. The BlackBerry suit settled for $612.5 million less than four weeks before the eBay argument, but until the settlement, public fears were palpable that the district court would enjoin BlackBerry use. Not only would an injunction deprive BlackBerry's Canadian owner, Research in Motion Ltd., of its huge investment in other, noninfringing aspects of its device, but it would shut down virtually all BlackBerry sales and service in the United States, home to the great bulk of the company's 4.3 million wireless-addicted users. (Although RIM announced that a noninfringing design-around of the patented invention could be installed in the event an injunction was issued, doubts arose about its ease of installation and, indeed, its immunity from further infringement claims.)

As in the *eBay* case, the trial in *NTP v. RIM*, produced a hefty damage award for the patent owners: $53.7 million for past infringement, and an 8.55 percent royalty for uses made prior to the entry of an injunction. Also, as with the MercExchange patents, the Patent Office's reexamination of the NTP patents while the court proceedings were under way cast doubt on the validity of the patents in issue. Nonetheless, and unlike his fellow Virginia trial judge in the *eBay* case, Judge James Spencer ordered an injunction against RIM, staying it only for the purposes of appeal. After his ruling was affirmed by the Federal Circuit, and the Supreme Court denied review, Judge Spencer left little doubt that if the parties did not settle the case, the prospect of entering an injunction did not intimidate him.

On May 15, 2006, the U.S. Supreme Court announced its decision in *eBay v. MercExchange,* unanimously holding that the Federal Circuit erred in enforcing a virtually categorical preference for permanent injunctions in patent cases and directing it in the future to require the plaintiff to pass, as it must in other fields of law, a four-factor test: "(1) that it has suffered an irreparable injury; (2) that remedies available at law, such as monetary damages, are inadequate to compensate for that injury; (3) that, considering the balance of hardships between the plaintiff and defendant, a remedy in equity is warranted; and (4) that the public interest would not be disserved by a permanent injunction."

The Court's formula, particularly the elements of irreparable injury and the inadequacy of damages, would appear to offer trial courts a well-calibrated tool to resolve the conflict between patent owners like drug companies, which require injunctive relief to support their research investments, and those like electronics companies whose typically modest investments and incremental advances can be adequately compensated with damage awards. But the justices were ambivalent on the point. In a concurring opinion authored by the chief justice, three justices took the position that, although injunctions are discretionary, the long practice of granting them in patent cases should weigh heavily in their favor. Four other justices, in a concurring opinion written by Justice Anthony Kennedy, thought that, whatever the force of history, "in many instances the nature of the patent being enforced and the economic function of the patent holder present considerations quite unlike earlier cases." Singling out business method patents as one category that may not deserve injunctions—"the potential vagueness and suspect validity of some of these patents may affect the calculus under the four-factor test"—these justices added that "when the patented invention is but a small component of the product the companies seek to produce and the threat of an injunction is employed simply for undue leverage in negotiations, legal damages may well be sufficient to compensate for the infringement and an injunction may not serve the public interest."

The *eBay* decision—and particularly the prospect that carefully exercised judicial discretion in grants of injunctive relief could meet the needs of both the electronics and pharmaceutical industries—relieved some of the urgency of contemporary reform efforts. (One of the more controversial proposals in pending House and Senate reform bills would have denied injunctive relief to a prevailing patent owner unless the owner could prove that it would suffer irreparable harm.) But other proposals, made in the Federal Trade Commission's 2003 report and the National Research Council's 2004 report, and variously put forward in congressional hearings, underline that other items on the reform agenda remain pressing: patent secrecy, all-or-nothing outcomes, and patent quality. As measures to decrease secrecy, the FTC report proposed legislation requiring publication of all patent applications eighteen months after filing, and further liberalizing third parties' ability to challenge patents immediately upon issue. The FTC report also recommended reducing the Patent Act's all-or-nothing aspect by exempting good-faith, independent inventions from liability in narrowly defined circumstances, and stiffening the proof of willful infringement required for increased monetary awards. To increase patent quality, the report proposed added funding for the Patent Office and tightening the legal standard of nonobviousness. (In April 2007, the U.S. Supreme Court performed the necessary tightening on its own.) Bills introduced in the House in spring 2005, and in the Senate in summer 2006, proposed generally the same avenues of reform, although with differences in detail.

Mapping Patent Change

The grand sweep of patent law, from the 1623 Statute of Monopolies to the reform bills introduced in the U.S. Congress at the turn of the twentieth century, reveals a cyclical pattern of strong and weak protection. The fact that both the Statute of Monopolies and the contemporary U.S. reform bills sought to trim the prevailing levels of protection implies not only that they were preceded by high protectionist policies, but also that they will eventually be followed by them. The perception at the threshold of the TNEC hearings that industry was using patent "monopolies" to suppress competition and, sixty years later, the demonization of patent "trolls" in the popular press and in congressional hearing rooms, were sure omens of pressure for change in Congress and the courts.

Business planning for patent cycles requires attention not only to the trends of public and political sentiment but also to prevailing industry tensions and their likely resolution. The contemporary face-off between pharmaceutical and electronics companies over the correct level of patent protection has delayed patent reform, but will not derail it, for existing legal doctrine can be applied to resolve seemingly impenetrable stalemates. Supreme Court Justice Anthony Kennedy's suggestion in the *eBay* case that trial courts should withhold injunctions in appropriate cases, and award only damages to the patent owner, is economically sensible, and seems likely to be followed by lower courts in cases where the validity of the patent in issue is suspect (as will often be the case with business method patents) or the patented invention is only a small part of the infringing product (as will often be the case with electronics patents generally).

3

Copyrights

Late in 2004, Google Inc. launched an audacious project—a company vice president called it the company's moon shot—to scan and store in the company's servers every book ever published, upward of thirty million volumes, in order to make the texts fully searchable by users around the world. A great many of these books, lent to Google by such major libraries as those at Harvard, Stanford, and Oxford, as well as the New York Public Library, are in the public domain, and no longer protected by copyright. But the fact that copyright still protects the majority of these works set off alarms among authors and publishers in the United States and elsewhere. On September 20, 2005, several writers, along with the Authors Guild, filed a copyright infringement lawsuit against Google for its unauthorized reproduction of their works; a parallel lawsuit by five major publishers followed on October 19, 2005.

The Google Library Project and the lawsuits it triggered underline two striking differences between copyright law and other intellectual property laws. One is the unique role that technological advance plays in the law's evolution. While all intellectual property laws expand their subject matter to accommodate new technologies, copyright law alone regularly engages technological advance as an occasion for extending rights and creating new markets. Over the course of the twentieth century, Congress and the courts extended the Copyright Act's public performance right to encompass first radio, then television, then cable and satellite performance of music and film, just as they extended the act's reproduction right to cover the production of phono records, photocopies, and, eventually, computer server copies of the sort made by Google. The lesson for businesses that produce or use copyrighted works is that while Congress generally extends copyright to encompass new technologies, it rarely does so completely; business risk and reward in these situations lie in gauging the width of the gap.

The second important difference between copyright and other forms of intellectual property is that while patent, trademark, and trade secret lawsuits are characteristically waged between competitors jockeying for market share, a great many copyright lawsuits (particularly those involving new technologies) find copyright owners battling their most natural allies—the very companies that disseminate their works to consumers. When, in the early 1900s, music publishers sued radio stations for the unauthorized performance of their works over the air, both sides knew that the dispute was not about market share, but about whether, and how much, the radio stations would have to pay for the music they broadcast. The same was true when music publishers sued the record companies for making unauthorized recordings; when movie studios sued the cable companies; and, possibly, when authors and publishers sued Google. (Indeed, another Google service, called the Google Book Search Partner Program, allies Google with American publishers—including several that are parties to the Google Library Project lawsuit—to use searches for passages from published books as a vehicle for marketing those books online.) The copyright lesson for managers is to view such copyright lawsuits as an occasion for partnership and licensing, not market exclusion.

For all of its undeniable cultural impact, copyright is essentially about commerce. It protects not only writers, composers, and artists, but also mapmakers, data compilers, and software designers. Copyright also protects the publishing, movie, record, and software companies whose investments bring the work of these creative people to market. Copyright is big business. A 2004 Economists Inc. analysis of industry data reported that core copyright industries—book publishing, recorded music, newspapers, magazines, motion pictures, broadcasting, software—added $626.2 billion, or 6 percent, to the U.S. economy in 2002. Less central copyright industries, such as fabric and architectural design, and the services that support the core copyright industries, added another $624 billion to the economy that year. Core copyright industries employed 5,484,000 workers, and all copyright industries employed 11,476,000 workers, roughly equal to employment in the leisure and hospitality business. Core copyright exports were $89.26 billion, substantially more than exports from such other major sectors as chemicals and aircraft.

The U.S. Copyright Act captures all of this value by granting five exclusive rights to copyright owners: the rights to reproduce their works, to adapt them, and to publicly perform, display, and distribute them. The act enables companies to divide and subdivide these rights with a finer hand than do patent, trademark, or trade secret law. As a result, opportunities abound for copyright owners to extract the highest possible prices from the most narrowly defined markets. So, too, do opportunities for assigning particular rights to the businesses best situated to exploit them—a novelist is not as well placed as a trade publisher to produce and promote his book; a trade publisher will not be as adept as a film studio at making and marketing a motion picture based on the novel; and the studio may lack a merchandiser's skill for producing and distributing knickknacks based on the movie. Copyright enables the copyright owner to allocate rights among these businesses and dozens more.

Copyrights are easier to obtain than patents, but harder to defend. While a patent requires a detailed application to the patent office of every country where a patent is sought (and examination for compliance with the applicable statutory standards), the very act of creating a copyrightable work—a story, a drawing, even a shopping list—instantly secures copyright for that work, and not only in the country where the work was created, but in more than 150 others around the world. At the same time, copyright protection is narrower than patent protection: patents can approximate protection for ideas, but copyright confines its protection to the *expression* of ideas. The writer Raymond Chandler may have invented the idea of a tough yet thoughtful private eye, but once he published the first story in his Philip Marlowe series, that idea became free for the taking, and bred a host of imitators. This explains the extreme price sensitivity of copyrighted works. Chandler's publisher would not think to charge more than the generally prevailing price for one of the writer's books for fear that an appreciable number of readers would defect to one or more of these imitators.

Technology not only creates new types of copyrightable works and new markets for all forms of copyrighted works, it also drives value in the copyright industries. Movie studios today divide the release times for feature films over a trajectory that will typically start with theatrical exhibition, followed months later by DVD release, then pay-per-view, cable, free network broadcast, then off-network, with foreign and ancillary releases such as airline play tied to the film's success in other markets. It is copyright law and its subdivision of exclusive rights that make possible these divisions over media and time.

Although theatrical release was at one time the economic linchpin of motion picture marketing, DVD and television distribution are today the key organizing forces of the release schedule, and theatrical releases alone will rarely if ever repay the cost of making and distributing a film. Instead, theatrical release has effectively become a marketing campaign for the DVD. (In 1994 the average window between theatrical and video release was six and a half months; by 2005, it was down to three to four months.) Internet delivery of movies will doubtless require further reshuffling of release windows. When filmmaker Steven Soderbergh announced that he would release his latest film to theaters, DVD, and high-definition cable on the same day, he added dryly that it was nothing new. "Simultaneous release is already here. It's called piracy."

Copyright rules sometimes hamper efforts at price discrimination. When a movie theater offers discounts to seniors because their demand for movies is weaker, or lowers ticket prices on Tuesdays because it is generally a slow day, it is price-discriminating to its advantage because lower admission fees are better than no fees at all. But price discrimination is not always as easy as asking to see a senior citizen's driver's license. Paramount Pictures discovered this in 1979 when it sought to capture relatively high prices from sales of prerecorded videocassettes to video rental outlets (which would pay the price because each cassette could produce a stream of rental revenues from customers), while at the same time distributing the videocassettes to retailers for sale to consumers at a substantially lower price. Of course, the program was doomed to fail. Video rental stores stopped purchasing (high-priced) tapes from Paramount and started buying (low-priced) tapes from retail outlets like Fotomat in order to increase their profit from rentals.

The reason Paramount's differential pricing program failed lies in copyright law's age-old first sale doctrine: once a copyright owner sells a copy of its work, it cannot control the resale or other transfer of that particular copy. In 1983 the film studios asked Congress for an exception from the first sale doctrine that would give them the right to control video rentals and consequently the leverage to bargain with rental outlets for a share of rental revenues. Grassroots opposition from video rental stores killed the effort, but fourteen years later Sumner Redstone, whose Viacom controlled both Blockbuster and Paramount Studios, devised a way to solve the problem without legislation. As Redstone saw it, the problem was that if Blockbuster, then the leading videocassette rental chain, had to pay $60 to $100 to purchase a videocassette, it could not possibly stock a sufficient supply to meet customer demand for popular films. But if it could instead pay as little as $6 or $7 for each videocassette, it could afford to give the film studios—which under the first sale doctrine were receiving no share of the video rental revenues—a 40 percent share. Effectively, Redstone's negotiated arrangement achieved through contract what Congress had rejected as a matter of legislation, producing greater revenues overall for the studios and for Blockbuster than they had enjoyed before.

Copyright owners regularly turn to self-help and to business strategies to overcome not only legislative inertia, but market obstructions. In the face of the daunting transaction costs of collecting payments from tens of millions of widely dispersed performances and reproductions of copyrighted works, copyright owners developed institutional mechanisms—like the musical collecting societies ASCAP and BMI, and the Copyright Clearance Center—to ensure that they are paid for these widespread uses. When Congress hesitated to bring computer programs within copyright, software vendors invented so-called shrinkwrap licenses (they persist today with their lines of unreadable, or at least unread, fine print) obligating purchasers who open the package to restrictions even more onerous than copyright law would have imposed, such as prohibitions on making personal copies for research purposes.

New technologies sometimes raise questions about the scope of copyright licenses. When in 1950 a film studio licensed to a television network "the right to perform the copyrighted work on television," did it by that phrase transfer the rights to the cable TV market, not foreseen at the time, or did it reserve the rights to itself? Such questions arise anytime a new technology appears. Before the advent of motion pictures, did a dramatist's grant of rights to produce his play on the stage include the right to transform it into a motion picture? (Some courts said yes, others no.) Did motion picture rights granted during the silent film era include the right to make "talkies"? (Again, some courts said yes, others no.) Copyright owners that have the required leverage will finesse the drafting problem by insisting on contract language giving them rights to exploitation "anywhere in the universe" by any "technological mechanism or electronic means, method or device now known or hereafter conceived or created." But even this prescription is not foolproof. In one 1993 decision, a federal appellate court ruled that this ostensibly all-embracing language failed to include the right to distribute a motion picture in the home video market.

Technology defined, and challenged, copyright from the very start. Until the invention of movable type, there was no need for copyright because the high cost of making copies consumed most of what purchasers were willing to pay. Only when copies became cheap and plentiful did exclusive rights in printed works begin to make economic sense as a vehicle for capturing the value of the content the copies contained. In the sixteenth and early seventeenth centuries, much as the English Crown dispensed monopolies over inventions, it also regulated the book trade by conferring grants of exclusive patents to print particular books. Later, in 1557, by vesting a printing monopoly in the Stationers Company, the

Crown managed to control virtually all publishing in the realm. Like true patents for invention, the Stationers' monopoly survived the massive parliamentary and judicial attacks on other Crown patents, such as those for salt, starch, and vinegar, but ultimately even this monopoly ended, effectively replaced by the world's first copyright act, the Statute of Anne in 1710.

Copyright lawmakers today respond far more quickly to new technologies than they did in Gutenberg's day. No sooner does a new technology appear—motion pictures, radio, television, cable VCRs, DVRs, photocopying, the Internet—than copyright owners rush to Congress and the courts to expand their rights lest a new, free use of their works displace established, paying uses. The authors' and publishers' lawsuits against Google, and the record and movie companies' outcries over Napster, Grokster, and other free file-sharing services are only the most recent of such complaints. New technologies create pressures not only for the expansion of rights, but also for the expansion of copyright subject matter. Photography, first popularized in the 1850s, came under copyright relatively quickly, in 1865. But while Thomas Edison invented the phonograph in 1877, Congress did not bring sound recordings into the Copyright Act until almost one hundred years later. Beginning in the 1960s, the great debate was whether computer software—a hybrid that was part technology, part creative expression—should be protected under patent law or copyright law, and even after amendments to the Copyright Act in 1980 brought computer programs into copyright, questions persisted over the proper scope for their protection.

Copyright industries suffer when the law accommodates new technologies at an uneven pace. Rights delayed are often effectively rights denied. If Congress waits too long to legislate, habits of free use may become so entrenched that it becomes politically impossible to enact a law that will reverse these habits. This is what happened with home videotaping off the air in the 1980s, and film companies have yet to establish a legal beachhead against home copying. Yet for Congress to legislate too soon after the emergence of a new and still undefined technology runs the risk that the law will fail to anticipate salient features that emerge only after the technology matures. This happened when in 1984 Congress passed legislation protecting semiconductor chip designs well before any pattern of unauthorized copying emerged; soon after, the industry shifted to more complex, higher-density chips that made the statute even less relevant than before.

A long-standing division between Congress and courts in copyright matters complicates business predictions of legal response to techno-logical change. Although Congress sometimes lags in its response to new technologies, its approach is characteristically to extend the reach of copyright—both to encompass new uses of copyrighted works, and to expand copyright subject matter. Courts, by contrast, have histori-cally been the more conservative branch, not only declining to expand copyright on their own—something they have regularly done for patents and trademarks—but also systematically wielding the judge-made fair use doctrine to excuse otherwise infringing uses.

This historical split between congressional and judicial lawmaking means that the question of whether copyright is expanding or contract-ing at any moment is complicated by the question of whether Congress or the judiciary is at that moment ascendant in copyright matters. Thus the great age of copyright expansion in America was the nineteenth century, not the twentieth, for it was over that period that beyond the eighteenth century's modest exclusive rights to print, publish, and vend copyrighted works, Congress added the robust contemporary rights encompassing performance, dramatization, and translation as well. It was also at the end of the nineteenth century that Congress for the first time brought the great body of English literature, along with other foreign works, under U.S. copyright control.

If the persisting challenge for copyright businesses is to evaluate copyright law's legislative and judicial prospects at any moment— How long will Congress take to bring a new technology into copyright? How extensively will courts cut back on statutory protection?—two guiding principles have proved true over time. First, when new tech-nological *uses* of copyrighted works emerge, lawmakers will sooner or later extend copyright to encompass these uses, and courts will cut back that protection only if—and only so long as—the transaction costs of negotiating a license to make the use are insurmountably high. The trajectory of protection for motion pictures over the course of the twentieth century, discussed below, illustrates the give-and-take between Congress and the courts in reconciling the principle of exclusive rights with the reality of transaction costs. Second, as new forms of technological *subject matter* emerge to claim copyright protection, Congress will, again, bring the new subject matter within copyright, while courts will take care to see that protection for the new subject matter extends only to those elements that have traditionally come within copyright. This lawmaking give-and-take between Congress and the courts led to intense debates over the scope of protection for computer programs, the so-called softwars of the 1980s and 1990s, also described below.

How the Movie Studios Used Copyright to Tame Their Distribution Partners

Over the course of the twentieth century, three successive technologies challenged the movie theater—and ultimately each other—as the principal venue for disseminating motion pictures: broadcast television, cable television, and the videocassette recorder. In the case of television, the studios' copyright control over the new market was unquestioned, and they wielded this control rigorously. Cable and VCR, by contrast, presented a legal challenge, for it was far from clear that these new uses fell within copyright's exclusive right. In the case of uncontrolled VCR use, the studios believed they were fighting for their economic life. (No matter that the VCR, and later DVD technology, turned out to be the greatest financial boon ever reaped by Hollywood.) Each of these encounters contained the seeds of the next, just as the last—copyright's encounter with the VCR—embodies the seeds of today's conflict between the studios and newer generations of technologies: personal video recorders, like TiVo and the Internet. And in every one of these lawsuits, the studios understood that a copyright victory did not mean that they would shut down their adversaries, as one might a competitor, but rather that they would enter into a license for expanded distribution of their films.

THE STUDIOS VERSUS TELEVISION

Because the film studios had absolute, unquestioned dominion over television broadcast of their works, they were able to withhold the thousands of works in their film libraries until the networks and stations grew large enough to pay them enough to offset the likely drain on theater profits. Although prime-time programming was on the air by 1948, the major studios began releasing films to television only in 1955, and even then the studios, under continued pressure from theater owners, would usually license only pre-1947 films. By the 1960s, though, television showed that it could more than compensate for the losses inflicted on theaters, and contemporary feature films began to appear on television prime time. In 1967, the industry's trade group, the Motion Picture Association of America, reported that product from Hollywood's major studios—not only feature films, but made-for-television series—filled 44 of 73.5 prime-time hours each week.

Copyright promotes competition, and while the major studios sat on their copyrights through the 1950s, second-tier studios and independents quickly filled the vacuum. Some of the movies, most notably B westerns, were old. William Boyd, who starred in the Hopalong Cassidy films in the 1930s, bought the television rights for $350,000 and, seeing their huge success on television, launched a new series of the westerns specifically for that medium. Also, as far back as the 1930s, farsighted producers had their eye on television as an eventual destination for new films. In 1936, when Walt Disney was renegotiating his theatrical distribution deal with United Artists, he insisted on retaining television broadcast rights to himself, and when United balked, he moved distribution to RKO, a decision that repaid his foresight many years later.

THE STUDIOS VERSUS CATV

As the film studios and television broadcasters were developing their new partnership in the 1960s, a new technology was emerging that would seriously challenge the economics of their carefully structured copyright licenses. Antennas were sprouting up everywhere to retransmit television signals from urban areas to rural locales physically cut off from broadcast signals, and the antenna operators refused to accept copyright control over their retransmissions. In the beginning, both broadcasters and copyright owners stood to gain from the new service: broadcasters earned their revenues from advertisers; advertisers paid more for larger broadcast audiences; community antenna television increased audience size; and as broadcast markets and revenues increased so too did the prices that broadcasters bid for copyrighted films. But as CATV, and later cable television, outgrew their early role and began importing distant broadcast signals into local markets and originating their own programming, local broadcasters objected. Film companies too saw the challenge to their revenue structure. Only by exercising copyright control over cable, the studios believed, could they hope to compensate for lost broadcast revenues.

The film studios pinned their hopes on a 1931 Supreme Court decision holding that a hotel's retransmission of radio broadcasts to its rooms infringed the music publisher's performance right in the music being broadcast. If, the copyright owners reasoned, transmissions inside a hotel infringed the performance right, so too did community antenna systems that retransmitted broadcast signals to individual homes. In its suit against one such community antenna operator, Fortnightly Corporation, United Artists Television persuaded both the trial court and the appellate court to agree, and to hold that Fortnightly's retransmissions infringed United Artists' performance right in its films.

The U.S. Supreme Court reversed the lower courts. In the words of one leading film lawyer, the decision "shook Hollywood." The Court framed its analysis of whether Fortnightly "performed," and thus infringed United Artists' films, by asking whether Fortnightly, with its tall antennas connected by cable to subscribers' television sets, was more like a broadcaster (which does perform) or a viewer (who does not). The Court came down on the viewer side of the line. Unlike broadcasters, which select their programming and sell time to advertisers, cable made no programming choices and earned its revenues from subscribers. "Essentially," the Court observed, "a CATV system no more than enhances the viewer's capacity to receive the broadcaster's signals; it provides a well-located antenna with an efficient connection to the viewer's television set."

Fortnightly illustrates the dilemma that copyright owners face when deciding whether to file a test case against a new technology. If they file too early, they run the risk that the technology, like Fortnightly's, will be in too primitive a state for a court to consider it a significant economic threat. But to wait for the technology to mature runs the risk that it will have become so widely entrenched among users that no court would be inclined to shut it down. (*Fortnightly* was not decided by the Supreme Court until about twenty years after the first community antenna system was installed, and not until eight years after the suit was filed.)

When, almost a year after the start of the lawsuit against Fortnightly, CBS and three other copyright owners filed an infringement action against Teleprompter and another CATV operator, they were able to choose defendants that, because they originated and selected programming, and sold advertising and imported distant television signals, looked far more like broadcasters than did Fortnightly. The trial court stayed the lawsuit pending the ultimate decision in *Fortnightly,* so that by the time the new case reached the Supreme Court, the Court's dividing line between broadcasters and viewers had become a compelling precedent against the copyright owners. Justice Potter Stewart, who wrote the Court's opinion in *Fortnightly,* also wrote for the Court in *Teleprompter,* holding that the cable system once again fell on the viewer side of the line. The system's additional functions, though they "may allow the [CATV] systems to compete more effectively with the broadcasters for the television market," ultimately made no difference. Recognizing that importation of distant signals might depress, if not obliterate, the fees that local stations would be willing to pay copyright owners for the same content, Stewart nonetheless concluded that even if copyright owners suffered economic injury, it had no bearing on whether the defendant's operation amounted to "performance."

As the Supreme Court recognized, the decision on whether and how to bring cable retransmissions into copyright was better left to Congress than to the courts (Justice Abe Fortas observed in his dissent in *Fortnightly* that "this case calls not for the judgment of Solomon, but for the dexterity of Houdini"), and by late 1971 the interested industries had worked out a "consensus agreement" that combined regulation by the Federal Communications Commission and legislation from Congress as part of its ongoing efforts at revising the 1909 Copyright Act. The FCC issued rules in early 1972, and in 1976 this regulatory approach laid the foundation for the new copyright act's treatment of cable television retransmission.

If the Supreme Court failed in the CATV cases to employ the wisdom of Solomon, Congress did not. The 1976 Copyright Act gave neither copyright owners an absolute right against cable retransmission, nor cable companies an absolute exemption from copyright liability. Instead, the legislators imposed a statutory license on cable retransmissions and prescribed the royalties to be paid by the cable companies for periodic distribution to the copyright owners. Congress had resorted to a statutory copyright license only once before, in the case of recordings of musical works. In the case of cable, the decision was in part motivated by the problem of transaction costs: "It would be impractical and unduly burdensome to require every cable system to negotiate with every copyright owner whose work was retransmitted by a cable system." But there was also a concern that because broadcasters competed with cable and had historically sought to stifle cable's development, they might use their exclusive rights in copyrighted programs as a predatory tool to curb cable's growth. Since the cable compromise, statutory licenses have become a popular legislative tool for accommodating copyright law's otherwise exclusive rights to new technological uses of copyrighted works.

THE STUDIOS VERSUS IN-HOME PERFORMANCES

Historically, to come within copyright control, a performance must be public. (The song "Happy Birthday" is still protected by copyright, but so long as it is performed privately, among family and friends, no copyright tribute need be paid.) To be public, a performance must either occur in a public place, like a theater, or must be transmitted to the public, as in the case of broadcast television and cable transmission of copyrighted works.

Thus defined, the public performance right has been more than adequate to secure performance revenues to copyright owners. But to anyone in the film industry observing the direction of future technologies, the requirement that the performance be public presented a fearsome prospect: if entertainment in the twenty-first century was to be beamed, on demand, from a "celestial jukebox"—a digital warehouse containing on its servers every film ever made—to the individual user who ordered up the entertainment for enjoyment in the privacy of his home, a court might consider this to be a private performance because its content is selected by the user, not the broadcaster, and the transmission is to a single individual, not a mass audience. If these performances are private, economically valuable uses of film and other copyrighted works will increasingly slip outside of copyright control; and as private performances consume the market for public performances, there will be no revenues to compensate for the loss. The studios thus needed a definition of "public" that would encompass the celestial jukebox.

This time, the major motion picture studios did not wait for the new technology to mature, but instead, in a series of test cases, took aim at an existing, comparable use of motion pictures, with the hope that the decisions in these cases could be employed as favorable precedents when the celestial jukebox finally emerged.

As is common in test case strategy, the studios' first target was the easiest: a video store, Maxwell's Video Showcase, in which customers could, for a fee, select a prerecorded videocassette, repair to a small private booth in the back of the store, and there view the movie transmitted from a VCR in the front of the store to a television screen in the private booth. Both the district court and, on appeal, the Third Circuit Court of Appeals agreed with the film studios that this constituted a public performance. The private nature of the booths was irrelevant, the court held: it was the store that was the relevant public place because "any member of the public can view a motion picture by paying the appropriate fee." (The fact that the video store dispensed popcorn and soft drinks to patrons didn't hurt the studios' case that the store was much like a movie theater.) As an alternative ground for decision, the court ruled that the transmission from the front of Maxwell's to the back was as much a transmission to the public as a broadcast by a television station into a home.

With the *Maxwell's* precedent on the books, and taking care to again file their action in the Third Circuit, where the earlier decision would weigh as direct precedent, the film studios next took aim at a slightly more difficult target—a business, Aveco, that located its VCRs not at the front of the store for transmission to rented, private booths, but in the booths themselves, where customers could play videocassettes they had rented or brought into the store on their own. Following its earlier decision, the court ruled that this too constituted public performance. "Maxwell's, like Aveco, was willing to make a viewing room and video cassette available to any member of the public with the inclination to avail himself of this service. It is this availability that made Maxwell's stores public places, not the coincidence that the video cassette players were situated in the lobby."

The studios' next case was a misstep. Instead of following the modestly staged strategy of the first two cases with another, only slightly harder case filed in the Third Circuit, the film companies filed an action in Hollywood's home circuit, the Ninth Circuit in California, targeting conduct that involved neither a public place, like a store, nor a transmission of video signals from one place to another. Instead the studios challenged a resort hotel's rental of videodiscs to its guests for viewing on players in individual guest rooms. But this, the Ninth Circuit ruled, did not constitute a public performance: a hotel room is a private, not a public, place, and a bellhop carrying a videodisc to a guest room could hardly qualify as a "transmission."

The next move was for a shrewd entrepreneur, On Command Video, to design a hotel video delivery system that in many ways mimicked the system allowed by the Ninth Circuit but stayed clear of the features condemned in the Third Circuit. (It was no coincidence that On Command was formerly named "End Run Communications.") The company's wired performance system connected hotel guest rooms to a centrally located console containing motion picture videocassettes and enabled guests to view the motion pictures whenever they wanted in the privacy of their hotel rooms. Next, On Command removed the test case strategy from the studios' hands. Instead of waiting to be sued in the Third Circuit, where the legal precedents were favorable to the studios, it filed its own lawsuit in the Ninth Circuit—where the case law was unfavorable to the studios—seeking a declaratory judgment that its performances were not "public."

On Command's strategy, though ingenious, just barely missed the mark. The trial court rejected the company's claim that, because the system would transmit performances from each videocassette to no more than one room at a time, none of its transmissions would be to the public. Hotel guests watching a movie in their rooms are, the court ruled, "members of the public" because "the relationship between the transmitter of the performance, On Command, and the audience, hotel guests, is a commercial, public one regardless of where the viewing takes place." For authority, the court relied on a definition that had been inserted into the bill that ultimately became the 1976 Copyright Act many years before, and that arguably anticipated the celestial jukebox: a transmitted performance is to the public, whether the members of the public capable of receiving it "receive it in the same place or in separate places and at the same time or at different times." Following the decision, On Command entered into a license arrangement with the studios.

THE STUDIOS VERSUS VIDEOTAPE

Although the Copyright Act requires infringing performances to be public, it imposes no comparable requirement on the unauthorized *reproduction* of copyrighted works; a copy can be made entirely in private and still infringe. Nonetheless, there is a widespread popular belief that private copies—a photocopy made for personal use, a television program copied off the air—are exempt from copyright liability. Also, copyright law's fair use doctrine, which excuses copyright infringement whose benefit to the public outweighs its cost to the copyright owner, offers courts a ready instrument to excuse private copying. Copyright owners consequently worry that unauthorized private copies will someday displace the market for public copies, just as private performances may one day cannibalize the market for public performances. A 1973 appellate court ruling, affirmed in 1975 by an equally divided (4–4) U.S. Supreme Court, that it was fair use for the National Library of Medicine to make photocopies for researchers, set off alarm bells for motion picture studios concerned that home videocassette recorders, introduced into the American market in 1975, would be the next candidate for judicial exemption from copyright control.

If the photocopying case taught the film companies anything, it was that it is hard to win a case against a technology that large numbers of consumers habitually use to make free copies. Yet 1975, when the videocassette market was still in its infancy, was not the ideal time for the studios to press Congress for a law expressly bringing VCRs under copyright control. Congress was at the end of an exhausting fifteen-year effort to revise the 1909 Copyright Act—one of its final achievements was to reach a compromise on the photocopying issue—and lawmakers were not disposed to take on a controversial issue that could undermine the many legislative compromises already struck. So the studios turned to the federal courts. In November 1976, two months after the new copyright act was signed into law, Universal City Studios, joined by Walt Disney Productions, and with a financial contribution from Warner Bros., filed a copyright infringement lawsuit in federal district court in Los Angeles against the Sony Corporation of America, charging that home copying of televised films was copyright infringement and that by selling its Betamax videotape recorders for home use Sony was contributing to the infringement of the studios' motion pictures. Sony, the studios argued, was as liable for the resulting off-the-air copies as were the home copiers themselves.

By filing their lawsuit before VCR use became widespread—there were only about fifty thousand Betamax recorders in the United States in 1976—the studios hoped to avoid the tactical problem of waging battle against a popular, widely entrenched technology. But by choosing to sue rather than to lobby Congress, the studios had to face another obstacle: the reluctance of federal courts, and particularly the U.S. Supreme Court, to extend copyright into what they perceived to be the private domain. Nonetheless, the studios were betting that their evidence that consumers were building personal video libraries from recorded feature films would dramatize the commercial implications of home copying. One witness testified that stores sold out their supply of blank videocassettes immediately before the television broadcast of *Gone With the Wind*, and Disney's chairman testified that his studio had turned down offers to broadcast its films because of fear that consumers would videotape the broadcasts.

In October 1979, District Judge Warren Ferguson ruled that the Copyright Act did not extend to private, noncommercial copies; that even if it did, such copying was an exempted fair use; that even if the use wasn't fair, Sony could not be held liable for copies made by others; and that even if Sony were held liable, it should not be subject to an injunction since that would harm the public more than denying the injunction would harm the studios. The three years that it took for the case to progress to decision did not help the copyright owners. By the time Judge Ferguson issued his decision, VCR producers had sold 475,000 machines into American homes.

The studios appealed, well aware that the Ninth Circuit Court of Appeals was at the time taking as long as three years to decide a case. To their relief, the court moved with unusual speed, releasing its decision in October 1981, eight months after hearing argument. The decision was a sweeping victory for Universal and Disney, with all three judges voting to reverse each of Judge Ferguson's holdings: Congress did not intend to exempt private copies from copyright liability; such copying was not fair use; and Sony was legally responsible for the activities of home users. The court did, though, take a cue from Judge Ferguson's reluctance to award injunctive relief. When great public injury would result from an injunction, the court wrote, a trial judge could instead award damages or a continuing royalty—effectively imposing a compulsory license—on the copyright user.

Two days after the court of appeals decision, bills introduced in both houses of Congress sought to reverse the result and exempt off-the-air home videotapes from copyright liability. Opposing bills, supported by the Motion Picture Association of America, would have subjected home copies to liability but, following the suggestions made by the district and circuit courts in *Sony*, would have replaced injunctive relief with a requirement that equipment and tape manufacturers pay a statutorily fixed royalty on every VCR and blank videocassette they sold. The MPAA's proposal of a $50 levy on each videotape recorder was politically shrewd. Not only would it eliminate the prospect of copyright police removing VCRs from stores and homes, it would also reward (predominantly American) film producers at the expense of (predominantly Japanese) VCR manufacturers.

In the slow waltz of copyright lawmaking, Congress usually postpones action if a Supreme Court decision is pending, as it did with the CATV cases. The bills limped to a halt when in June 1982 the U.S. Supreme Court agreed to hear Sony's appeal from the Ninth Circuit decision. The Supreme Court heard argument in *Sony v. Universal* in January 1983, and as the end of the Court's term approached without a decision, both sides had to wonder what result such protracted deliberations would produce. Until a decade later, when Justice Thurgood Marshall's court papers were opened to the public, no one outside the Court would know that a 7–2 majority had lined up in favor of the film studios shortly after the parties' argument, but that by the end of the term this majority had turned into a 5–4 one favoring Sony.

Without disclosing the shift in majorities, the Court put the case down for reargument the next term, and subsequently, in 1984, held that it constituted fair use to make copies off the air for purposes of "time-shifting"—watching a show at a different time than it was broadcast—but implied that it was not fair use to make copies for the purpose of creating a home film library. Also, so long as its VCRs had a "substantial noninfringing use" such as time-shifting, Sony would not be liable for the other, infringing uses of its equipment, such as compiling a library.

Although the Supreme Court observed that Congress in the past regularly filled the void when the Court ruled against copyright liability, it seemed unlikely that Congress would this time reverse the judicial result. In the year before the Supreme Court first heard arguments in the *Sony* case, the number of VCRs in American homes had risen to five million, VCRs had become a $3 billion a year business, and, according to one source, 9 percent of the population owned a video recorder and another 10 percent said they were very likely to buy one in the future. If the growing number of American homes with VCRs could influence a Supreme Court decision against imposing liability, it would certainly have that effect on Congress. Also, while imposing a levy on equipment and tapes might result in fewer sales by offshore manufacturers, it would also raise prices for American consumers.

In 1984, the film studios were not inclined to press the point, for they had begun to appreciate the VCR's silver lining, as a vehicle not only for making unauthorized copies off the air but also for playing authorized videocassettes rented and purchased by consumers. Prerecorded tapes first went on the market, and the first video rental store opened, in late 1977. (Twentieth Century Fox was the first to license into this market, charging $300,000 for fifty films from its library, a price that the licensee recovered in the first two months of release.) By 2000, sales of prerecorded videocassettes produced greater revenues than domestic box-office receipts. As they did with television, the studios would ultimately reconcile themselves—profitably—to a new dissemination technology.

THE STUDIOS VERSUS DIGITAL COPYING TECHNOLOGIES

The great success of prerecorded entertainment—first videocassettes, then DVDs—obscured the immediate impact of *Sony v. Universal*. But the long-term impact was unmistakable. Silicon Valley lawyers used the Supreme Court's decision to benchmark the legal risk presented by their clients' new digital products. So long as they could find a "substantial noninfringing use"—the Court's phrase—for the product, lawyers counseled entrepreneurs and venture capitalists that the investment was reasonably secure from copyright attack. The *Sony* rule opened the door to a broad array of private copying devices, not only for films, but for recorded music as well.

Of the new generation of home copying devices, none presented a deeper threat to the film companies than digital video recorders like TiVo. The studios and broadcast stations worried most about the DVR's ability to skip or fast-forward through advertising, but the technology produces other disruptions as well. One is that it erodes the economics of carefully planned broadcast schedules; another is that, as the DVR's storage capacity grows from dozens to hundreds of hours of programming, it will undermine the vital part of the television business that depends on syndication and reruns for profitability; and, of course, whole libraries of programming recorded on TiVo will compete with real-time broadcast television and other entertainment. As of 2006, TiVo had 4.4 million subscribers, and, according to one widely consulted study, nearly half of all U.S. television-owning households will have a DVR by 2014. Cable and satellite companies have ardently supported DVR technology for their own services.

As with other technology-driven market challenges, copyright owners responded to the DVR with business as well as legal strategies. Following the lead taken by feature films, television producers have experimented with product placement as a solution to DVR ad-skipping, integrating advertisers' products into broadcast programming. (Few solutions in Hollywood are new: in 1948 David O. Selznick proposed to television sponsor Liggett & Myers that, instead of standalone ads and endorsements for the company's Chesterfield cigarettes, packages of the cigarettes be placed strategically around the show's set.) By 2005, branded products were no longer appearing merely as props, but were being incorporated into the show's story line. One company offered a "virtual" product placement service that digitally retrofits products into programming, or removes them, to be replaced by another virtual product. Nielsen Media Research has introduced product placement measuring services.

The history of the motion picture industry's encounters with new technologies, from television in the 1940s and 1950s to TiVo at the turn of the twenty-first century, teaches two important lessons about the use of copyright to navigate relationships with future distribution partners. One is that because copyright fosters production of competing works, no copyright owner can hope to control the spigot that releases content to distributors. Copyright gave the creator of the first cowboy movie no monopoly over that genre, and if one film studio demanded too high a price for its horse operas, broadcasters and other media channels would turn to its competitors for content. When the major film studios withheld the films in their libraries until they decided that television was a big enough market to offset the drain on theatrical profits, any number of smaller competitors, like Walt Disney and William Boyd, helped to fill the airwaves with their own, less costly content.

The second lesson is that in law, as in life, timing is everything. The film studios, and sophisticated copyright owners generally, understand the parallel dangers of filing a lawsuit too soon—before the new technology appears to be sufficiently threatening to justify legal sanctions— and filing too late—after the technology has become so well-entrenched among users that no court or legislator will dare to shut it down. This is what happened with CATV in the *Fortnightly* and *Teleprompter* cases.

In the case of home copying, if the first technology to come before the Supreme Court had been not the comparatively primitive Betamax VCR, with its modest inroads on film revenues, but the sophisticated DVR, poised for a full-fledged assault on industry profits, the Court almost surely would have imposed liability, or at least drawn a loophole considerably smaller than "substantial noninfringing use." But with the *Sony* precedent on the books, any attack on the DVR will be a struggle. The studios struck on a more productive solution in the home-performance cases, filing their lawsuits before the technology of the celestial jukebox even emerged. By proceeding against conduct that raised comparable copyright issues but posed no direct threat to consumer habits, they succeeded in establishing precedents that will protect their copyrights now that on-demand, in-home programming is becoming a reality.

How the Computer Industry Used Copyright to Fight for Market Share

More than any other episode in copyright's long history, the battle over protection for computer software in the 1980s and early 1990s illustrates how the slightest nuance in judicial doctrine can affect billions of dollars in revenues and alter the course of a major industry. Three central copyright rules—the rule that copyright protects expression, but not ideas; that a work must be original to be copyrightable; and the fair use doctrine of *Sony v. Universal*—proved decisive in resolving the conflict between companies like IBM, Apple, and Sega that sought through copyright to control access to their established operating system platforms, and, on the other side, producers of competing and complementary equipment, such as Fujitsu Limited, Franklin Computer, and Accolade, Inc., that sought access for their equipment to those platforms. The legal reverberations of the battle were felt by businesses worldwide.

In 1993, as the software battles—called "softwars" by one IBM executive—were drawing to a close, Charles R. Morris and Charles H. Ferguson wrote in the *Harvard Business Review* that competitive success in information technologies "flows to the company that manages to establish proprietary architectural control over a broad, fast-moving competitive space." The "broad, fast-moving competitive space" is the platform—IBM's System/360 mainframe in the late 1960s, Microsoft's MS-DOS, released in 1981, and later Windows in 1990. IBM's copyright strategy for its mainframe business—soon to be followed by Digital Equipment Corp. for minicomputers, Microsoft and Apple for personal computers, and Sega and Nintendo for video-game consoles—had a single object: the creation of an operating system platform, access to which could be controlled by the platform's owner.

A platform can be open or closed. On an open platform, the products of one software or hardware provider can interoperate with those of any other provider. Interoperability confers on the platform provider and its users alike the benefits of the so-called network externalities that flow from being part of a large network, much as telephone companies and their customers benefit from a nationally interoperable calling system. Closed or proprietary platforms, whose owners restrict access to their operating systems, can also offer significant returns, much like the profits to be reaped from setting up a toll-booth on a well-traveled highway. If the closed platform's configuration has become a formal or de facto standard—much as if the highway were the only one in the region—the toll taker gets to earn monopoly profits. Copyright in interface specifications—the computer code that, like a toll gate, controls access to the platform—has value for providers of open platforms. For providers of closed platforms, it is absolutely crucial.

When IBM introduced its System/360 mainframe computer in 1964, it was an open system, and IBM widely released information about the structure and details of the operating system so that others could write applications to run on it. The system was also upwardly compatible—software developed for an early IBM model could be moved to a more advanced model without modification. These two features proved to be an extraordinary draw for customers: openness attracted other companies to produce applications and attaching equipment for the platform well beyond the number that IBM itself could have produced, and upward compatibility ensured that a customer could upgrade its applications and peripheral equipment without purchasing an entirely new system. But these features also meant that, having once bought into the System/360 platform with all its applications and peripherals, the customer was economically locked into it, for none of the costly equipment it leased or purchased would interoperate with mainframes offered by other manufacturers. (By 1977, customers had spent $200 billion on software designed to run on IBM systems, and by 1978 IBM controlled 65.2 percent of the world mainframe market.) But so long as the system remained open, the availability of interoperable equipment and applications from competitors kept prices competitive.

IBM's commitment to an open mainframe environment changed in 1978 when the company decided that software, not hardware, revenues would drive its System/360 strategy. For the first time, the company asserted copyright in its operating system software and began charging for its use. It sharply reduced the information that it made available to customers and competitors about the operating system's structure and details, and it significantly tightened the terms of its program licenses. IBM's claim to copyright in the operating system's interface specifications was critical to the new strategy to control the platform's architecture, for without knowing these specifications—the key that opened the platform's doors—competitors could no longer offer interoperable programs or equipment to a user community that was now effectively locked into the System/360 architecture.

Companies, in their quest for profitable platforms, strike the balance between openness and control differently, depending on their assessment of the marketplace. While DEC followed IBM's lead in asserting proprietary control over its minicomputer operating systems, IBM itself took an open-platform approach to the PC, relying on Intel for its microprocessors and Microsoft for its operating systems, and understanding that both suppliers would sell to competing PC producers as well. One result was the overwhelming market share won by the PC platform. But another result was to give Microsoft and Intel virtual control over the platform, leaving IBM with little more than sales of the boxes that contained the microprocessors and operating software, a commodity business with slender margins. Apple, by contrast, traded the prospect of a larger personal computer platform for the profits to be earned from complete control over its computers' architecture and operating system. All of these strategies—of DEC, Microsoft, Intel, and Apple—had one feature in common: their reliance on copyright to protect the platform's interface specifications.

SOFTWARS I: DOES COPYRIGHT PROTECT THE KEYS TO THE KINGDOM?

Copyright was by most measures an odd choice to protect computer software. As a technological invention aimed at achieving a prescribed result—the Copyright Act defines "computer program" as "a set of statements or instructions to be used directly or indirectly in a computer in order to bring about a certain result"—computer software might seem to fit better under patent or trade secret law. Indeed, for more than a century under the so-called idea-expression distinction, American courts expressly rejected copyright protection for such procedures, processes, systems, or methods of operation.

Why, then, did copyright become the principal vehicle for software protection through the 1980s and 1990s? One reason is that, ill-fitting as copyright was, other intellectual properties—patents, trade secrets—were even more deficient. Supreme Court decisions in 1972 and 1978 cast a shadow over the patentability of computer programs, and the Patent Office lacked the trained personnel to examine software applications. Trade secrets, which worked well for closeted, custom-designed technologies, were of far less use for publicly disseminated off-the-shelf products. And though proposals abounded for tailor-made laws fitted to the specific characteristics of software, they lacked the pedigrees of historical validation and international acceptance.

There was also an affirmative case to be made for copyright, at least by IBM and other companies interested in securing their operating system platforms. Protecting computer programs as literary works under the premier international copyright treaty, the Berne Convention for the Protection of Literary and Artistic Works, would ensure protection for these operating systems not only in the United States, but also, automatically, in every one of the dozens of countries belonging to the Berne Union. (It is no coincidence that when the United States finally adhered to the Berne Convention in 1989, more than a century after the treaty first came into force, it was at the height of IBM's campaign to get computer programs recognized as copyrightable literary works worldwide; an IBM representative was one of the thirteen witnesses who testified in support of Berne adherence at the 1988 Senate hearings.) Automatic worldwide protection was only one of Berne's advantages over its sister treaty for patents, the Paris Convention for the Protection of Industrial Property. Unlike the Paris Convention, which allows compulsory licensing across the full range of patent rights, the Berne Convention allows compulsory licenses only in highly limited circumstances—a valuable guarantee to platform owners that they would not have to open their platforms to competitors on the "reasonable" terms of a compulsory license.

The U.S. Copyright Office issued its first registration for a computer program in 1964, and in 1980 Congress expressly brought computer programs under the Copyright Act. But the legislation left unanswered several questions of importance to companies like IBM, DEC, and Apple, including that of whether courts would extend copyright protection not only to application programs but also to the computer operating systems that defined those companies' platforms. (Some argued that application programs were more like literary works than were operating systems, which worked more like circuitry.) Apple tested the waters with a lawsuit filed in 1982 in federal court in Pennsylvania, alleging that Franklin Computer had infringed the copyright in the Apple II operating system by copying the system's code as part of its plan to build a personal computer that would run applications designed for the Apple II, and that would compete on the Apple II platform generally. Franklin responded that producing a system on which Apple-compatible software could run required it to emulate the Apple operating system, which, as essentially a method of operation, was itself unprotectible.

Apple lost in the trial court, which questioned the copyrightability of operating system programs, but in 1983, on appeal to the Third Circuit Court of Appeals, Apple won a resounding endorsement for its position. (This was the court that, a year later, gave the motion picture studios their first victory in the test case strategy to establish the scope of the public performance right.) The court rejected Franklin's argument that as a process, system, or method of operation, operating systems were categorically excluded from protection under the Copyright Act. Instead it observed that "Apple does not seek to copyright the method which instructs the computer to inform its operating functions, but only the instructions themselves"—the implication being that the lines of code in a computer program constitute the programs protectible "expression," not its unprotectible method or "idea."

Welcome as the Third Circuit's decision was to Apple and other companies seeking to maintain control over their software platforms, it did not answer the crucial question of whether the interface specifications that govern access to an operating system were themselves copyrightable. Can copyright lock up an element so crucial to achieving interoperability—and competition—in the computer industry? As the motion picture studios did in staging their test cases for the public performance right, the software owners filed their next case in the same circuit, seeking to hammer home their initial victory. Although the new case, *Whelan Associates v. Jaslow Dental Laboratories,* involved not interface specifications but a program for administering the business of dental laboratories, the hope was that by adeptly positioning the facts and the law, a decision might result that endorsed a scope of copyright protection for computer programs that was broad enough to encompass interface specifications.

The broad protectionists prevailed. The district court ruled for the copyright owner and the Third Circuit Court of Appeals affirmed, holding that the copyright in the dental lab computer program covered not only the exact lines of the program's code but also, because of the expense of its development, the program's "structure, sequence and organization." The program's only unprotectible element, the court said, was its seminal concept—"the efficient organization of a dental laboratory." The platform proprietors cheered, for here was a judicially endorsed scope of protection broad enough to encompass interface specifications.

The stakes in *Whelan v. Jaslow* were greater than whether one dental laboratory system infringed another, and it was no coincidence that ADAPSO, the Association of Data Processing Service Organizations, dominated by companies favoring broad copyright protection for computer programs, filed an amicus curiae brief in support of Whelan. (ADAPSO, along with Microsoft, also filed amicus briefs supporting Apple in *Apple v. Franklin*.) Among the other trade associations that became active in the software debate, aligning themselves with IBM, DEC, and Apple, were the Computer and Business Equipment Manufacturers Association and the Information Industry Association. On the side of companies in the interoperability community opposing protection for interface specifications were Amdahl, StorageTek, and Unisys, among others, and the Computer and Communications Industry Association, eventually to be joined by the American Committee for Interoperable Systems. Copyright academics, with few exceptions, lined up behind the interoperability community, and in the years following the *Whelan* decision dozens of conferences and law review articles found academics, practitioners, programmers, and trade association representatives debating whether *Whelan* was good law or bad.

Advances in copyright law often occur by indirection, and the next crucial turn in the interoperability debate came not in a dispute involving interface specifications or even computer programs, but rather in a 1991 Supreme Court case, *Feist v. Rural Telephone*, dealing with telephone directories. In *Feist* the Supreme Court ruled that no matter how much expense and effort—"sweat of the brow"—the copyright claimant had invested in collecting names, addresses, and telephone numbers, if the effort did not result in creative expression (the alphabetical ordering of subscribers was not, in the Court's view, creative), it was not copyrightable. It did not require much subtlety to see the connection between the Supreme Court's decision in *Feist* and the Third Circuit's decision in *Whelan*. If effort and expense alone could not support copyright for telephone directory white pages, they would also not support *Whelan*'s protection of software structure, no matter how costly it was to develop, because it was insufficiently creative to qualify as copyrightable expression.

Feist's impact on the interoperability debate became apparent less than a year later in a dispute between the giant software developer Computer Associates and a smaller competitor, Altai, Inc., over an application program for IBM mainframe operating systems. Aided by amicus briefs—this time from the Software Publishers Association, supporting a loose standard for protecting computer programs, and from Compaq, Novell, Borland, and the American Committee for Interoperable Systems, arguing for a strict one—the Second Circuit Court of Appeals categorically rejected the Third Circuit's approach to copyrightability in *Whelan*. Relying on the Supreme Court's declaration in *Feist* that "the primary objective of copyright is not to reward the labor of authors," the court of appeals observed that "serious students of the industry have been highly critical of the sweeping scope of copyright protection engendered by the *Whelan* rule, in that it enables first comers to 'lock-up' basic programming techniques as implemented in programs to perform particular tasks."

Although the court in *Computer Associates* did not expressly consider interface specifications, its exclusion of protection for elements of a computer program "dictated by considerations of efficiency" or "required by factors external to the program itself " left no doubt about its intentions, and, thanks to the court's definitive, almost treatiselike approach, the decision for all practical purposes ended the debate over the copyrightability of interface specifications. Every circuit court in the country that subsequently addressed the question of the scope of copyright protection for computer programs chose to follow *Computer Associates* rather than *Whelan*.

SOFTWARS II: CAN A COMPETITOR COPY THE KEYS TO THE KINGDOM?

Establishing that interface specifications are not copyrightable was just the first battle for companies in the interoperability community. The second battle centered on how those companies could obtain access to the specifications so that they could copy them. Source code— the form in which programmers write computer programs—is comprehensible to humans but not to the computer that must execute a program. Object code—the form to which source code must be converted for it to be executed by a computer—is comprehensible to computers but generally not to humans. The problem is that software producers commonly market their programs only in the form of indecipherable object code; by guarding the underlying, and comprehensible, source code as a trade secret, they can conceal their interface specifications from the prying eyes of competitors.

Legally, it is permissible to reverse-engineer a trade secret. A perfume producer that analyzes its competitor's fragrance to determine its composition, and then manufactures and distributes an identical fragrance, will face no liability for trade secret theft. There is a reverse-engineering technique, called disassembly, by which an engineer can convert a computer program's object code into comprehensible source code. The engineer can then analyze the source code to pick out the program's underlying—and uncopyrightable—interface specifications, and thus obtain the key to achieving interoperability. But copyright presents an obstacle, for as an initial step, disassembly necessarily requires the competitor to make at least one copy of the program's entire object code. The persisting question in the United States and abroad was whether that interim copy constitutes copyright infringement.

The software battles were being fought in Europe as well as in the United States, and in 1989 the Commission of the European Community issued a proposal for a software directive that sought to resolve the three central questions of software protection: Should computer programs be protected by copyright? (The proposal said they should be.) Should interface specifications be protectible? (The proposed directive said no, at least where the interface had to be copied in order to achieve interoperability.) Should reverse engineering be allowed? (The proposal contained no express provision on the point.) Vigorous lobbying ensued—IBM, DEC, Apple, and Microsoft arrayed on one side against reverse engineering, and Groupe Bull, Olivetti, NCR, Unisys, and Fujitsu España on the other—efforts that, in May 1991, produced the proposal ultimately adopted for implementation by EC member countries: while computer programs would be subject to copyright, interface specifications would not, and reverse engineering would be permitted where "indispensable to obtain the information necessary to achieve the interoperability of an independently created computer program with other programs."

In the early 1990s, the U.S. Congress lacked the will to confront the reverse-engineering issue as directly as did the European Community, so once again, the task fell to the courts. And once again, the issue was presented on facts that fell outside the mainstream of the software debate. Through the 1980s, Sega Enterprises, one of the world's largest video-game producers, sought to restrict the market for video games capable of running on Sega consoles to their own games and to games of third-party licensees that agreed to Sega's terms. When Accolade, a Silicon Valley video-game producer, failed to obtain a license from Sega, it did what other software producers in the interoperable community had done before it: it copied and disassembled the object code of Sega's video games to identify the interface specifications that would unlock Sega's Genesis console, and then it incorporated this code into its own independently created video games so that Accolade games could be played on the Genesis console.

In October 1991, Sega sued Accolade for copyright infringement in San Francisco federal district court, and six months later obtained a ruling in its favor. Six months after that, the Ninth Circuit Court of Appeals reversed, holding that "where disassembly is the only way to gain access to the ideas and functional elements embodied in a copyrighted computer program and where there is a legitimate reason for seeking such access, disassembly is a fair use of the copyrighted work as a matter of law." Other decisions across the country confirmed the result. Fair use, that durable copyright safety valve that had excused time-shifting in the *Sony* case, now carved out an important exception in the interest of open platforms.

Mapping Copyright Change

The great mistake made by the owners of entrenched software platforms like IBM's System/360 and Sega's video-game platform was in believing that they could enlist copyright to obtain not only market share, but enduring market dominance. Copyright has historically rejected protection for ideas, particularly functional ideas, and it was no surprise to students of copyright history that courts ultimately rejected copyright protection for interface specifications or that, through fair use, they opened the door to competitors' unauthorized reproduction of computer code in order to identify those functional elements.

The greatest casualty of the softwars was copyright itself, and not because the judicial decisions in any way injured copyright principle—they did not—but because the debate ignited a skepticism about the value of copyright that was unprecedented in the law's long history. Harvard law professor, and later Supreme Court justice, Stephen Breyer set the tone with a 1970 article in the *Harvard Law Review*, "The Uneasy Case for Copyright," that was nothing less than an attempt to dismantle the centuries-long economic and moral justifications for copyright law. Other academics picked up this critical theme during the software battles of the 1980s, and have not dropped it since. No expansionist legislative initiative—from extending the term of copyright to shoring up the rights of movie and record companies—has failed to trigger a loud and critical academic response.

Any business that produces or distributes copyrighted context should attend to this new direction in the law, because the present tendency to constrain rather than expand copyright can be found among lawmakers as well as academics. The judiciary, which has historically supplied copyright's conserving force, has since the 1990s substantially enlarged the inroads on copyright, following first the Supreme Court's 1991 decision in the *Feist* case, raising the bar for copyright protection, and then the Supreme Court's decision in the 2 Live Crew parody case, with the lower courts enlarging the fair use doctrine to encompass even the most modest efforts at altering a copyrighted work. Congress too has displayed a newly conservative bias, enacting legislation that succeeded in extinguishing perennial copyright fires but charted no new ground in extending rights. The Internet will doubtless prove to be the most important force in determining how long copyright's current contraction lasts and how deep its effects will be. As U.S. Register of Copyrights Marybeth Peters observed, the Internet has for the first time brought copyright law and copyright users face-to-face, confronting users directly with the law's "stern list of do's and don'ts." If this confrontation leaves consumers with a poor view of copyright, the law's prospects for growth over the coming years will be seriously diminished.

4

Trademarks

American trademark law is in the midst of a great transformation. A law whose original object was to protect consumers from confusion about the source of goods has since branched out and will today also protect brand equity for its own sake, apart from any possibility of consumer confusion. One hundred years ago, the St. Louis brewer Anheuser-Busch could enjoin another brewery from putting the name "Budweiser" on its label because consumer confusion would result; but the company could not have stopped a tobacco producer from putting "Budweiser" on cigarettes, because no one would think the brewer was the source of the cigarettes. Whether or not purchasers would presently make that mistake, trademark law has so expanded its reach that Anheuser-Busch could today halt the unauthorized use of the Budweiser brand not only on beer and cigarettes, but on fast food and even glassware.

Trademark law's origins as a consumer protection doctrine lie in the English common law of fraud and deceit. If a nineteenth-century grocer told a customer that the crackers in a bin were fresh when he knew they were stale, the customer who relied on the deceitful misrepresentation would be entitled to legal relief. From this beginning, it was only a small step for courts in England and later the United States to develop a distinct tort of "passing off" to enjoin the grocer from misrepresenting not only the product's quality but also its source. A grocer would commit passing off if he told his customers that the crackers in the bin came from the well-regarded Smith & Co., when in fact they came from the ill-reputed Jones & Sons. When in the late nineteenth century grocers began to speak less, letting brand names and distinctive packaging assume the grocer's role of informing customers about the source and quality of the goods, it required but one more small step for courts to endow Smith & Co. with rights against Jones & Sons in the event Jones & Sons deceitfully affixed a "Smith & Co." label to its packages of crackers. Thus was trademark law born, protecting distinctive names and symbols against use by competitors to deceive consumers as to the source of goods or services.

The rationale for trademark law lies in the economics of information, and not in the more familiar economics of public goods associated with patent and copyright law. While the object of patent and copyright law is to give businesses an incentive to invest in producing new and better information-rich *goods,* the object of trademark law is to stimulate investment in producing information *about* goods. Nicholas Economides, of New York University's Stern School of Business, put it simply: "The economic role of the trademark is to help the consumer identify the unobservable features of the trademarked product." For example, "the consumer of NABISCO WHEAT THINS knows and cares little about source (manufacturer). Rather, the consumer identifies the trademark with the features of the commodity, including crispness, sweetness or lack thereof, color, and the like."

Although trademark law's origins, and legitimacy, lie in its protection of consumers, the law has always, and inescapably, protected producers as well, giving them an incentive to invest in differentiating their products and brands from those of competitors. If a competitor were allowed to mislabel its own sweeter or less crispy cracker as "Wheat Thins," not only would customers be hurt, but Nabisco would suffer too. Because such sales are usually at a lower price, the competitor's misbranding would over the short term divert consumers from the authentic Nabisco product. Over the longer term, the power of the "Wheat Thins" brand itself, and its consequent ability to attract purchasers, would diminish as buyers grew less certain about the qualities of the product they could expect to find in their next box of "Wheat Thins." Thus, while trademark law's credo was (and still is) consumer protection, the law has from the very start also protected the commercial interests of producers.

The great revolution in trademark law has been to elevate this incidental protection for producers into a full-fledged property right—much like patent or copyright—that has only the most attenuated connection to consumer confusion, and sometimes no connection at all. Few people would believe that DuPont makes shoes, that Buick makes aspirin, or that Kodak makes pianos, but a congressional report on 1995 "antidilution" amendments to the Trademark Act cites these unauthorized uses of famous brand names as instances of dilution that would be barred under the newly amended act. "The concept of dilution recognizes the substantial investment the owner has made in the mark and the commercial value and aura of the mark itself, protecting both from those who would appropriate the mark for their own gain."

Dilution doctrine did not emerge from trademark law all at once and fully developed. Nor is it the only doctrine to disconnect trademark law from its common-law moorings in deceit and confusion and draw it closer to the patent and copyright domain of public goods. Instead, dilution and these other doctrines evolved, case by case, from the two oldest and most central of trademark principles: the principle that trademark ownership depends on trademark *use*, and the principle that, for a trademark to be protected, it must be *distinctive*.

Trademarks and Consumer Confusion: The Use Requirement

Trademark rights in the United States require trademark use, and the company that is first to use its brand in connection with goods or services in the marketplace is the company that gets to own it. (The urban legend of the entrepreneur who registered several attractive brand names for marijuana in anticipation of its legalization is just that—a legend.) If Acme Co. is the first to come up with the name "Bravo" for detergent, but Best Co. is the first to affix the name to goods and to sell those goods in commerce, it is Best, not Acme, that would get the rights to the name, entitling it to stop anyone, including Acme, from using "Bravo" in sales of detergent. The reason for this result lies in the role that trademark use plays in consumer confusion: only when Best put "Bravo" brand detergent on the supermarket shelves were consumers first able to connect the name to a product and thus to develop expectations about product quality when buying the brand.

Trademark use, and consequently trademark rights, can be geographically circumscribed. If Cash, Inc. was the first to open a "Riverside National Bank" in California, and subsequently Dollar Ltd. was the first to open its own "Riverside National Bank" in New York, each would have the exclusive right to use the "Riverside" name in its own territory, but not beyond; Cash could keep Dollar's Riverside banks out of California, and Dollar could keep Cash out of New York. For Cash to secure exclusive rights to the Riverside name in New York, it would have to establish a branch in New York under that name before anyone else did, including Dollar. The logic behind the rule is that California customers will have one set of expectations when they enter Cash's Riverside Bank there, and New York customers will have their own expectations when they bank at Dollar's establishment there.

The principle of market segregation applies to product and service markets as well as to geographic ones. If Acme applied "Bravo" to detergent and Elite applied "Bravo" to motor oil, each company would have exclusive rights in the brand for its respective product. When Acme sells detergent under the name "Bravo," purchasers will pin their expectations of quality to that product and that name, just as they will attach a different set of expectations when they see the name "Bravo" on Elite motor oil. For Acme to obtain exclusive rights in "Bravo" for motor oil, it would have to enter the motor oil market under that name before Best or anyone else did.

For brand-name companies, a law that ties rights to use can be frustrating. One effect of the forced connection is to discourage investment in promoting a brand. Would Acme be willing to invest tens of millions of dollars building up the "Bravo" brand for detergent if it knows that the only way it could control the brand in the market for motor oil would be to enter that market before someone else? The use requirement effectively penalizes first adopters who lack the resources or business motive to immediately enter all of the natural markets for their brands, and rewards predators who wait for goodwill to develop around another company's brand in one market and then, at least so long as consumers are not confused as to source, trade on the brand's value by introducing it on a new product in a different market.

Use-based rules increase business risk. In January 1999, as part of a multimillion-dollar promotion of its Internet portal, the Go Network, the Walt Disney Company formally introduced what it thought was a new logo—a traffic signal with the word "Go" inside a green circle surrounded by a yellow square. Go Network placed the logo on virtually every product it offered. What Disney overlooked was that a year earlier, GoTo.com, a search engine company, had started using a logo consisting of the words "Go" and "To" inside a green circle. GoTo.com sued Disney for trademark infringement. Similarly, NBC spent fourteen months and $750,000 developing what it thought was a new logo—a stylized red-and-blue "N"—as part of its corporate identity program, and plastered the logo over its broadcasts and on its stationery, cameras, vans, trailers, and helicopter. Nebraska Educational TV, which had adopted a substantially similar logo six months earlier—at a cost of less than $100—sued NBC for trademark infringement.

In both cases, the trial courts ruled for David against Goliath. When a federal trial court granted GoTo.com a preliminary injunction against Disney, over Disney's objection that it would cost more than $40 million to abandon its logo, Disney settled the lawsuit by agreeing to stop using the logo and to pay GoTo.com $21.5 million. Nebraska Educational TV also obtained an injunction, prompting NBC to give the educational broadcaster $500,000 worth of new and used equipment and $55,000 to replace its logo with a new one. Nor will good faith save the subsequent user. As the Disney court observed, even if it "concluded that Disney was as innocent as a fawn with *no* intent to copy or appropriate GoTo's logo, it would prove nothing since no such intent is necessary to demonstrate a likelihood of confusion."

What do brand asset companies do to protect themselves against being blindsided like Disney, NBC, and countless others? A search of the U.S. Patent and Trademark Office's Trademark Principal Register is the least costly place to start, and the PTO maintains a registration database that, readily accessible and free over the Internet, provides instantaneous results.

However, because trademark rights in the United States depend upon use, not registration, search of the trademark register offers no guarantee of immunity from suit. In 1994, after obtaining a search report that revealed no federally registered trademark for either the name "Star Class" or the symbol of a star used in connection with clothing, fashion designer Tommy Hilfiger adopted the name and symbol for a new line of menswear. To the designer's later surprise, the International Star Class Yacht Racing Association had already registered the name and symbol for its Star Class boats, and was also using them for hats, clothing, flags, decals, pins, and jewelry. A federal appellate court not only approved the trial court's order that Hilfiger stop using the brand, it also directed the trial court to consider an award of punitive damages and an accounting for profits against Hilfiger for failing to follow the company trademark lawyer's suggestion that the company pursue its trademark search beyond Class 25, the clothing classification, of the Principal Register. Ultimately, the trial court found no bad faith, and so declined to award damages.

Best practice among companies introducing a new brand is to look beyond the Principal Register, and to commission searches of brand-name dictionaries, trade journals, telephone directories, industry and business directories, and, increasingly, comprehensive Web-based information services. Professional search services exist that conduct these searches with relative efficiency. The problem is not just that each additional level of search becomes progressively more expensive, but that there is virtually no end to the searches that can in fact be conducted. Even the most diligent company will draw the line somewhere, but always with the agonizing knowledge that if it had pressed the search just one level deeper it might have uncovered a prior use that would defeat its own.

In 1946, as part of its first overhaul of trademark law in forty-one years, the U.S. Congress introduced a provision that gave brand-name companies some, albeit limited, relief from the harsh inefficiencies of the use requirement. Henceforth, a company that marketed its brand on goods or services in interstate commerce could, if it promptly registered the mark, obtain exclusive rights not only in those places where it did business, but throughout the United States. So, in the earlier example, if Cash, Inc. opened Riverside National Banks in California and Oregon, and then registered the name on the Principal Register in the PTO, it would enjoy nationwide rights, and could stop Dollar Ltd. from subsequently opening a Riverside National Bank in New York or anywhere else. The shortcoming of the reform, which persists to the present, is that it gives the registrant, Cash, Inc., rights only against companies that first use the brand *after* its registration. Earlier users—say, a Riverside Bank that opened in Iowa before the effective date of the Cash, Inc. registration—could continue to exclude Cash, Inc. from its territory. Since a great many small businesses on tight budgets decide not to register their brands—even the simplest federal registration can cost $325 for a single class of goods with online filing and before legal fees—this happens far more often than the better-heeled brand-name companies would like, requiring them to continue conducting searches outside the register if they want to avoid the fate of Disney, NBC, and Tommy Hilfiger.

The enduring legal preference for use over registration separates American trademark law from that in the rest of the world, for other countries allow trademark rights to be acquired on the basis of registration alone. Any American company that has sought protection for its brands abroad knows that if its search of a country's trademark register reveals no conflicting registrations, it can as a rule market its branded goods in that country free of fear that a prior user will be able to stop it. And if, having searched the country's trademark register without finding prior registrations, the company promptly registers its own trademark on the register, it can also be confident that it will be able to stop any other company from exploiting the brand in that country. Although critics argue that such registration-based systems lead to "warehousing" of unused marks—like the mythical brands for marijuana cigarettes—in fact, most countries will remove a brand from the register if it is not used within a prescribed period, commonly three years.

Since foreign practice differs so dramatically from American practice, what happens when the two collide? In 1969, a Canadian company applied to register the trademark "Lemon Tree" for a powdered beverage mix in Canada; in May of that year, an American company started using the identical mark for a similar mix in the United States, and a month later applied for registration in the United States—a not unusual lag between use and registration. The Canadian company did not file for registration in the United States until the following September. Because, however, the United States has treaty obligations requiring American courts to honor the priority of foreign registrations, the Canadian company prevailed over the American company on the strength of its earlier Canadian registration, even though the American company used the brand first. Had the American company, like the Canadian company, been able to register "Lemon Tree" prior to use, it could well have enjoyed priority in *both* the United States and Canada, which is similarly bound to honor earlier foreign registrations.

In part because of the use requirement's prejudice to U.S. registrants in their competition with foreign registrants, Congress in 1988 dropped use as a requirement for *filing* a trademark application, even though it retained use as a requirement for ultimately *registering* the mark. Under this amendment, an American brand-name owner can file an "intent to use" application in the PTO, effectively reserving a mark without using it for as long as four years, at the end of which the trademark must either be used and registered or the filing abandoned. If this reform had been in effect at the time of the Lemon Tree case, it would have been possible for the American brand owner to obtain filing priority over the Canadian owner. And, even though a U.S. registration will still not issue until the applicant actually uses its mark, the 1988 reform gives companies the critical opportunity to invest in selecting a new brand without fear that a competitor will beat it to market and defeat its ability to register. But despite the 1988 amendments, American trademark law remains wedded to the use requirement, and a company that does no more than use a brand before another company obtains registration for the same brand will continue to enjoy exclusive rights in every market occupied by its use.

Use and Abandonment: The McDonald's Dilemma

The use requirement's continuing grip on American trademark law affects other business practices too. Like a car left by the side of the road, a trademark will be deemed to have been abandoned if its owner stops using it and lacks any intention to resume use. (The Trademark Act adds a formal calibration to this by providing that nonuse for three consecutive years creates a presumption that a mark has been abandoned.) Also, as with the abandoned car, use can revive ownership, and the first user who adopts the abandoned brand will acquire ownership of it. When in 1972 Humble Oil replaced "Humble" with "Exxon" as its principal brand name, it nonetheless continued making limited sales under the Humble brand. Two years later, an unrelated oil exploration firm began calling itself "Humble," and when Exxon sued, the exploration firm defended that Humble had abandoned its trademark. The court agreed, ruling that Exxon had abandoned the name and that it made no difference that the oil exploration company presumably adopted the Humble mark to gain some of the luster historically associated with the Humble name.

The more valuable a brand is, the more reason a company has to police its unauthorized use in distant markets. Yet the fact that, like other intellectual assets, brands can be exploited repeatedly by uncounted users around the world makes them far harder to secure from abandonment than tangible assets like automobiles. No company has exercised greater vigilance than McDonald's has in enforcing the "Mc" prefix. In the United States, the company has succeeded in opposing registration or use of such marks as McBagels for a bagel bakery and restaurant, McTeddy for handcrafted teddy bears dressed in Scottish clothing, McDental for a dental group, and McClaim for legal and consultation services. The company has enjoyed somewhat less success outside the United States, winning preliminary skirmishes with McFish in New Zealand and MacDog in Germany, but losing to McBeans in Canada, McAllan in Denmark, McChina in the United Kingdom, and MacTea, MacChocolate, and MacNoodles in Singapore.

McDonald's' successful lawsuit against Quality Inns International's "McSleep" economy hotels illustrates the legal dimension of attempts to protect against trademark abandonment. Quality Inns made four arguments to support its use of the "Mc" prefix for its new chain, but the court rejected each one. Against Quality Inns' argument that the name "McSleep" would not confuse consumers into thinking McDonald's was operating or franchising the new chain, the court relied on survey results in which over 20 percent of the respondents gave "McDonald's" as their answer to the question, "Who or what company do you believe owns or operates the hotel called McSleep Inn?" To the argument that McDonald's marks have been used in the fast-food business but not in the lodging business, the court observed that McDonald's had obtained registrations for a range of uses wider than just food services—including "McStop" for interstate travel plazas and "McShuttle" for ground transportation—and had named its own headquarters hotel "McLodge." This effectively gave the company a "family" of marks under the "Mc" prefix, and consequently a first claim on other such uses. Against the claim that McDonald's had acquiesced in use of the prefix by others—among them McHappy, McDonuts, McMaid, McPaint, McBud—at least implicitly abandoning rights outside the fast-food market, the court found that only four of these constituted significant uses, and that none was sufficiently prominent to diminish consumer identification of McSleep with McDonald's. Finally, the court rejected the argument that "Mc" had become a generic prefix meaning thrifty, consistent, and convenient, holding that the use of "Mc" by others always referred to McDonald's itself as a source.

What was Quality Inns thinking when it chose the McSleep name? According to the trial testimony of company CEO Robert C. Hazard, the name occurred to him at two o'clock one morning and he jotted it down at bedside (good evidence that middle-of-the-night ideas are rarely as good as they seem at the time). Although Hazard testified that he wanted a name that conveyed thrift and consistency, the court disbelieved the denial that he was thinking of McDonald's at the time he came up with McSleep. One damning piece of evidence may have been an interview he gave to the *Washington Post* at the time his company announced its new chain. "Obviously, [the name is] a takeoff on McDonald's and quality at a consistent price," and a bit of leg-pulling: "We think we're going to let McDonald's continue to use their name." The court also found it telling that Quality Inns' advertising agency demanded an indemnity agreement in order to protect itself against litigation by McDonald's—something the agency had never asked for previously.

Avoiding abandonment requires more of brand owners than just monitoring uses and registrations of their marks in markets where they may someday want to use the mark themselves. Yet suing to enjoin an unauthorized use of a brand name can have adverse consequences for a company's public relations. According to Shelby Yastrow, general counsel for McDonald's, even the use of the full McDonald's name may get a mild response if it is on no more than a single restaurant. "I can't let him do it," Yastrow told a *Corporate Legal Times* writer, "because pretty soon somebody else will open up a McDonald's restaurant. On the other hand, I don't want a reputation that this big, nice, family-oriented company, which has 200 Ronald McDonald Houses around the country, goes out and sues somebody in Green Bay who happens to be named McDonald." What does McDonald's do in such cases? "We'll tell him we know he has some money invested, so here's $20,000 to change your sign and your stationery, and maybe some more money to advertise the new name." There are some uses over which the company actually enthuses because it establishes the brand as a gold standard for fast food. One is the *Economist* magazine's "Big Mac Index," which uses the price of a Big Mac in different countries to identify distortions in currency exchange rates.

The Use Requirement and Trademark Licenses

Because neither patent nor copyright law has a use requirement, few patents and copyrights are lost by abandonment. (A patent or copyright owner who ignores an unauthorized use will lose rights, but only against that particular infringer, and only after the statute of limitations expires.) Trademark owners suffer another comparative disadvantage in their dealings with unauthorized users. While a patent or copyright owner will frequently enter into a license with an infringer, and thus expand its market, a trademark owner, like McDonald's in the McSleep case, will be concerned that such a license might bring its brand into the wrong market at the wrong time. Also, unless the trademark owner imposes strict quality controls in the license agreement, the brand can fall victim to the vagaries of another company's quality control practices. Indeed, it constitutes trademark abandonment for a company to license its brand without quality controls. (The source of this rule is not so much the use requirement as it is trademark law's overarching aim to secure consumer expectations of consistent quality.) Thus, for McDonald's to preserve its "Mc" brand, its license with Quality Inns—had it decided to grant one—would not only have to include quality controls for McSleep operations, but McDonald's would have to police McSleep facilities much as it does its own franchise operations.

Courts differ in the rigor they require of quality control by licensors. In one leading case, a federal appellate court ruled that Dawn Donuts Company had not abandoned the mark "Dawn" for donuts even though it failed to include in its license agreements any system for inspection and control of the licensee's production practices and offered only the slenderest evidence at trial that its traveling sales representative conducted regular inspections. But another court held that when First Interstate Lending licensed use of the name "First Interstate" to a realty company, it abandoned all rights to the name because the license imposed on the realty company only the most general restrictions—that the licensee be a real estate broker in good standing—and ceded to the realty company sole responsibility for supervising its agents. The court concluded that "[b]ecause the quality of the work provided under the trademark could vary widely under the terms of the agreement, it can only be considered a naked license which results in the abandonment of the trademark."

Trademarks and Consumer Confusion: The Distinctiveness Requirement

Use is one traditional requirement for trademark protection in American law. The other is distinctiveness. Trademark law protects a brand only if and to the extent that the brand distinguishes, or at least is capable of distinguishing, the goods or services of one company from those of another. "Cheerios" is a distinctive brand for an oat cereal; "Oat Cereal" is not. Like the use requirement, distinctiveness has been a part of American trademark law from the beginning. And, like the use requirement, its role is changing. Just as Congress in 1946 gave trademark registrants rights in geographic markets they had not yet reached, so in 1995 it gave trademark owners rights in product markets—"Cheerios" for donuts as well as for breakfast cereal—they had not yet entered. Congress accomplished this not by tinkering with the registration process, as it did in the case of geographic rights, but rather by expanding the role of distinctiveness, effectively providing that highly distinctive or "famous" marks will enjoy rights in distant markets even though consumers are not confused by their use.

There are grades of distinctiveness. "Kodak," an arbitrary, made-up name for photographic equipment and supplies, is inherently distinctive. So is "Dial," a brand for soap that does nothing to describe the product. Because they are arbitrary and inherently distinctive, both marks were protectible from the day their owner first applied them to goods and released them to the marketplace. At the other end of the spectrum, "Camera" as a brand for cameras, or "Soap" as a brand for soap, are inherently descriptive and incapable of distinguishing source, and no amount of advertising or exposure in the marketplace will qualify either name for trademark protection. Although made-up marks like "Kodak" and "Dial" have their attractions, consumer product companies often choose terms that lie midway on the spectrum between distinctiveness and descriptiveness—words, such as "Pure" or "Palmolive" for soap, that are partially descriptive of the product, or words that at least suggest the product's qualities, such as "Ivory" or "Irish Spring"—because these terms, with their built-in meanings and associations, require less advertising to attract customers than do arbitrary marks like "Dial."

To give one company exclusive rights in even a partially suggestive term may deprive a competitor of words that it needs to describe its own product accurately. The Trademark Act reconciles the competing interests of the two companies by barring registration for marks that, when used in connection with the applicant's goods or services, are "merely descriptive" of them, unless the mark "has become distinctive of the applicant's goods in commerce." How does a merely descriptive mark become distinctive? Not surprisingly, given American trademark law's predilections, it can become distinctive through use: the Trademark Act treats an applicant's use of a mark exclusively and continuously for at least five years as strong evidence of the mark's distinctiveness.

Over a shorter period, other evidence that can establish distinctiveness includes large advertising campaigns and extensive sales. The act applies the same balancing formula to geographically descriptive terms, such as "Lackawana" for coal, and surnames, such as "McDonald's" for fast-food services, that, though not initially distinctive, may become so with time and use.

Apart from a disqualification for "immoral, deceptive or scandalous" marks, American trademark law will protect virtually anything as a trademark—a word, a name, a symbol, a color, a package design—so long as it is distinctive. This has not always been the case in the United States, and is still not in a great many other countries, although most are moving in this direction. Even after the 1946 reform legislation overhauled American trademark law, extending protection to any distinctive "word, name, symbol, or device or any combination thereof," the Patent Office at first read the formula narrowly. The office refused, for example, to register 3M's well-known and highly distinctive sleigh-shaped dispenser for cellophane adhesive tape on the ground that "device" in the statute meant not a mechanical device like a tape dispenser but an artistic figure, like a heraldic emblem. By the late 1950s, however, the office relented and began registering such distinctively shaped packaging as the classic Coca-Cola bottle. (In Coca-Cola's early days, when it was sold alongside other bottled drinks from bins under layers of ice, a purchaser could identify the soft drink only by the blind feel of the familiar—and distinctive—Coca-Cola bottle.)

Registrable trademarks today are limited only by the imagination of brand asset companies in choosing marks to distinguish their goods and services. The Patent Office has issued registrations for sounds, such as the NBC chimes; cartoon characters, such as Mickey Mouse and Bugs Bunny; slogans, such as GE's "We Bring Good Things to Life"; colors, such as pink for Owens Corning's fiberglass insulation; location on goods, such as Levi Strauss's rectangular bit of fabric sewn onto the hip pocket of its garments; buildings, such as the Fotomat kiosk; and even scents—a "high-impact fresh floral fragrance reminiscent of Plumeria blossoms" infused in embroidery yarn.

And holes from some of America's leading golf courses? In 1991 a company called Tour 18 opened a golf course incorporating well-known holes from championship courses around the country, among them the third hole from a course at Pinehurst Country Club, the fourteenth hole from Pebble Beach, and the eighteenth hole from Harbor Town Golf Links on Hilton Head Island. The three course owners sued, claiming trademark infringement of "the shapes of plaintiffs' golf holes, the length and width of the holes, the placement and shape of sand and water hazards, the size and shape of the greens, the slope and elevation of the holes, and the golf holes' surrounding vegetation." The trial court ruled against Pinehurst and Pebble Beach on the ground that the holes were not sufficiently distinctive to qualify for protection, but held that Harbor Town's eighteenth hole qualified because of its inherently distinctive red-and-white-striped lighthouse. The court also ruled that Tour 18's use of plaintiffs' trademarks on promotional materials and scorecards wrongly confused consumers into thinking that the course owners sponsored or approved Tour 18's operation.

The most important exception to this generally open-armed approach to registration of distinctive marks is the statute's exclusion of functional marks on the principle that their registration will constitute an unreasonable barrier to entry for competitors. Thus an auto parts manufacturer would be unable to register the color red as a trademark for an automobile brake light, and a farm equipment manufacturer could not register the color green for a tractor, because drivers expect all brake lights to be red and farmers prefer to have all their equipment match; giving one manufacturer an exclusive right to the color green would make it harder for other manufacturers to sell to a farmer who already has equipment in that color.

Distinctiveness and Genericide: The Thermos Dilemma

The great trademark risk for a consumer brand company today is not that its chosen trademark will be insufficiently distinctive to qualify for protection, but that, in promoting its mark and acquiring distinctiveness, the company also succeeds in identifying the mark with the class of goods generally—"Thermos," say, becoming the generic term for a vacuum-insulated bottle—and forfeiting any trademark rights in the term. (Trademark lawyers call this "genericide.") Of course, the irony is that genericide occurs at the very moment a product manager's dream comes true and the product brand becomes synonymous with the product itself. Some years ago, as part of its advertising campaign to forestall generic use of the term "Xerox," Xerox Corp. commissioned cartoonist Charles Addams to depict a graveyard with the tombstones of marks that had fallen to genericide. Among the victims: "Escalator," "Trampoline," "Raisin Bran," "Linoleum," "Yo-Yo," and "Shredded Wheat." The advertisement's headline was: ONCE A TRADEMARK, NOT ALWAYS A TRADE-MARK.

Brand-name owners can take steps to reduce the risk of genericide, but the ultimate legal fact—whether people use the mark generically as a noun or a verb—lies in human behavior that falls outside the trademark owner's control. Starting in 1907, when the American Thermos Bottle Company first applied for registration of the "Thermos" mark as applied to vacuum-insulated bottles, the company advertised its product as a "Thermos bottle," a usage that dangerously invited generic use by consumers. Not surprisingly, and as early as 1910, the public began to use the term as a synonym for a vacuum-insulated bottle. American Thermos viewed this opportunity as an "enormous amount of free advertising." However, following a judge's observation in a 1922 case that the trademark status of the "Thermos" mark "is not absolutely free from doubt," the company started using the words "vacuum bottle" or "vacuum jug" along with "Thermos"—the use of "vacuum" was intended to dispel the force of "Thermos" as a noun—and included a reference to its trademark registration. In 1935, the company hired a clipping service to monitor generic uses of "thermos" in advertising and trade literature, but until 1959 made no particular effort to monitor generic uses in nontrade publications.

American Thermos's efforts were too little, too late. When in 1958 its successor, King-Seeley, sued Aladdin Industries for threatening to sell vacuum-insulated containers under the name "thermos," Aladdin defended that the "Thermos" mark had been abandoned and was free for use by all. According to the court's findings, 12 percent, only a small minority, of consumers appreciated the trademark significance of "Thermos." Although the court held that the trademark was still valid, it circumscribed King-Seeley's rights: Aladdin was free to use the term "thermos" in lowercase if it was preceded by the possessive "Aladdin." But once the public gets into the habit of using a term generically, it is almost impossible to reverse its collapse, and inevitably "Thermos" slipped further into generic use. In 1963 a federal appellate court ruled that "whether the appropriation by the public was due to highly successful educational and advertising campaigns or to lack of diligence in policing is of no consequence; the fact is that the word 'thermos' has entered the public domain beyond recall."

Oliver P. Howes Jr., whose law firm represented American Thermos throughout the litigation, has observed that the company's central mistake was failing to adopt a rigorous trademark strategy from the start. The company was surely mistaken—as a matter of trademark law, if not marketing practice—to use "Thermos" generically in its advertising. Instead, it should have given early and equal prominence to a descriptive term such as "vacuum bottle," much as Kraft did with "Jell-O" brand gelatin, or as Coca-Cola did after "cola" was held to be a generic term, leaving the company with rights in the aggregate term "Coca-Cola" as well as in "Coke."

Some of the most successful brands are—precisely because they are successful—particularly susceptible to genericide, and best practice among their owners includes monitoring use in all media, alerting editors and dictionary publishers to their concerns about use of their brands in a generic sense, and, perhaps less effectively, taking out ads in media-oriented publications. A single issue of *Writer's Digest* contained advertisements warning off writers and editors from generic use of such terms as "Xerox," "Rolodex," "Weight Watchers," and even "Realtor." Kimberly-Clark paid for a full-page ad for "Kleenex": "To all the writers and typists and proofreaders and editors who help us protect our trademark Kleenex® by always starting it with a capital K followed by l-e-e-n-e-x and following it with a proper generic, be it tissue or diaper: Kimberly-Clark says Bless You!" But a request is one thing, compliance another. If writers, editors, and publishers—and the public generally—continue to use the term generically, there is nothing a brand-name owner can do, for no amount of legal ingenuity has yet devised a lawsuit to stop a dictionary's usage board from calling a tissue "kleenex" or to stop a consumer from referring to an inline skate as a "rollerblade."

Trademarks Without Confusion: Brand Extension and Dilution Doctrine

Just as the increased use of product brands in the late nineteenth century accelerated the need for an efficient federal trademark law and trademark register, and reduced the need for passing off lawsuits against deceitful merchants, so did the growth in the twentieth century of corporate brands increase business pressures for a trademark doctrine that would extend a company's rights beyond the individual goods or services with which it used the brand. Brands identified with particular goods continue to be important in the twenty-first century. "Coca-Cola" continues to rank number one in *Business Week*'s annual list of most valuable brands. But corporate brands that encompass a broad range of goods and services are valuable too: the next three spots on the *Business Week* list belong to Microsoft, IBM, and GE.

Trademark law moves slowly, and for decades the law's use requirement, confining a brand owner's exclusive rights to the goods or services that the company actually marketed, stood as an obstacle to protection for broader-reaching corporate brands. In one early case, unfathomable in today's environment of brand extension, the court refused to give an injunction to Borden's Condensed Milk Company, which used the brand "Borden's" on its condensed milk, against Borden Ice Cream Company's use of the "Borden's" name on its ice cream, because Borden's Condensed Milk was not itself using the brand in the ice-cream business. Trademark is, after all, a consumer protection law, and since—or so the reasoning went—Borden's Condensed Milk Company was not in the ice-cream business, no consumer would be confused into thinking that Borden Ice Cream's product came from Borden's Condensed Milk Company. Effectively, a company's brand extension strategy, if it had one, could at any time be undermined by another company's decision to enter the target (ice cream) market first, capturing for itself the built-up value of the brand in the adjacent (condensed milk) market.

But what if a brand became sufficiently distinctive and well-known that its fame, if not its use, spread to other markets? By the 1920s, courts began to appreciate that trademark law's use and distinctiveness requirements were reciprocal and that the distinctiveness requirement could do some of the work traditionally performed by the use requirement. Prestige goods companies like Rolls-Royce of America, Alfred Dunhill of London, and Tiffany & Co. that enjoyed renown outside their actual fields of use argued that the high degree of distinctiveness their brands enjoyed should be allowed to substitute for use in adjacent, and sometimes even distant, markets. It was on this theory that Rolls-Royce won an injunction against another company's use of the Rolls-Royce brand on radio tubes, that the Alfred Dunhill tobacco firm obtained relief against use of its name on men's shirts, and that the Tiffany jewelry firm was able to shut down use of "Tiffany" as a brand for motion pictures. It is no coincidence that the three brands all enjoyed prestige as well as fame, for courts in these pioneering cases were as much concerned with the likelihood that the defendant's possibly shoddy goods might tarnish a valued name as they were with the probability that a purchaser of a Dunhill shirt or a Rolls-Royce radio tube would be confused into thinking it had been manufactured, or at least licensed, by the British trademark owner.

The *Rolls-Royce*, *Dunhill*, and *Tiffany* cases were legal foundation stones for a doctrine (dilution) and a practice (brand extension) that, if skillfully executed, can produce extraordinary returns. One brand-name consultant used the example of Crest: "Crest is not a brand of fluoride toothpaste. Crest identifies and differentiates the source of the promise that you will die with your own natural teeth. And if there is a new, improved way of delivering that promise, it should come from Crest. If Crest is just a brand of fluoride toothpaste, then we could not have Crest mouthwash. If Crest is the promise of healthy teeth, we can have Crest mouthwash and a Crest toothbrush." Dilution doctrine converts a brand from a source identifier for a single product into a platform for a linked array of goods and services.

The genius of brand extension is that it enables the owner of an admired brand to obtain instant, virtually costless attention for new products under the same brand umbrella. If the *Borden's* case first arose today, the condensed milk company would easily prevail over the ice-cream company. Without reducing the value of the "Porsche" brand for automobiles, Porsche can extend its marque's value to watches, sunglasses, and leather goods that maintain the brand's reputation for style and quality. But if the advantages of brand extension are great, so are the risks, for a poorly calculated or executed product entry will not only fail to win customers for the new product, it can also erode the value of the brand in its heritage market, as when Rolls-Royce allowed Austin to use the Rolls-Royce brand to promote an inexpensive limousine with a Rolls-Royce engine, apparently tarnishing the brand. Overexposure too can destroy a brand. The aim of decisions like *Rolls-Royce, Dunhill,* and *Tiffany* is not so much to prevent tarnishment or blurring through overexposure as it is to allow brand owners to make these mistakes for themselves. Better for Rolls-Royce to decide whether Austin can use its name than for Austin to make that decision unilaterally, without consent from Rolls-Royce but to Rolls-Royce's injury.

More was needed than a patchwork of judicial decisions like *Rolls-Royce, Dunhill,* and *Tiffany* to sustain the delicate practice of brand extension and to prevent watchful predators in adjacent markets from taking a free ride on valuable brands. Despite continuing pressures from brand-name companies for Congress to grant a broad-ranging right against trademark dilution, the first statutory prescription came from the states, with Massachusetts enacting the first antidilution statute in 1947 and more than half the states following, with legislation giving brand-name owners relief "notwithstanding the absence of competition between the parties or the absence of confusion as to the source of goods and services." In principle, at least, the owner of a well-known brand could recover against an interloper if the products sold by the two were sufficiently close that consumers would associate the defendant's product with the plaintiff, blurring the significance of the plaintiff's brand.

Finally, in 1995, Congress amended the federal Trademark Act to provide a remedy for the dilution of "famous" marks, defining "dilution" as "the lessening of the capacity of a famous mark to identify and distinguish goods or services, regardless of the presence or absence of (1) competition between the owner of the famous mark and other parties, or (2) likelihood of confusion, mistake or deception." Although the 1995 amendments require fame to be determined through a judicial weighing of several factors, courts set the bar remarkably low, characterizing as famous some marks that, doubtless, were barely known outside their neighborhoods—among them "Intermatic" for electrical products, "Lexington" for investment advisory services, and "Nail-tiques" for fingernail care products. Amendments in 2006 raised the fame bar by requiring that the mark be "widely recognized by the general consuming public of the United States as a designation of source of the goods or services of the mark's owner."

If courts have been lax in how they define fame, they have been rigorous in how they formulate dilution. One federal appellate court ruled that the brand "Polo" used as the name of a magazine did not dilute Ralph Lauren's multibillion-dollar Polo mark for goods as diverse as apparel, accessories, and home furnishings. To be sure, *Polo* magazine was the direct successor to a periodical that had been devoted to polo and endorsed by the United States Polo Association. But in Lauren's favor, the periodical had more recently repositioned itself as a lifestyle magazine aimed at Lauren's customer base, and as part of its promotion the new publisher had sent a free copy of the magazine to customers of Neiman Marcus, one of Lauren's largest retailers. Because, however, there was no evidence that Lauren's Polo mark would actually be diluted by its unauthorized use on magazines, the court ruled against the company's dilution claim.

As the *Polo* decision suggests, dilution's boundaries are inherently ill-defined. As a consequence, brand-name owners will often minimize their risk by turning to private agreements to allocate their rights in distant markets. But even these contracts are not free from doubt, particularly when the markets involved are in transition. Starting in 1968, Apple Corps Ltd., the successor to the company founded by the Beatles to exploit their recordings, obtained registration in Britain, the United States, and elsewhere for the name "Apple" and a number of apple logos used in connection with sound recordings and sound recording apparatus. Nine years later, Apple Computer incorporated and subsequently obtained registration for the Apple name and logos used in connection with computers and computer programs in the United States, the United Kingdom, and other countries.

Then, in 1980, the inevitable happened. An Apple Corps lawyer wrote to Apple Computer that its use of the "Apple" trademark infringed Apple Corps' rights. Observing that Apple Computer must be "only too well aware of the enormous expense which could be involved in trade mark litigation," the letter asked "whether there is any room for negotiating towards a settlement" that would draw a line between the activities of the two businesses. Apple Computer responded favorably, and in 1981 the two companies agreed that Apple Computer could use the "Apple" name in connection with computers, monitors, software, printers, and other peripherals, but not in connection with "goods being specifically adapted for use in recording or reproduction of music or of performing artist works." Apple Computer also paid Apple Corps $80,000.

The $80,000 was just a down payment. The parties' settlement agreement included Apple Computer's undertaking not to use the Apple mark in connection with equipment designed for synthesizing music. But the revolutionary Macintosh computer introduced in 1984 contained a chip enabling the computer to record and synthesize sound; by the late 1980s Macs were widely used for mixing music in recording studios around the world. Apple Corps again complained, two years of unproductive negotiations ensued, and in 1989 Apple Corps filed suit in Britain alleging that Apple Computer had breached the 1981 settlement agreement and seeking a worldwide injunction against the sale of Macintosh computers under the Apple name and logo. Two years of trial proceedings and more negotiations followed, the parties finally entering into a new settlement agreement that divided between Apple Computer's field of use (generally electronic equipment) and Apple Corps' field of use (generally music). Money again changed hands, with Apple Computer paying $26.5 million to Apple Corps along with a significant sum for legal fees.

The 1991 settlement agreement, like the 1981 agreement, was short-lived, this time because it failed to anticipate the revolutionary impact of the Internet on the delivery of musical works. When in spring 2003 Apple Computers added an online music store to its free iTunes program, making 200,000 songs available for paid downloads, Apple Corps once again filed suit in Britain charging that the iTunes program breached the 1991 agreement. This time there were strong arguments that could be made on both sides, and as the judge hearing the case observed, if the parties' intention "was to create obscurity and difficulty for lawyers to debate in future years, they have succeeded handsomely." When the case finally came to trial in 2006, the court ruled that Apple Computer had not breached the settlement agreement because the iTunes music store operated as a retailer, not as a record label, and the "relevant customer" would not think it was a record label. In February 2007 the parties again settled, this time on terms that gave Apple Computer, which had recently renamed itself Apple Inc., full ownership of the Apple name and logo, subject to a license back to Apple Corps permitting its continued use of the marks.

As treacherous as brand extension rules are for a company like Apple Computer that finds itself ensnared at the periphery of another trademark owner's rights, these rules also impose a substantial legal burden on the trademark claimant. Under the trademark doctrine of abandonment, a brand-name owner that fails to proceed promptly against a second user, even one in a distant product or service line, faces the risk that it will lose rights to its brand not only in the distant market, but also in the market where it first acquired goodwill. (The Trademark Act defines abandonment to encompass any course of conduct, "including acts of omission as well as commission," that causes the mark "to lose its significance as a mark.") It is no answer to an abandonment claim that the trademark owner had more important business on its agenda than suing poachers on its good name, or even that it was unaware of the unauthorized use. When, as in the Apple case, the user occupies a distant field, the consequences of the abandonment rule can seem particularly harsh. Porsche AG may have no present or even future plans to enter the nightclub market, and would be hard-pressed to justify the legal expense of monitoring and enforcing its brand in this market. Yet if the company fails to detect the use of its name on a chain of nightclubs—and to prosecute the unauthorized user when discovered—it is at risk of a legal judgment that it has abandoned its brand, and not only in the nightclub market but in markets it already occupies.

Beyond Dilution: Initial Interest Confusion Doctrine

Even apart from Congress's elimination of the competition and confusion requirements for "famous" trademarks, federal courts have on their own expanded the traditional boundaries of trademark protection to encompass unauthorized uses that only marginally trade on the value of a brand. The most powerful engine for expansion has been a doctrine called "initial interest confusion," and the most fertile venue has been the Court of Appeals for the Second Circuit, which, centered in New York City, enjoys considerable influence in intellectual property matters across the country. Where trademark law traditionally requires a brand owner to prove that a competitor's use of its mark confused consumers into purchasing the competitor's product rather than its own (the lunch counter patron who orders Coca-Cola but is served the house brand instead), initial interest confusion doctrine holds that it is enough for the brand owner to show that consumers were initially confused as to source, even though their confusion was dispelled by the time they made their purchase (a Coca-Cola sign hangs behind the lunch counter, but the counterman announces that only the house brand cola is available.). In a seminal 1975 case, the Second Circuit ruled that the defendant's "Grotrian-Steinweg" brand for pianos infringed the plaintiff's "Steinway" piano brand, not because a potential purchaser looking into the Steinweg brand would purchase it thinking it was a Steinway, but because the name "would attract potential customers based on the reputation built up by Steinway." Such "initial confusion," the court said, "works an injury to Steinway."

This notion of poaching on a trademark's aura and associations—in a later case, the Second Circuit ruled that the use of "Pegasus" as the name of an oil trading business infringed Mobil Oil's flying horse trademark even though there was no ultimate confusion among customers—distends trademark protection even more dramatically than does dilution doctrine, and is but a step away from colliding with long-standing doctrines that not only tolerate but encourage referential, albeit unauthorized, uses of brand names. For example, trademark law's fair use doctrine entitles competitors to use trademarks descriptively: "Fish Fry" on packages of coating mix for fried foods does not infringe "Fish-Fri" for the same product; "Bob's Volkswagen Repair" for a shop that services Beetles does not infringe the "Volkswagen" brand; and a defendant who purchases "Coty" brand face powder and repackages it in a compact is free to use the "Coty" name in marketing its product. Indeed, a producer of smell-alike perfumes may refer to a well-known fragrance brand in describing its product as being like or identical to the branded fragrance—so long as it in fact is, just as Pepsi-Cola can compare its soft drink to Coca-Cola.

Businesses are entitled to use a trademark not only to describe their own goods and services but also to refer descriptively to the trademark owner itself. A newspaper or a novel can freely refer to a product by its brand name, even—or perhaps especially, under free speech principles—to criticize the product. An automotive reporter can rate the safety of "Ford" automobiles and a character in a movie can complain that "Coca-Cola" is too sweet. Even a competitor can invoke an otherwise protected brand. In one case, where a newspaper solicited readers to use a profit-making 900 number to phone in their choices of the sexiest individual member of a then-popular musical group, New Kids on the Block, the court ruled that the paper could in doing so refer to the group by name, even though the newspapers were in competition with the group, which had its own 900 numbers. All the newspaper had to show was that the group was not readily identifiable without using its name, and that the paper did nothing to suggest that the group sponsored its service.

Only a lawyer could locate the dividing line between a doctrine, initial interest confusion, that says it is trademark infringement to use another's brand to bring attention to your own, and a doctrine that says it is not trademark infringement to use another's brand in describing your own. And, as will be seen in chapter 6, recent case law on initial interest confusion on the Internet has almost entirely obliterated that line. If courts apply these Internet precedents to bricks-and-mortar conflicts—and there is no reason to believe that they will not—it will introduce yet another source of instability into planning for the competitive use of brand names.

Merchandising Rights

Dilution doctrine, because it disconnects trademark law from its historical requirements of trademark use and consumer confusion, effectively protects brands apart from any product or service to which they may be attached. Indeed, dilution doctrine protects brands as if they are themselves the relevant goods. Even apart from dilution, a merchandising industry devoted to exploiting the economic power of brand names has long existed, with annual revenues running into tens of billions of dollars in the United States alone. When a clothing manufacturer puts a university's name on its sweatshirts, or a sports team's emblem on its caps, few consumers think that the university or the team manufactured, or even sponsored, the product in the sense that they think that Nabisco stands behind "Wheat Thins" or McDonald's stands behind the "Big Mac." For decades, university and team owners made little effort to control the unauthorized use of their emblems and symbols. But, beginning in the 1970s, a handful of judicial decisions, including one in a lawsuit filed by the National Hockey League and thirteen member teams against the unlicensed sale of emblems bearing the trademarks of NHL teams, opened the door to licensed trademark merchandising by turning the traditional concept of trademark confusion on its head. As the court put it in the NHL case, the confusion requirement in these cases "is met by the fact that the defendant duplicated the protected trademarks and sold them to the public knowing that the public would identify them as being the teams' trademarks." Simply put, in the court's view an emblem is both a protectible trademark and the very good whose origin the trademark signifies.

As a commercial proposition, there is not much difference between Porsche AG exploiting the hard-won value of its brand through carefully managed brand extensions, or the NHL merchandising team names, or a celebrity profiting from the value associated with his or her name or likeness in the sale of goods or services. Certainly, in a celebrity-worshiping culture, the value of associating a product or service with Elvis Presley or Tiger Woods can easily rise to the same level as connecting it to a prestige brand. Trademark law has been at least modestly accommodating, and courts have given common-law trademark rights to Vanna White against Samsung's use in an advertisement of a lookalike robot at a *Wheel of Fortune* game board, and to singersongwriter Tom Waits against Frito-Lay's use of a soundalike in a Doritos commercial. Celebrity cases have not yet followed dilution law's widening path and granted property-like rights, free of any required showing of competition or confusion, and a celebrity will as a rule win a trademark case only if he or she can show that the defendant confused consumers into believing the celebrity had authorized the use. Thus, Johnny Carson lost his claim against a port-a-potty company for selling and renting its portable toilets under the name "Here's Johnny" ("The World's Foremost Commodian") because Carson could not demonstrate a likelihood that consumers would think he endorsed or sponsored the product.

One reason federal trademark law has not so far awarded full-fledged property rights to celebrities is that state lawmakers already have. In the 1950s, state courts and legislatures began to fashion the rudiments of a new property right, called the right of publicity, that would require none of trademark law's traditional indicia of use, distinctiveness, or confusion as a condition to relief. In 1977 the new right received the imprimatur of the U.S. Supreme Court in a case involving the unauthorized taping by a television news program of Hugo Zacchini's fifteen-second human cannonball act. No fewer than twenty-eight states today recognize the right of publicity, either by statute, judge-made law, or both. These laws protect not only a celebrity's name and likeness but, depending on the governing state law, the celebrity's voice, signature, and—at the outer margins— gestures, mannerisms, and other elements associated with his persona. In one case, the court ruled that a professional race car driver could sue for the unauthorized advertising use of a distinctively decorated race car with which he was identified. In some states, the right of publicity dies with the celebrity, but in others it passes to his estate. In 2004 media entrepreneur Robert F. X. Stillerman paid Lisa Marie Presley $100 million for an 85 percent stake in Elvis Presley Enterprises, Inc., which licenses the singer's name and likeness.

Mapping Trademark Change

At the end of a century of doctrinal expansion, brand-name protection in the United States today consists of two separate but intertwined strands. One, rooted in the economics of information, seeks no more than to secure consumers' expectations about the source of goods and services. The other, aligned with the economics of public goods, seeks to protect brands for their own sake, much as patent law protects inventions and copyright law protects entertainment and information. Because this second strand is still evolving, it offers not only new opportunities to exploit brand values, but also presents a higher degree of legal risk than do the more traditional trademark rules. The principal source of legal risk lies in the application of rules, fashioned a century or more ago to serve the needs of consumer protection, to a property right that has no particular concern for consumer deception. Rules based on trademark use and consumer confusion, though essential in one setting, are obstacles in the other.

The application of old trademark rules to new trademark uses will in some cases result in the underprotection of brand names. For example, once trademark law treats a brand name as itself an information product, the law will have no greater need for an abandonment doctrine than do patent or copyright law. More frequently, though, application of traditional trademark rules will *over*extend the new rights in brand names. One example is the availability of injunctive relief. Traditionally, once a trademark owner proves infringement, injunctive relief automatically follows on the premise that, if a court denied an injunction, consumer confusion would necessarily result. By contrast, courts in patent and copyright cases have at least indicated the desirability of withholding injunctions in circumstances where a damage award alone will better serve the public interest. Will brand-name owners continue to enjoy automatic injunctive relief when, like patent and copyright owners, they are asserting a property right and consumer confusion is no longer at stake? In time, Congress and the courts can be expected to ask that question, and their answer may seriously disrupt trademark practice.

Trademark protection has always been perpetual, on the premise that there is no statute of limitations on consumer confusion. When in 1998 Congress added twenty years to the statutory term of copyright protection, critics charged that it was a plot by the Walt Disney Company to extend the life of Mickey Mouse, whose copyright was soon to expire; a popular bumper sticker of the time read "Free Mickey." What the critics overlooked was that Mickey Mouse was already enjoying perpetual protection in the United States and around the world under trademark law. Congress may someday decide to reconsider whether trademark protection should be perpetual in cases that do not involve consumer confusion. Similarly, as a matter of copyright law, commentators, parodists, and satirists are free to make unauthorized use of the Mickey Mouse character under copyright law's freewheeling fair use defense; contemporary trademark law's comparatively constrained parody and comment defense can be expected to expand in the same direction.

A doctrine aimed at protecting consumers from deceptive practices in the marketing of goods and services will attract few social critics. Who, after all, would complain about increasing the quality of information concerning goods and services? But a law that grants property rights, enabling advertisers to manipulate consumers' fears and aspirations, will be a natural target of attack, and these excesses may at some point attract sufficient public and political attention to trigger reform. As early as 1899, Thorstein Veblen inveighed against "features which add to the cost and enhance the commercial value of the goods in question, but do not proportionately increase the serviceability of these articles for the material purposes which alone they ostensibly are designed to serve." In the same tradition, contemporary critics like Naomi Klein argue that "many of today's best-known manufacturers no longer produce products and advertise them, but rather buy products and 'brand' them"; consequently, "this corporate obsession with brand identity is waging a war on public and individual space, on public institutions such as school, on youthful identities, on the concept of nationality and on the possibilities for unmarketed space." Klein has also disparaged the "radical shift in corporate philosophy [that] has sent manufacturers on a cultural feeding frenzy as they seize upon every corner of unmarked landscape in search of the oxygen needed to inflate their brands. In the process, virtually nothing has been left unbranded."

If social criticism provides the political climate for moderating trademark law's new property dimension, it is political pressure that will effect the changes. Patent and copyright lawmaking has long reflected the tugs and pulls of contesting interest groups, and the result has inevitably been a balance struck between property incentives for intellectual property producers and free access for intellectual property users. Proprietary pharmaceutical companies press Congress for expanded patent protection, and electronics and software companies push for more limited protection. Book publishers and motion picture and music companies ask Congress to extend the reach of copyright, and, on the other side, librarians, educators, and home consumer electronics companies petition Congress to exempt their activities from copyright tribute. Trademark law, by contrast has had no established lobby for curtailing rights, and it is only in the most recent hearings that the voices of critics, such as media companies and the American Civil Liberties Union, have been heard, expressing concern that newly expanded trademark rules will inhibit free speech. The new property dimension of trademark law, as well as the congressional history of patent and copyright law, suggests that these critics are just the vanguard of a movement for limiting trademark rights that will ultimately be as numerous—and clamorous—as those that lobby Congress for limitations on patent and copyright.

5

<hr>

Trade Secrets

Agreat deal of innovation in companies large and small falls outside the neatly parceled categories of patent, copyright, and trademark. Some information—how to configure an overnight air delivery service; the format for a television reality program; the idea for a new brand—will often be too simple to trigger patent, copyright, or trademark protection. Particularly in the case of inventions, markets may be either too transitory to survive the three years or more it takes to prosecute a patent, or too long-lasting to be fully captured by the twenty-year term of a patent. Although the recipe for Coca-Cola syrup, first formulated in the nineteenth century, was presumably patentable at the time, the company evidently thought it would do better financially by keeping the formula secret than by obtaining a patent, which would have published it and then cast it into the public domain at the end of the patent term. Even when a company decides to follow the patent route, it will invariably treat its preapplication research and development efforts as a trade secret; and, after the patent issues, many companies will restrict access to the technical know-how that licensees may need to practice the invention.

Undisclosed information can, depending on the company and the industry, approach or exceed in value all of a company's patents, copyrights, and trademarks combined. Biotech pharmaceutical companies that routinely obtain patents on their products also regularly sidestep the patent system in protecting the highly complex processes employed in manufacturing these products, keeping them secret instead, so that when the product goes off patent twenty years later, producers of generic substitutes must still invest in developing the necessary manufacturing processes. Secret databases cataloging customer preferences and credit ratings can be enormously valuable in giving a company an advantage over its competitors. A bid on an upcoming project will be worthless if it leaks out. Even more personalized information can take the form of human capital, the intellectual asset that results when an employee's background and training combine with the practices of his particular company—for example, the most effective way to trade commodities, to stack crates in a warehouse, or to perform an innovative surgical technique.

For an intellectual asset manager, the most important fact about these aggregates of information is not that they possess enormous value nor that companies capture this value outside of patent, copyright, and trademark law. Rather, it is that legal rules play a relatively modest role in the organization and management of this information. At least historically, it is not law but *norms*—the accumulated patterns of personnel, security, and contracting practices, as well as the business culture in an industry or region—that shape and are shaped by the daily flow of secret business information. By predicting the practices of other firms in an industry or region, norms offer a company some expectation of reciprocal behavior when it undertakes security measures, hires and fires employees, and decides whether, when, and whom to sue and whether and on what terms to settle litigation. In the case of patent, copyright, and trademark, it is legal rules that define business practice; in the case of trade secrets, it is business practice that defines legal rules.

There is, to be sure, a law of trade secrets, and it applies when behavioral norms break down. But the Uniform Trade Secrets Act, presently in force in forty-two states, offers little more than a framework for legal decision. While the Patent Act fills 101 pages in the U.S. Code, the Copyright Act 199 pages, and the Trademark Act fifty pages, the Uniform Trade Secrets Act occupies a scant three. It is norms—the actual practices of companies in managing their secret information—that put meat on the law's bare bones. Norms answer the one prescriptive question that every hard trade secret case boils down to: What is reasonable behavior?

Trade secrets are different from trade secret law. Trade *secrets* embody the proprietary information that, through security measures and personnel practices, a company has secreted from the prying eyes of competitors and others. Trade secret *law* begins at the point where secrecy ends, and protects companies that, though their security and personnel practices were not entirely successful in keeping this valuable information secret, at least made a reasonable effort to preserve its secrecy. The purpose of trade secret law is to protect business information from poaching by faithless employees and unwanted intruders, and to do so without requiring absolute secrecy or security as the price of protection. Trade secret law is in this sense a safety net, but one whose outer edges are defined by the fact of secrecy itself.

Because trade secret law centers on behavioral norms rather than universal rules, the protection it offers is more circumstantial, and consequently more variable, in organizing and managing proprietary information than are patent, copyright, and even trademark. This explains why trade secret law is comparatively weak in protecting valuable information possessed and practiced by a company's employees. It is never an easy task to separate the residue of information that came from the employee's own training and skills from the information imparted by the employer. Also, courts are slow to grant injunctions against employees who wish to improve their prospects by moving to another company. Another variable behavioral norm is reverse engineering, the competitive practice of dissecting marketed products and services to see what makes them tick. Although trade secret law exempts reverse engineering from legal liability, it is sometimes unclear whether the defendant's conduct was legitimate reverse engineering or unlawful prying, and the court will consult reasonable business practice to determine whether to accept the legal defense of reverse engineering in the case before it.

At least three contemporary forces, none of them likely to be reversed, promise to test trade secret law's boundaries over the coming years. One is the increased pace of employee mobility, not only in high-technology industries, and not only in the United States. The contemporary trend toward serial job-taking, consulting arrangements, and outsourcing seems likely to weaken the bonds of worker loyalty around which trade secret norms developed over the course of the twentieth century, and courts in the future will be even less inclined than they presently are to enjoin departing employees. Second, the use of licenses to profit from the scalability of intellectual assets—a long-standing practice among patent, copyright, and trademark owners—will require crisp boundary lines to replace the behaviorally blurred edges of trade secret assets if these assets are to support fluently administered licenses. Many patent licenses include transfers of associated know-how, and for these licenses to be effective, their trade secret subject matter should, like the patent subject matter, be clearly delineated so that licensor and licensee can each be certain about their entitlements. Third, where trade secret law presently draws for its content on regional as well as industry norms—and in the United States on the rules applied by the fifty states—globalization will require harmonized definitions of rights that can be easily licensed across borders.

Judged both by the nature of these impending demands and the trajectory of early responses to them, it seems likely that the newly emerging trade secret law—if it is even called that—will depend far less for its substance on behavior and norms, and far more on property rules and entitlements of the sort contemplated by patent, copyright, and, more recently, trademark law. In some respects trade secret law's reconfiguration along property lines is already under way, as extensions of existing intellectual property rules have begun to colonize areas previously protected under trade secret law alone; patents for business methods and copyright protection for source code are two economically salient examples. Other developments are only beginning to come into focus, but all point in the direction of increased property rights. In many ways, trade secret law stands today where trademark law stood decades ago: as a regulatory, behavior-based doctrine that is on the verge of evolving into a system of property rules comparable to patent and copyright.

Trade Secrets as Competitive Strategy:
Cadence v. Avant!

No case better illustrates the use of civil and criminal trade secret litigation as a harsh competitive tool than a 1995 lawsuit filed by Silicon Valley software producer Cadence Design Systems against start-up rival Avant! The case started quietly enough. It should have been a tip-off to Cadence, at the time the country's leading producer of the software used in designing computer chips, when in early March 1991 four senior employees left the company to found design rival ArcSys, but refused to sign documents confirming their earlier agreement not to disclose confidential company information. However, Cadence showed no concern until three years later, when Gerald Hsu, the senior executive in charge of a Cadence project aimed at overtaking ArcSys's place-and-route software, told Cadence CEO Joe Costello that he was leaving the company. Hsu denied rumors that he was moving to ArcSys, but days later Costello learned not only that Hsu had moved to ArcSys, but that he had agreed to become its CEO.

By late August 1995, Cadence discovered why the four departing employees had declined to sign exit agreements: a new ArcSys product whose striking similarities to Cadence software—including an unnecessary comma that Cadence code writers had years before misplaced in Cadence code—suggested that ArcSys had achieved its stunningly rapid entry into the market for place-and-route chip design through theft of Cadence code. Adding to the company's concerns, that same month, Mitsura "Mitch" Igusa, yet another Cadence employee responsible for place-and-route software, left the company. When Cadence security officials discovered that Igusa had transferred large computer files from the company's headquarters to his home, they alerted the Santa Clara County District Attorney's Office; in the course of searching Igusa's home, investigators found computer source code identified as belonging to Cadence.

In October 1995, a partner from Cadence's law firm met with Deputy District Attorney Julius Finkelstein, the chief prosecutor in Santa Clara County's High Technology Crimes Unit, to review Cadence's evidence of trade secret thefts by ArcSys. In November 1995,

ArcSys, which had gone public in June 1995, merged with Integrated Silicon Systems, Inc. to become Avant! Two months later, local police and FBI agents searched Avant!'s headquarters, where they seized an electronic log indicating that one of the four executives who left Cadence in 1991 had taken with him a copy of a basic place-and-route program. Within twenty-four hours, Cadence filed a civil suit against Avant! alleging misappropriation of trade secrets as well as copyright infringement, unfair competition, conspiracy, breach of contract, and false advertising. The raid and civil suit occurred the day after expiration of the six-month lockout period following Avant!'s initial public offering, the first day on which company insiders could sell their stock. News of the raid and the civil action pummeled Avant! shares; by December 12, 1995, a week after the raid, the stock price was down almost two-thirds from the previous month's high of $45.

Avant! struck back, filing a countersuit the following month, charging Cadence with securities fraud, claiming that Costello and others in the company knew in advance of the raid on Avant! headquarters and used this information to short-sell Avant! stock. As evidence that Cadence insiders knew something was up, Avant! observed in its complaint that 376,000 Avant! shares changed hands on the day before the raid, as against a daily average of 60,000 shares the previous month. The Avant! countersuit also alleged that Cadence had sown fear, uncertainty, and doubt among Avant! customers, violating federal antitrust, racketeering, and false advertising laws.

On April 11, 1997, the Santa Clara district attorney filed criminal charges against Avant!, Gerald Hsu, five other Avant! executives, and Mitch Igusa, alleging conspiracy and theft of Cadence trade secrets. In trading the next day, Avant! stock lost roughly half its value. In early September 1997, federal judge Ronald Whyte stayed proceedings in the civil trade secret case while the county's criminal case law went forward. The criminal case came to an end on May 22, 2001, four years after the District Attorney's Office first filed charges, with all of the defendants entering into plea bargains with the prosecutor, including a dismissal against one of the defendants, jail sentences for four, and a prison term of up to six years for another. In addition to Avant!'s agreement to pay $27 million in fines and $190.4 million in restitution to

Cadence, Gerry Hsu agreed to a $2.7 million fine, but received no jail time. According to Deputy DA Finkelstein, "It's a very common story when you go after a criminal enterprise, the people at the top are the hardest to convict."

Settlement of the criminal case opened the door to settlement of the civil suit on November 13, 2002, a result no doubt foreshadowed by Avant!'s acquisition in December 2001 by Synopsys, Inc., the country's second-largest producer, after Cadence, of electronic design automation software. In return for the parties' agreement to dismiss all pending claims against each other, Cadence received $265 million and Cadence, Avant!, and Synopsys granted each other "reciprocal licenses covering the intellectual property at issue in the litigation." Adding in $47 million for settlement of a shareholder suit, Avant!'s total liability amounted to over half a billion dollars. The company also bore a disproportionate share of legal expenses; almost six years into the litigation Avant! had spent nearly $50 million in legal fees and Cadence $15 million.

Synopsys completed its acquisition only after meticulous due diligence in which, among other steps, it retained two successive teams of lawyers to evaluate the litigation risk. According to General Counsel Steven Sherick, "This was the most legal-intensive deal we've ever done at Synopsys. We wanted to make sure that two sets of independent lawyers have a consensus view." Effectively, the company financed the litigation risk by purchasing a litigation protection insurance policy at the time it acquired Avant! to cover monetary awards including attorneys' fees arising out of the litigation. For a premium of $95 million, Synopsys bought a $500 million policy with a $240 million deductible prefunded by itself.

Secrecy Law and Secrecy Norms

Trade secret law in America first took shape in the late nineteenth century, in part as a response to the forces of the Industrial Revolution, and was at the time considered to be a true property doctrine akin to patent and copyright. An 1868 decision from the Massachusetts Supreme Judicial Court, *Peabody v. Norfolk,* established trade secret law's property pedigree. Observing that "it is the policy of the law, for the advantage of the public, to encourage and protect invention and commercial enterprise," and that "if a man establishes a business and makes it valuable by his skill and attention, the good will of that business is recognized by the law as property," Justice Horace Gray concluded that one who "invents or discovers, and keeps secret, a process of manufacture" has "a property in it, which a court of chancery will protect against one who in violation of contract and breach of confidence undertakes to apply it to his own use, or to disclose it to third persons."

At least in nineteenth-century America, common-law notions of property rested on assumptions about actual possession and physical control, requirements that could readily be met when the contested information was truly a secret locked away in the company's office or factory safe. But as businesses grew, increasing numbers of employees necessarily came into possession of these once closeted secrets. The question of how many people can know a secret before it is no longer a secret also arose as goods entered the channels of commerce, where they often revealed their embodied secrets to innocent users as well as to prying intermeddlers. As absolute secrecy yielded to the exigencies of the marketplace, trade secret law in the early twentieth century evolved away from rigid conceptions of property rights and toward a new focus on individualized relationships of contract and loyalty in protecting proprietary information. Secrecy was still important, but only in the form of a watered-down requirement that, before filing suit, and as a token of its seriousness of purpose, the trade secret claimant must have adopted reasonable security measures to protect its information.

Trade secret law works through a small handful of general rules that prescribe the kind of information that will be subject to protection, the standards—principally a diluted requirement of secrecy—that the information must meet in order to qualify for protection, and the conduct of competitors that will subject them to liability for trade secret theft. A separate but related set of rules specifies the extent to which companies can protect their secrets through contracts, called covenants not to compete, that bar employees from moving to rival firms. And, in a comparatively recent move, the U.S. Congress has imposed criminal sanctions for trade secret theft. The law in each of these legal settings draws its content from industry and regional norms, and as a consequence, the law's safety net becomes necessary only when a company or its employees depart from these norms.

The Uniform Trade Secrets Act defines a "trade secret" as "information, including a formula, pattern, compilation, program, device, method, technique, or process that derives independent economic value, actual or potential, from not being generally known to, and not being readily ascertainable by proper means by, other persons who can obtain economic value from its disclosure or use." This statutory formula expands the scope of trade secret subject matter to include two valuable forms of information not previously protected under judge-made law. One is episodic information such as the knowledge of a specific marketing plan or a secret bid. The other is so-called negative know-how—the knowledge of a company's *un*successful research paths that, if known by a competitor, would save the competitor the expense of failing too.

The Uniform Trade Secrets Act, although it requires a trade secret claimant to undertake efforts to preserve the secrecy of its information, relaxes the strictures of absolute secrecy by requiring only that the efforts be "reasonable under the circumstances." Local norms in the relevant industry will determine what constitutes reasonable efforts. Reasonable security norms will also vary with a firm's size and sophistication. Because, for example, high-tech companies are more likely to mark proprietary data for security purposes, departures from this norm may be penalized among these companies more readily than among others. Similarly, because, according to a 2002 study by ASIS International, large companies are more likely than small ones to destroy sensitive information after it is no longer needed, they will be more likely to have their claims measured against this norm. Other measures that will bear on the determination of whether a company has made reasonable efforts include company policies on the marking, copying, and retention of documents; the use of guards, camera surveillance, and computer firewalls and restrictions on visitors to the workplace; encryption of data and the deployment of audit trails tracing user access to computer-based projects; maintenance of secure clean rooms; limitations on access to sensitive information to workers with a need to know; and procedures for employee entrance and exit interviews. These measures will vary from industry to industry and locale to locale.

Like trademarks, trade secrets enjoy a potentially perpetual life; just as trademarks expire when they lose their distinctiveness, trade secrets expire when their subject matter is no longer secret. No secret lasts forever. Mobile employees are one source of leakage. Reverse engineering by competitors is another, for it is the rare secret formula or code that cannot be discovered by diligent experimentation and tinkering with the publicly available product in which it is embedded. (Coca-Cola's legendary secret formula may be just that—a legend.)

The unauthorized acquisition of a trade secret will be actionable under the Uniform Trade Secrets Act only if the acquisition is by "improper means"—specifically, theft, bribery, misrepresentation, espionage, or breach of confidence. According to the 2002 ASIS study of Fortune 1000 corporations and small and midsized companies belonging to the U.S. Chamber of Commerce, the four principal risk factors for information loss, ranked in order of significance, were former employees, foreign competitors, on-site contractors, and domestic competitors.

Conduct that constitutes theft or breach of confidence in one context may not in another, and, as in the case of reasonable efforts to preserve secrecy, regional and industry norms will control. Courts will presumably take a more laissez-faire attitude to departing employees in California's Silicon Valley, where it is difficult to find a start-up that was *not* founded by the former employees of an industry leader. (One widely circulated genealogy chart for semiconductor companies begins with Bell Telephone Laboratories, whose departing employees in 1956 started Shockley Semiconductor, which in turn, with the departure of eight employees, begat Fairchild Semiconductor in 1957, which provided National Semiconductor with a new CEO in 1967 and Intel with its founding employees in 1968, and so on down through the generations.)

Risk factors will also vary with the size of the company and the nature of its business. The ASIS study reports computer hacking as a significant risk for service and finance companies and companies with annual revenues over $15 billion, while service companies and $6 billion–$15 billion companies reported vendors and suppliers as a significant risk. Current employees are an important risk for manufacturing companies, and foreign intelligence services are an important risk for high-technology companies.

Unlike patent law, trade secret law permits a rival to replicate protected information independently and, if the rival keeps its own discovery secret, to itself enjoy legal protection as a trade secret. Reverse engineering is also allowed. Thus the chemist who successfully analyzed a sample of Coca-Cola syrup in order to reconstruct its recipe would be free to produce and market a cola drink from that formula, but—thanks to trademark law—not as "Coca-Cola"! Manufacturing processes are particularly difficult to reverse-engineer from their end products, and particularly so in the case of biological products and semiconductor chips, which is one reason leaders in these industries depend so heavily on trade secret protection for this information.

Courts rely on local and industry norms in calibrating the scope to be given to the reverse-engineering principle. For example, while it might constitute an improper appropriation for chemical producer B to bribe a construction worker for details on the design of competitor A's chemical plant under construction, the answer would not be so clearcut if instead B hired a pilot to fly over the partly built plant to take photographs that offered clues as to the secret processes used by the competitor. In one such case, involving a DuPont plant under construction, the aerial photographer argued that his conduct was not improper because the flyover was in public airspace. The court was not persuaded: "'Improper' will always be a word of many nuances, determined by time, place and circumstances. We therefore need not proclaim a catalogue of commercial improprieties. Clearly, however, one of its commandments does say 'thou shall not appropriate a trade secret through deviousness under circumstances in which countervailing defenses are not reasonably available.'" The court was sensitive to the need not to overburden DuPont with the expense of secrecy. "Perhaps ordinary fences and roofs must be built to shut out incursive eyes, but we need not require the discoverer of a trade secret to guard against the unanticipated, the undetectable, or the unpreventable methods of espionage now available."

As should be evident from the DuPont case, by permitting rival B to disassemble manufacturer A's product in order to figure out the secret that makes it work—and, having discovered this information, to produce goods of its own embodying A's secret—trade secret law will inevitably influence investment decisions by both A and B. Manufacturer A will weigh applicable norms and legal rules in deciding how much to invest in producing secret information and on how high to build the walls that will keep it secret, while B's decision will weigh these same norms and rules in assessing the comparative costs of reverse-engineering A's secret or creating the secret information independently.

Secrets and Crimes

The Economic Espionage Act, passed by Congress in 1996 with strong bipartisan support, added criminal sanctions to the civil and criminal liability already imposed under state law. Congressional concern for trade secret theft by foreign companies dated to an FBI sting operation fourteen years earlier against senior executives of the highly respected Hitachi Ltd. and Mitsubishi Electric Corporation for conspiracy to steal and transport IBM secrets to Japan. As trade wars with Japan abated, so did congressional interest in the issue, but the concern revived in the early 1990s with FBI and CIA reports of extensive espionage by foreign governments—China, Cuba, France, Israel, and Russia among them—aimed at U.S. high-technology companies. The parade of horrors presented to Congress included the tale of an Air France first-class cabin bugged to capture secrets discussed by American executives on their way to Paris.

The Economic Espionage Act closely tracks the definition of trade secrets employed by the Uniform Trade Secrets Act, encompassing all forms of secret financial, business, scientific, technical, economic, and engineering information, and imposes penalties for trade secret theft that include fines up to $500,000 and ten years' imprisonment for individuals, and a fine up to $5 million for organizations. Although it was fears of foreign espionage that triggered passage of the EEA, prosecutions under the act have been almost exclusively aimed at individuals, not governments, and there have been many more prosecutions of company insiders and former employees than of outsiders and competitors.

It is one thing for a victim of trade secret theft to cooperate with prosecutors, quite another for it to see its trade secrets exposed as part of the prosecution. In an early prosecution under the Economic Espionage Act for attempted theft of Bristol-Myers Squibb's secret method for producing the anticancer drug Taxol, the trial court ruled against an attempt by government prosecutors to delete secret information that they were required to give to the defendant. An order to redact the information, the court ruled, would relieve the government of its duty to prove the existence of a trade secret and deprive defendants of their constitutional right to cross-examine witnesses and otherwise conduct their defense. Although the ruling was overturned on appeal, the appellate court implied that it might require such disclosure of secret information in a case in which the defendant had been charged with actual, and not just attempted, theft of trade secrets.

Companies are as reluctant to have their secrets disclosed in civil proceedings as in criminal ones. While a lawyer's demand letters to a poacher can be an effective shot across the bow, full-scale trade secret litigation is only rarely a good idea. Valued customers may become ensnared in the lawsuit, and firms that gain a reputation for suing departing employees may have a hard time recruiting new ones. Also, secrecy and litigation are natural enemies: the legal process may disclose trade secrets and other proprietary information not only to the defendant, but to other competitors as well. Although U.S. courts will issue protective orders in order to guard a company's secrets, the realities of wide-ranging discovery will often make leakage all but inevitable. In some foreign jurisdictions, even protective orders and closed trial proceedings may be unavailable. One study that combined field research with a review of the literature concluded that these "huge litigation costs" lead to a situation in which employers will usually sue only "for extreme cases of trade secret violations as in the case of former CEO's, CTO's, or in cases of corporate raiding."

Mobile Employees and Restrictive Covenants

Companies regularly turn to contracts to overcome the limitations of trade secret law. During the heyday of the 1990s high-tech boom in California's Silicon Valley, a prospective employee, investor, or consultant could barely have coffee with a start-up company without being asked to sign an agreement not to disclose the information he received. Even more common, and with a far longer history, are agreements under which an employee promises not to compete with his employer in the event he leaves the company. When they are enforceable, these noncompete covenants offer stronger protection than does trade secret law, since by barring the former employee from taking a position with a rival company, they relieve the trade secret owner of the need to prove that the employee in fact disclosed the trade secret to his new employer.

From the viewpoint of the former employer, the problem with employee covenants not to compete is that they are so often difficult to enforce. Courts and legislatures balance interests in promoting investment in innovation (which they perceive to favor the former employer) against society's interests in employee mobility (which favors the former employee), but the ultimate decisions usually tip toward the employee. This judicial and legislative bias dates to fifteenth- and sixteenth-century English court decisions striking down restraints that masters imposed on their apprentices to prolong their period of noncompetitive, and usually wageless, service. Although at one time courts struck down offending covenants in their entirety, today they let these covenants stand, but trim them so that their impact is not unreasonable. In doing so, courts consult regional and industry norms to determine a covenant's reasonable breadth, duration, and geographic scope.

Courts in most states will ask whether the post-employment restraint is broader than is necessary to protect the employer's legitimate interests. Among the factors they weigh are the duration of the restraint (context matters: a five-year restraint has been upheld, but a two-year restraint has not); its geographic scope (the restraint should generally be no broader than the market in which the employer does business); whether the employment is at will (at-will employees are treated more sympathetically than those with fixed-term contracts); the nature of the employee's work (because of the direct impact of the loss of customers, sales employees get less favorable treatment than other employees); and whether the employer contributed to the employee's training (the employer who contributes will receive more favorable treatment).

Trade secret law also figures in decisions on the enforceability of post-employment covenants. Courts will assess the reasonableness of a noncompete covenant's breadth by asking whether the covenant is any wider than is required to protect against disclosure of the former employer's trade secrets along with some interstitial, otherwise unprotectible, technical information. Also, in determining whether the covenant is of reasonable length, courts often employ the same measure they use in determining how long a trade secret injunction should run—the time that it would take a competitor to lawfully reverse-engineer the former employer's protected methods.

If trade secret norms give substance to legal rules, the reverse is also true: trade secret rules contribute to the evolution of trade secret norms. For example, the fact that, as a legal matter, California almost entirely outlaws post-employment covenants not to compete and takes a stinting approach to trade secret protection generally, has had an unmistakable impact on trade secret norms in the state. AnnaLee Saxenian, a close student of entrepreneurial patterns in Silicon Valley, credits the region's intimate information network, built on the proximity between technology companies in the Palo Alto–San Jose corridor and shared educational and social connections to Stanford University, with nourishing the entrepreneurial process there. A key element of this seamless information web has been the high degree of employee mobility across Silicon Valley companies, with average annual employee turnover in the 1970s over 35 percent for electronics firms generally, and as high as 59 percent in the smaller firms. Another Silicon Valley observer reported wide use of temporary labor and independent contractors, rapid job mobility, and weak loyalty to individual firms. Yet while these employment patterns may have contributed to a norm of easy movement of information across company lines, so too do applicable legal rules. As Stanford law professor Ronald Gilson has observed, California's legal prohibition against post-employment covenants not to compete played a significant part in this relatively free flow of human capital in Silicon Valley. In Gilson's view, "legal rules are one of the poles around which the shape of the business culture is formed."

The Evolving Contours of Trade Secret Law

Mobility, scalability, and globalization are the most salient forces pressing for change in trade secret law. Few features of traditional trade secret law can be expected to survive an economy that is characterized by a highly mobile workforce and business interests in leveraging intellectual assets across domestic and global markets. These new demands place trade secret law at the threshold of wrenching changes that will in time reduce the difference between it and other forms of intellectual property, such as patent and copyright, that are more explicitly framed around property rights. The trend toward greater job mobility— serial job-taking, consulting arrangements, and outsourcing—will heighten pressures to substitute licensable property rights for increasingly ineffective employee covenants not to compete. Interests in leveraged exploitation of these valuable assets will similarly press to reconfigure trade secret law along the dimensions of scalable property rights.

According to one study, a young American with two years or more of college training will on average change jobs at least eleven times over a forty-year working life. Shorter job tenure and higher employee mobility in the United States and elsewhere will not only weaken historic norms of secrecy and bonds of loyalty, it will also increase the inclination of courts to overturn noncompete covenants that they might have tolerated in times of long-term employment. Forcing an employee to the sidelines of his specialty for two years, or even one, after his being employed for no more than three or four, will doubtless appear unjust, particularly since any know-how the employee possesses will as likely be the product of his own training and work experience as of any information imparted by the employer.

A tug-of-war between the Texas Legislature and the Texas Supreme

Court in the 1990s illustrates the competing equities in an environment of short-term labor, and the instability that characterizes trade secret rules in transition. In 1989, the state legislature, concerned that a string of state supreme court decisions in the late 1980s made it difficult to enforce employee noncompete covenants and were consequently discouraging business investment in the state, passed a law to overrule the decisions. Ten months later, the Texas Supreme Court decided that the new statute did not apply to employees at will—workers with the most precarious job tenure—but in 1993 the legislature responded with an amendment making these covenants enforceable against at-will employees as well. A year later, applying the amended statute for the first time, the Texas Supreme Court construed the 1993 amendment narrowly and once again declined to enforce the covenant against an at-will employee.

If, as seen from the Texas experience, post-employment covenants continue to diminish in force, businesses will look for other ways to protect valuable information, leading to arrangements for alternative, property-like transactions between the company that loses an employee and the company that hires him. Such arrangements will shift the focus from injunctions against employees to license payments for information. Such licenses, unencumbered by limitations inherent in employment contracts or confidential relationships between employer and employee, can rationalize the transfer of information that occurs when an employee leaves one company for another, and can level the playing field between the two companies by requiring one to compensate the other for its loss of informational advantage. This practice already exists when companies license their patents as part of a package that includes consultation services or temporary outplacement of employees who possess the know-how that is needed to practice the patented inventions, and it is but a small step to extend the practice to situations where a patent is not part of the package.

The genius of patents, copyrights, and trademarks lies in scalability, giving their owners the exclusive right to exploit these intellectual assets in every market where the asset may have value. Trade secret law, by contrast, terminates its protection at the very moment information first becomes public; unlike patent, copyright, and trademark law, which aim at the widespread exploitation of intellectual assets, the goal of trade secret law is to manage the leakage of secret information in its inevitable brushes with the public marketplace. Some secret information will always remain local and particularized to the operations of the company that created it. But other information, such as business databases and methods, can possess value across companies and even industries if it is not constrained by trade secret law's strictures of secrecy. Economic pressures to exploit such assets in public markets will inevitably create a legal environment conducive to new, nonsecret modes of protection; indeed, in the case of databases and business methods, these new modes have already emerged.

Global markets will also place new, possibly unsustainable demands on a trade secret law that depends so heavily on the peculiarities of regional norms and the relations between employers and employees. Until the 1994 TRIPs Agreement established an international standard for protection of trade secrets among World Trade Organization member countries—as of 2007 there were 150—few countries possessed a trade secret doctrine that was even as developed as the relatively rudimentary Uniform Trade Secrets Act. Inclusion of the new TRIPs provision was part of an initiative by economically developed economies to erect an international legal infrastructure that can foster technology transfers from industrialized countries to economically less developed countries. As this infrastructure matures, so too will the pressures for harmonizing the legal definition of the assets that are the subject of these transfers.

Mobility, scalability, and globalization will cast a harsh light on some of trade secret law's long-accepted deficiencies, further propelling the forces of change. One long-standing complaint is that trade secret law's emphasis on secrecy unproductively skews investment toward those innovations that can most effectively be kept secret. Also, the uncertainties of trade secret litigation force companies to invest significantly in negotiating nondisclosure agreements in the hope that these will obviate litigation. Another criticism is that, since few secrets last long, trade secret protection, though an effective tool for obtaining lead time advantage measured in months, is hardly a prescription for investment in the more substantial innovations that require a longer period to repay their investment. And it is possible that as courts further dilute non-compete covenants, companies will increase the inefficient secrecy practices—tight security, divisions of labor, and need-to-know access—that trade secret law was intended to meliorate. Such backward steps can only increase the pressures for alternative property-based systems to protect this information.

As trade secret law evolves over the next several decades, its transformation is likely to implicate substantially expanded property rights. Unlike trademark law, in which the evolution toward property rights has moved in a single, straight line, trade secret law will move along several sometimes winding trajectories. Two such trends are already evident: the colonization by patent, copyright, and trademark law of areas previously regulated under trade secret law, and the expansion of trade secret law itself to extend property rights in recurring, expedient circumstances. It is too early to discern the precise outlines of these property prospects, but it seems certain that trade secret protection in twenty-first-century America will not return to the simple property theory that marked its birth in the nineteenth century.

Paradoxically, it is the most dramatic incursion of property rules into trade secret law's traditional domain that has been the least observed. Business method patents, which have flourished more vigorously in the United States than elsewhere, can best be understood as a legal response to business frustrations over the limitations of trade secret law in supporting the exploitation of such valuable business methods as stock hedging strategies and tax-reduction techniques. Some of the business method patents that have become enmeshed in high-stakes litigation—such as computerized systems for managing mutual fund investments—encompass subject matter that historically has been protected exclusively under trade secret law.

Copyright too has moved into trade secret territory. Software companies commonly shroud their computer source code in secrecy, treating these trade secrets as crown jewels. However, as became evident in the "softwars" of the 1980s and 1990s, software companies also deploy copyright law as their first line of defense to protect these secrets against reverse engineering. The great question for copyright in the 1990s, whether reverse engineering of object code in order to discover its underlying source code constitutes fair use, was fundamentally a test of copyright law's capacity to guard trade secrets—a test that, outside the limited area of secret interface specifications, it passed with high marks.

Trade secret law's limitations in achieving scalability are nowhere more evident than in the case of data collections such as customer information and financial databases. In many cases, copyright law will protect both the arrangement and content of these databases. When Jose Ignacio Lopez de Arriortua, the automotive procurement whiz, left General Motors for Volkswagen in 1993, he allegedly delivered to his new employer, among other copyrighted prizes, a 3,350-page printout listing 60,000 parts, their suppliers, and prices and delivery schedules for GM Europe. A lawsuit for copyright as well as trade secret infringement was filed in March 1996. After months of failed negotiations, the suit was settled on terms that included a payment by Volkswagen to GM of $100 million and Volkswagen's agreement to sever all ties with Lopez and to purchase $1 billion in GM parts over seven years.

In many cases, the value of a database will lie not in its organization—which copyright will protect—but in the specific facts collected—which copyright will not protect. Computer hacking has undermined the already limited capacity of trade secrets to protect databases, and U.S. law presently offers few effective protections for nonsecret data. Misappropriation doctrine, created by the U.S. Supreme Court in 1918 to give property-like protection—the Court coyly called it a "quasi property"—to the Associated Press news service against poaching by the International News Service of wartime news items collected by AP reporters, has since been limited by some courts to hot news, as in the *AP* case itself. However, other courts have applied the doctrine more expansively. In 1983 the Illinois Supreme Court handed down a decision that is a high-water mark in the application of misappropriation doctrine, giving Dow Jones & Company exclusive rights in the Dow Jones Industrial Average against the Chicago Board of Trade's use of the index as the underlying commodity in a commodity futures contract.

The problem with misappropriation doctrine as a solution to trade secret law's inadequate protection of databases is that it is only spottily applied around the country, and is far too limited in the fourteen states that do apply it to support licenses effective across state, much less national, borders. Database providers have sought to promote the exploitation of these increasingly valuable assets through national, property-like legislation that, under treaty arrangements, could support transborder licensing and enforcement. In 1996 the European Union adopted a database directive that extends protection to the facts collected in databases and has since been implemented throughout the European Community. However, the EC directive rests on the treaty principle of reciprocity, which means that database companies headquartered outside the Community will receive protection inside the Community only if their own country offers comparable protection to data collections coming from the Community. Database protection bills have been introduced in the U.S. Congress since 1996, but none has yet won sufficient support to ensure passage.

Trade secret law itself may evolve to offer some limited prospect of property-like rights in valuable information. The Uniform Trade Secrets Act offers relief not only against departing employees who disclose secret information to others, but also against those whose new positions merely *threaten* such disclosure, giving rise, but only in a handful of states so far, to the doctrine of "inevitable disclosure," which requires neither breach of confidence, unlawful appropriation, nor even a contractual undertaking.

A 1994 lawsuit by PepsiCo indicates some of the promise, and practical limits, of inevitable disclosure doctrine in protecting information assets. In November 1994, William Redmond Jr., a ten-year company veteran, resigned his post at PepsiCo to join Quaker Oats as vice president–field operations for Gatorade. (Redmond had been assiduously courted by Gatorade's president, Donald Uzzi, who himself left a senior post at PepsiCo at the beginning of 1994; the courtship began two months after Uzzi left PepsiCo.) Since his job as general manager of the business unit covering all of California involved coordinating PepsiCo's sports and New Age drink business, Redmond was understandably familiar with PepsiCo's strategic plan, market initiatives, annual operating plan, selling and pricing architecture, and delivery system —all of which PepsiCo maintained as trade secrets. Less than a week after Redmond gave notice to PepsiCo that he had accepted an offer from Quaker, PepsiCo filed suit in federal district court in Chicago to enjoin him from starting work at Quaker and from disclosing PepsiCo trade secrets.

Did Redmond's acceptance of a position at a direct competitor constitute a "threatened appropriation" of a trade secret, as required by the Uniform Trade Secrets Act? Acting quickly—a month after the lawsuit was filed—the federal district ruled that it did, and on appeal the circuit court affirmed under the "inevitable disclosure" doctrine. Recognizing the tension in trade secret law between encouraging firms to innovate and allowing their employees to pursue their livelihoods, the appellate court agreed with the district court that "unless Redmond possessed an uncanny ability to compartmentalize information, he would necessarily be making decisions about [Quaker's] Gatorade and Snapple [marketing] by relying on his knowledge of [PepsiCo's] trade secrets." In the court's view, PepsiCo was right to be concerned that Redmond would inevitably rely on PepsiCo trade secrets as he helped plot Quaker's new course for Gatorade and Snapple, and that these secrets would give Quaker a substantial advantage in "knowing exactly how [PepsiCo] will price, distribute and market its sports drinks and new age drinks, and being able to respond strategically."

One limitation on the inevitable disclosure doctrine is its requirement that the trade secret owner prove that the former employee deviated from applicable norms of good conduct. The PepsiCo court attached substantial weight to Redmond's "lack of forthrightness on some occasions, and out and out lies on others, in the period between the time he accepted the position with defendant Quaker and when he informed plaintiff that he had accepted that position." In the court's view, Redmond "could not be trusted to act with the necessary sensitivity and good faith under the circumstances in which the only practical verification that he was not using plaintiff's secrets would be defendant Redmond's word to that effect." Another obvious limitation of the doctrine is that, because it effectively does little more than replicate the post-employment covenant not to compete, states like California that prohibit enforcement of such covenants also disfavor the doctrine. Courts in the great many states that restrict noncompete covenants to two or three years have shown no willingness to enter inevitable disclosure injunctions any longer than that; indeed, few such injunctions have exceeded a year.

A remedy ordered in one inevitable disclosure case may point the way to a licensing solution for these standoffs that makes better business sense than either an absolute injunction or no injunction at all. In that case, the court ordered a one-year injunction against an employee who left his job at an annual $29,000 salary for a new job at $50,000. But, as the price of the injunction, the court directed the former employer to pay the employee $3,300 per month for the duration of the injunction, effectively splitting the difference between the two employers. Such licenses may of course be negotiated without the benefit of a court order, and more commonly the payments will move in the opposite direction. In November 2005, Nortel Networks, the Canadian telephone equipment maker, effectively paid Motorola $11.5 million in order to hire away its chief operating officer as its new chief executive. The payment came following Motorola's filing of a lawsuit seeking to enjoin the employee's departure to its competitor.

Mapping Trade Secret Change

Trade secrets are by nature the most subterranean of all intellectual assets. Not only do secrecy and confidential relationships keep trade secrets out of view, but their value often lies in the interstices, rather than on the surface, of business operations, in the form of know-how that lubricates business practice and data collections that animate planning, marketing, and sales. Trade secrets are, in a phrase, business as usual, and it is only when a firm, its employees, or an outsider departs from regional or industrywide norms of secrecy and confidence that trade secrets erupt into daylight as they did in the *Cadence v. Avant!* civil and criminal cases.

Best practice for company trade secrets is to watch for the breach of security norms and to act quickly when they occur. (It should have been a tip-off to executives at Cadence when four departing senior employees refused to confirm their earlier nondisclosure agreements.) Smart trade secret practice also means paying close attention to evolving legal regimes for exploiting traditionally secret information without the requirements of secrecy—for example, using patents and patent licenses to exploit business methods and practices formerly protected by trade secret law, and being alert to other legal doctrines that over the coming years will inject property-like rights into what has long been the domain of norms and relationships.

6

======

Intellectual Assets on the Internet

I f the defining attribute of intellectual assets is that they can be used
by countless numbers of consumers across national borders and never
be exhausted, then the Internet may be the first distribution technology to fully capture this unique quality. By detaching inventions, entertainment, and advertising from the physical products that embody
them, the Internet, even more than television and radio before it, enables the transmission of content at virtually no cost.

It is, of course, this unfettered use that represents the Internet's
greatest challenge to intellectual assets. The early battle cry of Internet
activists, "Information wants to be free!" captures the essence of the
challenge. Habits of free access to a seemingly endless stream of information and entertainment breed the belief that the content itself is—or
can be—free. Yet as the motion picture studios discovered with the VCR
in the 1980s, once habits of free use become entrenched, they cannot be
reversed by legislation, because Congress is simply disinclined to pass
laws that people will not obey. The fact that intellectual assets are public
goods is the main reason for intellectual property law's chronic instability; habits of free use on the Internet only add to that burden.

The Internet has accelerated the evolution of patent, copyright, and
trademark law along their individual trajectories of change. In the case
of patents, the Internet has heightened the problem of patent thickets

and thus increased pressures to reduce the number of patents and to trim their scope. For copyright, while popular attention has centered on the problem of uncompensated copying, an equally important challenge has emerged for Internet intermediaries like eBay, Google, and Yahoo! whose operations inevitability entangle them in copyright's liability net. The use of domain names has accelerated the trend in trademark law to treat brands as protectible properties apart from any showing of consumer confusion; new advertising strategies have also helped to push consumer confusion from center stage. And in the background is the drumbeat of the open-source movement, raising—for academics at least—the question of whether, and to what extent, intellectual property is needed in an Internet environment where cooperative effort has emerged as a new and entrancing norm.

Patents on the Internet

It is no coincidence that the U.S. Supreme Court's 2006 decision in *eBay v. MercExchange*, which unanimously overturned the principle of automatic injunctions in patent cases, involved an Internet patent. The patent in question, encompassing eBay's "Buy It Now" feature, dramatized how patent enforcement on the Internet can bring a wide swath of e-commerce to a standstill. Also, because Internet patents typically involve software technology or business methods, or both, they suffer from the overbreadth and poor quality that characterizes these largely uncharted fields. In 2004, an auction by a bankrupt software company of thirty-nine patents covering such basic Internet activities as the use of electronic documents to automate the sale of goods and services raised concerns that the winning bidder would use the patents to extract excessive license fees for uses already widely practiced in Internet commerce. Another company, which overwhelmingly led a 2004 Electronic Frontier Foundation poll seeking nominations for the worst Internet-related patents, owned five patents on streaming audio and video technologies that, according to a company executive, were integral to use of the most common media players on the Internet.

The enforcement history of U.S. Patent No. 5,960,411, for a system of "1-Click" online purchases, granted on September 28, 1999, to

Amazon.com founder Jeff Bezos and a number of coinventors, illustrates how potent an Internet patent can be as a competitive weapon. The heart of the claimed 1-Click advance was that it enabled customers to order an item on the Internet with a single click of a computer mouse, obviating the several additional steps required by the older "shopping cart" model of Internet purchase. From the viewpoint of patent law's nonobviousness requirement, there were any number of nonelectronic antecedents to Amazon.com's 1-Click model, from a bartender's willingness to run a tab for a regular customer to purchases made from a vending machine. Nonetheless, on October 21, 1999, less than a month after the 1-Click patent issued, Amazon.com filed a patent infringement lawsuit against rival BarnesandNoble.com for its "Express Lane" service, requesting a preliminary injunction pending trial, and on December 1, 1999, at the height of the holiday shopping season, the court barred Barnes and Noble from using its Express Lane system.

Ultimately, the Court of Appeals for the Federal Circuit vacated the injunction, holding that while Amazon had "made a showing that it is likely to succeed at trial on its infringement case," Barnes and Noble had raised "substantial questions" about the patent's validity. (The preliminary injunction attracted substantial press and triggered widespread attacks on business method patents; in March 2000, the Patent Office announced more rigorous review for this class of patents.) But the appellate decision did not come until February 2001, well after Barnes and Noble had been deprived of the Express Lane system for yet another Christmas shopping season. The case subsequently settled. But there is an old adage about glass houses and throwing stones: late in 2006, after four years of failed talks aimed at negotiating a license, IBM sued Amazon.com in the rocket dockets of Tyler and Lufkin, Texas, for infringing what IBM described as key patents, including inventions for ordering items using an electronic catalog and storing data in an interactive network.

Other Internet technologies ramify even more widely than Amazon's 1-Click. In the early 1990s, researchers at the University of California–San Francisco developed a tool for a Web browser that enabled interactivity with individual pages on the World Wide Web—as described in their 1994 patent application, a "distributed hypermedia method for automatically invoking external application providing interaction and display of embedded objects within a hypermedia document." In plain terms, the tool enabled developers to embed interactive programs in their Web pages for a wide variety of personal and commercial uses, from playing video games to conducting virtual tours of real estate.

After the patent issued, more than four years later, UC's licensee, Eolas Technologies, sued Microsoft and won a federal jury verdict that Microsoft's Internet Explorer browser technology infringed the UC patent. The Chicago jury awarded Eolas $520.6 million—$1.47 for each copy of Windows containing the Explorer browser. Although the court could have enjoined Microsoft from continuing to use the infringing technology, it entered a more limited decree that embraced only future, not past, releases, and new or newly released versions of Microsoft's Windows operating system that contained Internet Explorer. The court also gave Microsoft a seventeen-week lead time to devise noninfringing technology, and stayed the injunction pending the appeals that followed.

Carefully crafted as it was, the Microsoft injunction was only the start of an unraveling skein. A great many interactive music, video, and document services on the Internet had been designed to interoperate with the infringing Microsoft code, and their vendors now had to rewrite their own code to conform it to the new, noninfringing version of Microsoft's browser. Countless Web pages too had to be modified, because the patented technology had become a standard feature in the software for coding these pages. In October 2003, two months after the jury award, the World Wide Web Consortium, an Internet standards-setting organization, wrote to the director of the Patent Office urging reexamination— and hopefully invalidation—of the UC patent "to prevent substantial economic technical damage to the operation of the World Wide Web." The next month the director ordered review of the patent, but, years later, in June 2006, the Patent Office issued a reexamination certificate confirming the patentability of the original UC claims.

The Internet not only suffers from overbroad, low-quality patents, but also offers an unparalleled vehicle for challenging them. Years before the World Wide Web Consortium urged reexamination of the UC browser patent, it issued a call across the Internet to uncover prior art that might be used to invalidate a patent that threatened to interfere with the Consortium's open standard for implementing privacy measures on the Internet. In April 2004, the Electronic Frontier Foundation launched its "Patent Busting Project," soliciting nominations for potentially invalid patents that were being used to chill Internet innovation; the EFF would then research the patents and, as appropriate, request their reexamination by the Patent and Trademark Office. And in May 2006, the same month the Patent Office ordered reexamination of Amazon.com's 1-Click patent, the office held a public meeting to discuss a proposal for Web-based peer review of patent applications. As conceived by New York Law School professor Beth Noveck, an online global community of volunteer reviewers would receive electronic notification of pending patent applications and, as appropriate, forward relevant prior art to the Patent Office for its consideration. The goal, Noveck said, was to get a thousand eyeballs to examine a single application.

Copyrights on the Internet

The Internet has transformed the business of copyright more than that of patent or trademark. Music, which as recently as the 1990s required a trip to a local record store or depended on the programming whims of a local radio station, is today available over the Internet in hard copies, through streaming, or on demand. As bandwidth expands and compression technologies improve, motion pictures and other audiovisual content are increasingly available at the viewer's pleasure. Books too can be downloaded, and the economics of the Internet have made on-demand publishing practicable for smaller niche markets than could sustain a traditional publishing venture. The great fear of entertainment companies from the 1990s forward has been that widespread digital dissemination of their works over the Internet would not only devastate their existing markets, but would itself elude the reach of copyright.

THE PEER-TO-PEER PROBLEM

Napster, the Internet music-sharing service invented in 1999 by eighteen-year-old college dropout Shawn Fanning, combined existing digital technologies—search engines, instant messaging, file sharing, digital compression—to enable subscribers quickly and easily to share digital musical files over the Internet. Anyone with a computer and a connection to the Internet could freely copy the music residing on the computer of another Napster subscriber; effectively this meant that a subscriber could copy virtually any recorded music he desired. As Napster flourished—at its height, the service claimed to have over seventy million subscribers—the music companies suffered. According to data collected by the industry trade group the Recording Industry Association of America, the number of CDs shipped in 2001 dropped 6.4 percent from the number shipped in 2000; 2002 saw a further drop of 8.9 percent, and 2003 a 7.1 percent drop. (The industry's critics said that it was poor product, not free file sharing, that caused the decline.)

The record labels mounted a three-pronged attack to protect their existing distribution channels and clear a secure path for authorized online distribution in the future. One line of attack, initiated even before Napster was launched, had the companies encrypting their recorded music to prevent unauthorized copies. But because encryption only invites disencryption—as one academic hacker put it, encryption is at best a speed bump, not a traffic barrier—the companies also sought legislation making disencryption unlawful. Together with allies from other copyright industries, the record companies succeeded in obtaining passage of the 1998 Digital Millennium Copyright Act outlawing the circumvention of any technological measure that "effectively" controlled access to, or copying of, copyrighted content.

The companies' second line of legal attack, initiated in fall 2003, was to file lawsuits against people who uploaded songs to peer-to-peer file-sharing systems like Napster. The first wave of lawsuits targeted

261 defendants, and the Recording Industry Association promised thousands more. It was essentially a campaign of intimidation—under the Copyright Act's provision for so-called statutory damages, the record companies would be entitled to recover, at a minimum, $750 for *each* of the thousand or more songs that any particular defendant copied, although cases quickly settled with aggregate payments in the $2,000–$3,000 range. The industry received bad press for suing twelve-year-olds and unwitting grandmothers, but the campaign evidently had an effect. According to a Pew Internet and American Life poll conducted two months after the lawsuits began, the number of Americans downloading music files dropped by half; at the same time, growing numbers of users were purchasing downloads from authorized services such as Apple's iTunes.

Even before the record companies started suing individuals, they opened another front against the companies, like Napster, that distributed file-sharing software, a decision that eventually brought them, along with music publishers and motion picture studios, to the U.S. Supreme Court. The legal strategy rested on the Supreme Court's 1984 ruling in the *Betamax* case that the manufacturer of equipment like Sony's Betamax VCR could be held liable for copyright infringements made with its equipment if the equipment had no substantial noninfringing use. In December 1999, the record companies, eventually joined by music publishers and several recording artists, filed their first lawsuit, against Napster, in San Francisco federal district court.

In late July 2000, federal district judge Marilyn Hall Patel granted the copyright owners' motion for a preliminary injunction, effectively shutting down Napster until a trial could be held. Judge Patel ruled that Napster was a contributory infringer—"one who, with knowledge of the infringing activity, induces, causes or materially contributes to the infringing conduct of another"—because it knew or should have known about its subscribers' copying, and because without Napster's software and the servers that Napster used to index subscribers' songs, subscribers' copying of the songs would have been difficult, if not impossible. The court rejected Napster's claim that its service, like Sony's video recorders, had substantial noninfringing uses. The court of appeals upheld the injunction, but narrowed it so that Napster did not bear the entire burden of monitoring infringements on the system.

If Napster's legal vulnerability lay in its maintenance of a music directory on its servers, the lesson for later peer-to-peer services such as Kazaa and Grokster was to separate themselves from such servers and, for that matter, from any other involvement in their subscribers' activities. When in early October 2001 the record companies, joined by movie studios, sued Kazaa and Grokster in Los Angeles federal court, the two companies defended that they could not be held contributorily liable for their subscribers' infringements because their operations were not subject to centralized control; both services were truly peer-to-peer. The district court and the court of appeals agreed, holding that the difference in the systems' architecture required a legal result different from *Napster*.

The trial and appeals court decisions in *Grokster* underlined the copyright owners' deepest fear, that the Internet would one day confront them with tens of millions of infringements, yet no one to sue. (Lawsuits against twelve-year-olds and grandmothers were a scare tactic, not a long-term litigation strategy.) The companies went to Congress seeking passage of an "Induce Act" that would dramatically expand the scope of liability of Internet equipment and service providers, but there met vigorous opposition from such Internet stalwarts as Yahoo!, Google, and CNET. Political efforts slowed when the U.S. Supreme Court agreed to hear the *Grokster* appeal and stopped entirely when in 2005 the Court overturned the lower court decisions and handed a victory to the entertainment companies, holding that "one who distributes a device with the object of promoting its use to infringe copyright . . . is liable for the resulting acts of infringement by third parties using the device, regardless of the device's lawful uses."

The irony of the lawsuits against Napster, Grokster, and their kin was that the record companies were suing the very companies that were their most logical allies in distributing music over the Internet. Early in the Napster litigation, the venture capital firm Hummer Winblad invested in the file-sharing service, and entertainment and publishing giant Bertelsmann lent the company $85 million, with the specific aim of transforming Napster into a licensed, legitimate distributor of music to its tens of millions of subscribers. (Bertelsmann found itself in the unusual position of lending money to a company that one of its divisions, BMG Entertainment, was suing.) But when Hummer Winblad partner Hank Barry, who was serving as Napster's interim CEO, approached the record companies for licenses, they rebuffed him in order to protect both their existing bricks-and-mortar distribution channels and the two struggling online music services that they themselves had established.

The movie studios learned from the record companies' mistake. When a 2006 industry study revealed that more than one-third of the film industry's $6.1 billion losses to piracy were attributable to Internet copying, the studios accelerated their dealmaking for the online distribution of feature films and television programming. The most eye-catching transaction was Warner Bros.' agreement to distribute over two hundred movies, including recent blockbuster releases and television programs, through peer-to-peer service BitTorrent. BitTorrent users had for years been the target of lawsuits from the studios, including Warner Bros., and the file-sharing service opened the way to the eventual deal by agreeing with the studios to remove unauthorized links to copyrighted files from its Web site. Warner Bros. Home Entertainment Group president Kevin Tsujihara was quoted in the *New York Times* as saying, "We've been struggling with peer-to-peer technology and trying to figure out a way to harness the good in all that the technology allows us to do. If we can convert 5, 10 or 15 percent of the illegal downloaders into consumers of our product, that is significant."

FROM INFRINGERS TO PARTNERS

If peer-to-peer services like Napster and Grokster infringed copyright by aiding and abetting their subscribers' activities, what of search engines like Google and Yahoo!, which provide the means for locating possibly infringing material, or online auctions like eBay, which host infringing content posted by others? In 1998, Congress struck a balance between copyright owners and Internet service providers by carving out "safe harbors" to protect service providers from monetary liability so long as they comply with prescribed conditions. One condition is that they implement a policy to terminate any users who are repeat copyright infringers. Another is prompt removal of copyrighted material as soon as the service provider receives notice that it is infringing. For their part, copyright owners can communicate the notice that triggers liability through a prescribed "notice and takedown" procedure: once the copyright owner notifies the service provider of infringing material on its system, the provider must remove or block access to the material. The 1998 amendments also carve out a more ample safe harbor for common carriers, such as telephone companies, that are less able to exercise control over content passing through their services.

A recurring problem with copyright legislation like the 1998 safe harbor statute is that, drafted with current technologies in view, it will inevitably be applied to future, often quite different, technologies as well. In September 1995, when the bill proposing the safe harbors was first introduced, it contained a provision that would have excluded relief for any Internet service whose workers had knowledge of infringing Web sites. The condition meant little to Internet directories like Lycos and AltaVista that used electronic "spiders" to compile their Web site directories. But to a company like Yahoo! that relied on human "surfers" to compile its directory of Web sites, the condition was potentially devastating since the company's search staff would unavoidably acquire the sort of knowledge that would defeat safe harbor protection.

Yahoo!, which was hardly three years old at the time the safe harbor bill was introduced, had not been monitoring the legislation. Indeed, the company knew nothing of the peril that awaited until late March 1998, when General Counsel John Place got a telephone call from a staffer for Congresswoman Zoe Lofgren, who represented a neighboring district, telling him that after months of unproductive negotiations on the safe harbor provisions, Orrin Hatch, chairman of the Senate Judiciary Committee, and responsible for copyright matters in the Senate, had ordered representatives from the warring Internet and copyright communities to agree on a finished draft of the bill within a week. In the course of the conversation, the staffer alerted Place to the bill's language exempting only Internet service providers that neither knew nor had reason to know of infringing activity.

Years later, Place reflected, "Ideally, management would understand that some amount of resources has to be put into public policy, somehow keeping your finger on Washington's pulse and having some kind of avenues to make your points of view known in Washington, but I seriously doubt that is a lesson that most start-up CEOs are going to have the luxury of learning. As smart as they were, and as supportive of me as the management team at that time at Yahoo! was, this just would have been an impossible sell. Being in a start-up situation, if you haven't been there, it's really hard to understand what it's like. It takes really basically every fiber of your being. It's a very intense environment. Every head has to count, every head has to have a high level of productivity to it. And the management teams of most high-tech start-ups have little or no experience when it comes to the importance of dealing with Washington. So for a CEO of a start-up to recognize the importance of dedicating resources—i.e., money!—to someone to deal with public policy is probably too much to ask."

Place promptly went to work, first engaging a Washington lawyer, and then a lobbyist, to navigate the legislative process. After more than a week of constant meetings and phone calls with congressional staffers, it became clear that the language of the bill could not be altered without upsetting the great many delicate compromises that had already been made. But there might be another way for Yahoo! to get what it needed. In construing a statute, courts will often consult the legislative reports that accompany the statute, and it might be possible to get language favorable to Yahoo! included in the reports accompanying the safe harbor bill. Over the next several weeks Place worked with his new Washington team, getting well-timed assists from company cofounder Jerry Yang, and talking not only with lawmakers and staffers on Capitol Hill but also with the other lobbyists involved in the bill's passage. At the same time, Place understood that he could not exaggerate the problems that the existing language might create for Yahoo! "I thought, 'I have to be really careful about this. I can't be running around like Chicken Little in public and saying this is horrible for Yahoo!, because that would have an effect on Wall Street's perceptions and shareholders' perceptions.'"

Yahoo!'s efforts paid off, and language appeared in both the House and Senate reports acknowledging that human editors and reviewers will sometimes be involved in compiling online directories and that, though they would not qualify for the safe harbor if they turned "a blind eye to 'red flags' of obvious infringement," the knowledge standard "should not be applied in a manner which would create a disincentive to the development of directories which involve human intervention." Indeed, the reports gave what could only be construed as a lifesaving endorsement of Yahoo! practices: "Directories are particularly helpful in conducting effective searches by filtering out irrelevant and offensive material. The Yahoo! directory, for example, currently categorizes over 800,000 on-line locations and serves as a 'card catalogue' to the World Wide Web, which over 35,000,000 different users visit each month. Directories such as Yahoo!s usually are created by people visiting sites to categorize them. It is precisely the human judgment and editorial discretion exercised by these catalogues which makes directories valuable."

As subscriber-driven Web sites like MySpace and YouTube increase by orders of magnitude the quantity of copyrighted content posted and shared over the Internet, the notice and takedown procedure of the Copyright Act's safe harbor provisions will become increasingly onerous for the film and record companies that must use it. Web site operators understand this, and have been improving and adopting technologies that can electronically identify infringing content for copyright owners. The cooperative spirit is no coincidence. Subscriber sites are big business and everyone understands that if the safe harbors prove too cumbersome, the copyright owners will go to Congress for more effective relief. It is also no coincidence that, with these sites now being run by established businesses—MySpace is owned by News Corp., YouTube by Google— the ultimate resolution will be licensing and not lawsuits for piracy. When in November 2006 Universal Music Group, owned by the French media conglomerate Vivendi, sued MySpace for the unlawful uploading of music videos, most observers understood that it was only a tactical step in its negotiations to license content to MySpace, just as it had done earlier with YouTube.

Lost to most observers in the tumult surrounding enactment of the safe harbor provisions was one startling fact. Like any other intellectual property right—indeed, like property rights generally— copyright law has historically embodied the principle that anyone who wants to use a protected work must first seek out the copyright owner and obtain permission, or, if he does not, must risk the prospect of paying damages and profits for past infringements and being enjoined from future infringements. The safe harbor provisions effectively reverse that principle, requiring the copyright owner to identify infringing uses and to seek out the user—in this case the Internet service provider—in order to object to the use; the copyright owner will obtain monetary relief for past infringements and receive an injunction for the future only if the service provider fails to comply with the copyright owner's notice.

Few copyright owners or Internet service providers today object to the safe harbor provisions, for they have so far effectively balanced the relative needs and abilities of each to patrol and control online infringement, and have contributed to the fluent regulation of infringing uses on the Internet. But if copyright owners have accepted the practical desirability of safe harbors, they have grown increasingly concerned over the logic of the expedient they embody, a logic that could entirely transform copyright—and, for that matter, patent and trademark law—from a property system that requires individuals to seek permission to use a particular intellectual asset, to a system that effectively casts these assets into the public domain, free for use by all, unless the asset's owner specifically requests that it be excluded.

Trademarks on the Internet

Trademark law at the end of the twentieth century consisted of two strands: one studded with age-old doctrines to protect consumers against confusion as to the source of goods and services, the other advancing new doctrines, such as dilution and initial interest confusion, to protect brand-name owners against the unauthorized use of their marks, whether or not consumers are confused. A wave of trademark protectionism on the Internet has drawn this second strand forward, reflecting a concern among brand owners, evidently shared by at least some courts, that forms of trademark free-riding that have long been tolerable in the world of bricks and mortar will dangerously engulf brand values in the digital environment.

Domain names were the first battlefield. (A domain name identifies a place, effectively the Web address, where the domain name registrant's Web site can be located.) Because domain names direct commercial traffic on the Web, they can have substantial value and yield extraordinary margins. In 2005, the resale market for domain names reportedly produced sales of 5,851 names for a total of $29 million. In 2006, "On.Com" sold for $635,000, "Macau.com" for $550,000, and "Sex.com" for a record $12 million. In none of these cases did the initial registration cost more than a few dollars.

The singular competitive use of domain names on the Web is not so much to confuse consumers about the source of goods and services as it is to divert them from the brand owner's Web site, which the consumer was presumably expecting to reach, to a site maintained by a competitor or by a critic of the brand owner (a so-called gripe site). For a company to register "Panavision.com" as a domain name and to use the site to misrepresent it as a legitimate source of Panavision brand camera equipment would likely confuse consumers about the source of the advertised equipment—the classic case of trademark infringement or passing off. If, however, the object of the registrant's Web site is to criticize Panavision equipment, or to advertise a different brand of camera equipment, there would be no consumer confusion, and trademark law's traditional formula would not apply. The central trademark question in the early years of the Internet was whether such uses of brand names should constitute trademark infringement.

The first cases involved cybersquatting—maintaining an empty Web site under the name Panavision for the sole purpose of selling the domain name to the owner of the Panavision trademark. At first, trademark owners who sued for trademark infringement when their names were hijacked this way lost for one or more of three reasons: the cybersquatter was not competing with the trademark owner; it was not making a commercial, trademark use of the mark; or it was not confusing consumers. But in 1998 in a case against cybersquatter Dennis Toeppen, who had reserved 240 domain names—including not only "panavision.com" but "deltaairlines.com," "crateandbarrel.com," and "ussteel.com"—a federal appeals court ruled, in an action brought by Panavision International, that Toeppen's use of Panavision as a domain name constituted unlawful dilution under the 1995 antidilution amendments to the federal Trademark Act. Evidently recognizing that it was stretching the concept of dilution beyond the doctrine's established boundaries, the court as much as said that this was dilution because it *ought* to be dilution: "Potential customers of Panavision will be discouraged if they cannot find its web page by typing in 'Panavision.com,' but instead are forced to wade through hundreds of web sites. This dilutes the value of Panavision's trademark."

A year later, Congress passed the Anticybersquatting Consumer Protection Act to bar the use of marks and personal names in situations that traditional trademark law might not reach. The act gives a brand owner rights against anyone who, with "a bad faith intent to profit" from its mark, "registers, traffics in, or uses a domain name that . . . is identical or confusingly similar to" a distinctive mark, or that is "identical or confusingly similar to or dilutive of " a famous mark.

Private initiative has supplemented judicial and legislative action against cybersquatting. The same year that Congress passed the Anticybersquatting Act, the nonprofit Internet Corporation for Assigned Names and Numbers introduced a privately administered "Uniform Domain Name Dispute Resolution Policy" that offers a less costly, more streamlined and global procedure for resolving these disputes, usually online. The policy operates as a contract between an accredited domain name registrar and each of its domain name registrants; among other requirements, the policy obligates the registrant to answer for any unauthorized trademark use in mandatory arbitration proceedings brought by the trademark owner and conducted by an ICANN-approved dispute resolution provider. A trademark owner who can show that the domain name registrant's name is confusingly similar to its mark, that the registrant has no rights in it, and that the domain name was registered and used in bad faith can have the domain name canceled or transferred to it.

The Anticybersquatting Act and the UDRP address the easiest problem. But there are more vexing concerns. One is that while many trademark owners around the world can and do own rights in the same name for the same or different businesses, only one can use that name in a particular domain. Delta Airlines, Delta Financial, and Delta-Comm Internet Services each owns the "Delta" brand in its respective line of business—not to mention the owners of the 644 other federally registered "Delta" marks for goods and services in the United States alone. Which Delta company is entitled to the delta.com domain? (DeltaComm Internet Services was the first to obtain the domain name registration; it subsequently sold the name to Delta Financial, which then sold it to Delta Airlines.) The "Scrabble" mark for board games is owned by Hasbro in the United States and Canada, but by Mattel in the rest of the world. A prospective buyer interested in the game who goes to scrabble.com will find that Hasbro and Mattel have created a gateway site enabling the user to link to the site of the company that owns the mark in that user's part of the world. Had the two companies not reached this Solomonic solution, the first of them to register the trademark as a domain name would have enjoyed exclusive global ownership worldwide at the scrabble.com address.

Domain names were only the first, and bluntest, instruments for appropriating brand names on the Internet. Search devices such as metatags and keywords offer more varied opportunities for diversionary use. A metatag is a piece of code embedded in a Web site so that it is detectable only by a search engine and not by its user. Although they are no longer widely used, metatags at one time commonly included popular trademarks in order to attract users interested in a particular brand of goods to a Web site offering competing or complementary goods. If, for example, a Web-based searchable database for film aficionados operates under the name "MovieBuff," the owner of a chain of video rental stores might bury the word "MovieBuff" as a metatag in its Web site so that when a user enters "MovieBuff" in its search engine in order to reach the film database, his search will bring him not only to the intended MovieBuff site, but to the video rental site as well. Keywords—ordinary search terms such as "camera," "autofocus," and "photography"—which are sold by search engines like Google to advertisers, such as camera companies Canon and Nikon, so that links to their sites will appear when a user enters the keyword as a search term, have substantially displaced metatags, but raise the same question as metatags when trademarks, rather than descriptive words, are used as search terms.

Do these unauthorized diversionary uses amount to trademark

infringement? Some courts have answered yes, relying on the initial interest confusion doctrine innovated in the *Steinway* case discussed in chapter 4. In 1999, in the "MovieBuff" case, a federal appellate court ruled against defendant West Coast Video's use of plaintiff's "MovieBuff" trademark as a metatag because "Web surfers looking for Brookfield's 'Movie Buff' products who are taken by a search engine to 'westcoastvideo.com' will find a database similar enough to 'Movie Buff' such that a sizeable number of consumers who were originally looking for Brookfield's product will simply decide to utilize West Coast's offerings instead."

The "MovieBuff" court used an example from the bricks-and-mortar world to support its reasoning: "Using another's trademark in one's metatags is much like posting a sign with another's trademark in front of one's store. Suppose West Coast's competitor (let's call it 'Blockbuster') puts up a billboard on a highway reading—'West Coast Video: 2 miles ahead at Exit 7'—where West Coast is really located at Exit 8 but Blockbuster is located at Exit 7. Customers looking for West Coast's store will pull off at Exit 7 and drive around looking for it. Unable to locate West Coast, but seeing the Blockbuster store right by the highway entrance, they may simply rent there. Even consumers who prefer West Coast may find it not worth the trouble to continue searching for West Coast since there is a Blockbuster right there. Customers are not confused in the narrow sense: they are fully aware that they are purchasing from Blockbuster and they have no reason to believe that Blockbuster is related to, or in any way sponsored by, West Coast. Nevertheless, the fact that there is only initial consumer confusion does not alter the fact that Blockbuster would be misappropriating West Coast's acquired goodwill."

Five years later, the same court extended this questionable reasoning to search engine Netscape's use of plaintiff Playboy Enterprises' trademarks "Playboy and "Playmate" among over four hundred keywords to trigger banner ads for adult-oriented companies. One of the court's three judges, Marsha S. Berzon, concurred, but expressed reservations about the "MovieBuff" precedent, using a bricks-and-mortar metaphor of her own: "Suppose a customer walks into a bookstore and asks for *Playboy* magazine and is then directed to the adult magazine section, where he or she sees *Penthouse* or *Hustler* up front on the rack while *Playboy* is buried in back. One would not say that *Penthouse* or *Hustler* had violated *Playboy's* trademark. This conclusion holds true even if *Hustler* paid the store owner to put its magazines in front of *Playboy's*."

Not all American courts agree that brand names should enjoy expanded coverage on the Internet, nor, as Judge Berzon's observation suggests, do all agree that the implications of real-world analogs are unambiguous. (Surely it is less inconvenient for a shopper to be momentarily diverted from one expected Web link to another than to be diverted from one highway exit to another.) Since, historically, Congress generally acts to expand, not contract, trademark rights, there is small likelihood that it will act to curb this trend. The next big question for brand-name companies and their competitors is whether these expansionary rules crafted for the Internet will migrate from this setting into trademark law's mainstream, and contribute to the broadening of trademark law generally.

Intellectual Assets Without Property?

There is much theorizing, but scant empirical evidence, on whether the inducements offered by intellectual property are essential to the production of intellectual assets. Would basement inventors create new products without the promise of patent protection? Would novice writers create new works without copyright? Anecdotes abound that amateurs need no promise of property rights to spur their efforts. But would businesses be willing to invest the sums required to reduce an invention to practice, to produce and launch a motion picture, or to develop and market a new brand without the promise of exclusive rights? There is less theory, and no empirical evidence at all, on the question whether intellectual property laws stimulate the economically *optimum* quantity of intellectual assets.

The Internet, with its hundreds of millions of linked users, gives unique force to these questions. Napster and Grokster put Internet file sharing in the headlines, but the Internet's communal infrastructure enables users to create information as well as to steal it. By early 2007, according to its Web site, Wikipedia, the free online encyclopedia, had more than seventy-five thousand active volunteer contributors working on over five million articles in over one hundred languages. Linux, the open-source operating system, is but one of many valuable but freely accessible software products created, debugged, and modified by thousands of programmers around the world, each contributing his time over the Internet. Consumer goods companies as large as Procter & Gamble tap into wired communities of volunteers for feedback on products and suggestions for design alternatives. And since these are all information products, with the Internet as the medium of transport, capturing their value requires no investment in material or machines.

As it turns out, intellectual property as an instrument of control has as important a role on the Internet as off it. Linux, for example, embodies a fundamentally simple idea, but an institutionally complex implementation, and illustrates the important place that property rules occupy even in the communal development of an intellectual asset. Introduced in 1991 by Linus Torvalds, a young university student in Helsinki, and improved and enhanced by volunteer programmers over the Internet, the Linux operating system is distributed under the so-called General Public License, which means that, unlike commercial operating systems, its source code is freely available to the public. Although Linux itself is noncommercial, it is distributed commercially by such established firms as Novell and Red Hat; it runs on Intel's proprietary chip architecture; and it operates on software platforms maintained by Fujitsu, Hewlett-Packard, IBM, and Sun Microsystems. Although Linux today has a significant share of the server market, its inroads into the PC market, dominated by Microsoft's Windows, have so far been modest. (Since applications written for Windows will not run on Linux, Linux distributors must convince the vast installed base of Windows PC users to change their applications.)

Apart from its communal origins, the key distinguishing feature of Linux is that it is free. As Torvalds explains in *Just for Fun: The Story of an Accidental Revolutionary*, "I didn't want to sell Linux. And I didn't want to lose control, which meant I didn't want anybody else to sell it, either." Since, "as the copyright owner, I got to make up the rules," Torvalds included a copyright policy in his first release: "You can use the operating system for free, as long as you don't sell it, and if you make changes or improvements you must make them available to everybody in source code" (rather than inaccessible object code). Torvalds later reflected on the extent to which, in creating Linux, he had himself relied on software tools freely distributed over the Internet, the most important of which was a compiler distributed under the Free Software Foundation's General Public License. Impressed by the GPL, which imposed no bar on commercial use, "I dumped my old copyright and adopted the GPL."

Since Linux is free, companies like Novell and Red Hat profit by offering enhancements to streamline and support the operating system's use. Among other products, they sell interoperable databases and integration software as well as services for Linux servers. The standard intellectual property tactic for a company in this business would be to add to the free content some copyrightable or patentable content of its own—a copyright fig leaf of sorts—charging customers for the entire package. But the GPL requires that any modification of GPL-licensed source code like Linux itself also be licensed under the terms of the GPL, which is why the GPL is called a "viral" license. When in February 2004 Red Hat launched a Linux enhancement enabling several functions to occur simultaneously on a single processor, competitor Novell was free to copy the upgrade from Redhat's Web site and, within a week, introduce it as part of its own Linux operating system.

"Free" does not mean uncontested, and Linux—and the open-source movement generally—promises to become as contentious a battleground as interoperability was during the softwars of the 1990s, described in chapter 3. The prize in both is the same: a dominating platform. The battle, so far, finds Microsoft defending its widely entrenched Windows operating system, much as it did in the 1990s, but IBM, which during the softwars had allied itself with—indeed led—the dominant companies, now promoting Linux, along with a number of other well-established companies including Dell, Hewlett-Packard, and Intel. In January 2005 IBM agreed to make five hundred software patents available free to Linux as well as other open-source software projects, and it is unlikely that Linux would have achieved its current prominence without these powerful patrons.

Nor does "free" mean unprotected by intellectual property law. Just as Linus Torvalds asserted copyright in Linux from the start, so the GPL presupposes copyright in all of its licensed content. Indeed, copyright is the lever that the GPL employs to extract undertakings of free use by its licensees; if a user violates the license, the copyright owner can sue for copyright infringement. Also, to preserve the integrity of Linux distribution channels, authorized Linux distributors in the open-source community have registered the brand as a trademark and opposed its registration by others.

And "free" does not mean unencumbered by the claims of intellectual asset owners from outside the open-source community. Intellectual property is ubiquitous, particularly on the Internet, and it is difficult for Linux developers to escape entirely the spiderweb of intellectual property rights that are not subject to the GPL. In March 2003, SCO Group, a seller of Linux and Unix products based in Lindon, Utah, sued IBM in Utah state court alleging that IBM had misappropriated SCO trade secrets from the Unix operating system and incorporated them in an IBM Linux product. The lawsuit, which also asserted unfair competition, breach of contract, and tortious interference with contract, sought more than $1 billion in damages.

Commentators puzzled as to why SCO based the lawsuit on Utah's trade secret law rather than on federal copyright law, for which infringement is much easier to prove. One reason may have been that, as a Utah company, SCO was hoping for a home court advantage in state court there. (If this was its strategy, IBM promptly defeated it by having the case removed to federal district court in Salt Lake City.) Another possible reason for choosing trade secret over copyright may have been SCO's uncertainty as to whether it in fact owned the copyright in the allegedly purloined code. Unix was initially developed by AT&T, which later sold the intellectual property rights in it to Novell Networks, which in turn sold some of these interests to a predecessor of SCO. What was in dispute was whether the transfer from Novell included the relevant Unix copyrights.

One way to pressure an accused intellectual property infringer to settle is to warn its customers that they too may be held liable for infringement. In May 2003, two months after filing the lawsuit against

IBM, SCO sent letters to fifteen hundred major Linux users alerting them to their potential liability for using its intellectual property; subsequently, SCO filed lawsuits against users DaimlerChrysler and auto parts supplier AutoZone. Sowing fear, uncertainty, and doubt is a common tactic in the software business—IBM itself was known to spread FUD during the softwars—and major Linux suppliers like Novell and Hewlett-Packard responded by agreeing to indemnify their customers against losses from any such lawsuit. Open Source Development Labs, a consortium dedicated to promoting Linux, set up a $10 million legal defense fund with contributions from Intel and IBM, among others. Nor was SCO without support in the battle. In late May 2003, just after it released its warning letters to major Linux users, Microsoft purchased a Unix license from it for $13 million, bolstering the legitimacy of SCO's intellectual property claims and adding to its war chest.

Software economics make for changing bedfellows, and late in 2006 rivals Microsoft and Novell announced a collaboration to ensure that Microsoft's Windows operating system could interoperate with Novell's version of Linux on corporate servers. As part of the deal, Microsoft agreed not to file patent infringement suits against customers purchasing Novell's version of Linux.

In a February 9, 2005, decision, U.S. district judge Dale A. Kimball rejected IBM's motion for summary judgment, but left no doubt of his skepticism about SCO's claims. "It is astonishing," Judge Kimball wrote, "that SCO has not offered any competent evidence to create a disputed fact regarding whether IBM has infringed SCO's alleged copyrights through IBM's Linux activities." Judge Kimball was puzzled by SCO's continued ambivalence as to whether it was in fact making a copyright claim against IBM, for "it clearly has alleged such a claim."

In late June 2006, a magistrate judge assigned to the case reviewed 198 of SCO's 294 claims and dismissed all but eleven of them, using a bricks-and-mortar analogy to make his point about the vagueness of the claims: "Certainly if an individual was stopped and accused of shoplifting after walking out of Neiman Marcus they would expect to be eventually told what they allegedly stole. It would be absurd for an officer to tell the accused that 'you know what you stole. I'm not telling.' Or, to simply hand the accused individual a catalog of Neiman

Marcus' entire inventory and say 'it's in there somewhere, you figure it out.' In essence," the judge said, "IBM is left to wade through all the code found in the operating systems, and then ask SCO are you claiming line X in the Read-Copy-Update method found in Linux because there is a somewhat similar line in the Read-Copy-Update in AIX? Such an endeavor seems like a waste of resources and time because under the court's orders SCO should have already identified such information."

The ubiquity of intellectual assets on the Internet—not just copyrights, but patents, trademarks, and trade secrets—together with the ever-widening embrace of the viral General Public License, means that no software or online business can ever be entirely free of concern for intellectual property claims. In 2003, the same year SCO sued IBM, a former sister company of SCO, Lineo, agreed to settle a copyright infringement lawsuit in which Monte Vista, a Linux software company charged it with copying, and removing copyright notices from, code appearing in Monte Vista's GPL-licensed software. An executive of the investment firm that formerly controlled Lineo blamed the infringement on an Indian company to which it had outsourced the work. The executive, who was also the chairman of SCO, told a *New York Times* reporter, "SCO picked a big fight and it flowed over to the Linux environment and we found ourselves in an awkward position. For better or for worse it's one of the cautions and dangers and flaws for the model. It happened to Lineo and has happened to several others."

The great success of Linux and other collaborative online efforts does not presage the decline of copyright as a policy instrument for organizing investment in the production and dissemination of literary works. Apart from the fact that Linux and the GPL generally depend on copyright to enforce compliance with their rules of use, the fact that open systems are iterative and widely dispersed limits their attractions to a particular kind of information product. It is no coincidence that the two best-known online collaborations—Linux and Wikipedia—involve, respectively, a computer operating system and an encyclopedic collection of facts, for it is in the nature of functional and factual tools like these that their efficiency and accuracy will be improved by small doses of constant, repeated attention. By contrast, few lasting works of

music, art, film, or literature owe their origins to such widely dispersed—
and democratic—collaborations, or their perfection (if perfection were
even desirable) to such repeated attentions from masses of contributors.

Mapping Intellectual Asset Change on the Internet

Any intellectual asset company that does business on the Internet—
which means any company that does business—will over the coming
years encounter two irreversible facts: the Internet has changed intellectual property law, and intellectual property law has changed the Internet. The *Playboy* and *MovieBuff* trademark cases are examples of
how courts have perceived Internet practices as requiring the expansion of property rights beyond the boundaries set in the bricks-and-
mortar world. The case of *eBay v. MercExchange,* which overturned
the principle that injunctive relief is automatically available in patent
infringement cases, is an example of how the U.S. Supreme Court understood Internet technologies to require the contraction of property
rights. Companies need to monitor such changes not only on the
Internet—the setting where they arose—but in the bricks-and-mortar
world as well, for precedents established in one setting inescapably migrate to cases decided in other settings.

A more revolutionary change may alter copyright law, on and off
the Internet. The safe harbor provisions, for which Yahoo! and other
Internet service providers lobbied, effectively depart from the historic
copyright principle that a user must request permission from the
copyright owner or face liability for infringement, replacing it with
the opposite principle, that a copyright owner can obtain relief only if,
after the owner asks the user to remove infringing copies appearing
on its site, the user refuses to do so. Google has argued for a comparable reversal of copyright principles in rejecting criticism from publishers and authors over its Library Project, described in chapter 3.
Under Google's approach, it would be free to copy onto its servers any
copyrighted works it wants, and would be obligated to remove them
only if the copyright owner so requested within a prescribed period.
A victory for Google would revolutionize copyright practice on the
Internet and, over time, in the bricks-and-mortar world too. Such a

change could lead to reconsideration of the foundations of patent, trademark, and trade secret law as well.

Intellectual property practice has also changed the Internet, mainly by curbing otherwise unlicensed individual and collaborative uses. Copyright owners have, for example, digitally encrypted the music they release on the Internet as part of a three-pronged strategy that also includes lawsuits against service providers and individual users. Vast collaborative enterprises like Linux that aim to harness the power of the Internet to increase the reach and efficiency of works created online, though "free," rely on copyright as a means to perpetuate their originators' notions of freedom. But these efforts are also prey to incursions by technologies produced outside the collaborative venture, typically in the form of lawsuits for patent infringement.

7

Intellectual Assets in International Markets

No intellectual asset owner can ignore the global imperative of scalability. If sales can be multiplied threefold or more with little additional investment, then the surest way to grow profits is to exploit the company's intellectual assets around the world. Some intellectual asset owners view profits earned in foreign markets as a windfall. But many multinational companies, from film studios to pharmaceutical producers, will from the outset proportion their investments in creating intellectual assets to the revenues they anticipate from all markets, domestic and foreign. The more thoughtful companies will also adjust their expectations to the contours of foreign legal cultures and to differences in the pace, cost, and stability of local intellectual property enforcement.

Even the most sophisticated companies encounter legal surprises in their foreign ventures, particularly if the company is habituated to sometimes idiosyncratic U.S. intellectual property rules. Trademark rights in other countries are acquired by registration, not by use as in the United States, and more than one American company has lost foreign rights in its brand because its application arrived too late at the local trademark registry. Patent-based companies must discipline their researchers to defer publishing their results until after the company has applied for a patent; because other countries do not have the one-year grace period of American law, patents must be applied for promptly upon reducing the invention to practice. So-called moral rights—giving authors the right to object to the distortion of their works—are generally ignored in the United States, but may bar the broadcast abroad of a film that was colorized in the United States or edited to make room for commercials. Even rules on the permissibility of price discrimination may differ, and an intellectual property owner may find that the price it set in one country is being undermined by imports from another country where the selling price is lower.

Careful drafting of intellectual property licenses can inject some degree of certainty into transborder commerce. Inclusion of so-called choice of law and choice of forum clauses, common in most commercial international transactions, can usually ensure that the law of a single jurisdiction selected by the parties will govern performance of the license anywhere in the world—"The parties agree that any disputes arising under this agreement shall be governed by the statutes and case law of England"—and that the forum in which the dispute is adjudicated or arbitrated will be one that is acceptable to the parties—"The parties agree that any dispute under this agreement shall be tried in the courts of Belgium." Of course, contract clauses govern only the conduct of the contracting parties, not of infringers, whose conduct will instead be controlled by the law of the country where the alleged infringement occurred.

Territoriality and the Trade Economics of Intellectual Assets

Why does U.S. law not govern the rights of American companies wherever they may exploit their intellectual assets? A centuries-old principle—territoriality—drives not only the law, but also the economics of international protection for intellectual property. There is no such thing as an international patent, copyright, trademark, or trade secret. Subject to treaty arrangements with other nations, every country gets to decide for itself what intellectual assets to protect within its borders, as well as the extent—if any—to which it will protect the intellectual assets of foreign nationals. The force of U.S. patent, copyright, trademark, and trade secret law ends at the U.S. border. For protection abroad, American intellectual asset owners must look to the law of the country in which the asset is being exploited.

The territoriality principle played a short-lived but important part in the BlackBerry patent infringement litigation discussed in chapter 2. Research in Motion, BlackBerry's Canada-based maker, argued that although most users of the wireless device lived and worked in the United States, the system's all-important relay servers—through which BlackBerry e-mails travel—were located in Waterloo, Ontario, the company's home base, and thus fell outside the territorial scope of the U.S. patents owned by its adversary, NTP. In an unusual move, the Canadian government filed an amicus brief with the Court of Appeals for the Federal Circuit supporting RIM's position and arguing—ultimately unsuccessfully—that the court's decision against the company violated the "integrity of the operation of Canadian intellectual property laws" by requiring activities entirely inside Canada to conform to U.S. law. To criticisms that his government was seeking favor for a local company, a spokesman for Canada's Department of Foreign Affairs and International Trade answered that the government was simply concerned that the court was intruding U.S. law onto Canadian soil.

Countries, most notably the United States, regularly violate the territoriality principle. In 1972 the U.S. Supreme Court ruled that it would offend territoriality for it to hold that Deepsouth Packing Company manufactured its shrimp deveiner in America, and thus infringed Laitram Corp.'s U.S. patent on the device, when in fact the company did nothing more on U.S. soil than to ship components of the deveiner for assembly and use in other countries, such as Brazil. If a U.S. inventor wants patent protection in foreign markets, the Court ruled, he should "seek it abroad through patents secured in countries where his goods are being used." But, twelve years later, Congress overruled the Supreme Court decision and intruded U.S. patent law onto foreign territories by amending the Patent Act to make it infringement simply to supply a substantial number of the components in or from the United States, if doing so actively induces the components' combination outside the United States "in a manner that would infringe the patent if such combination occurred within the United States."

There are powerful economic reasons for countries like the United States, which are net intellectual asset exporters, to extend their intellectual property rules into countries like Brazil, which are net intellectual asset importers. Historically, net intellectual asset importers saw little reason to protect intellectual goods coming from abroad. For Brazil to give patent protection to a foreign producer of shrimp processors would require its nationals to pay higher prices for this equipment than they otherwise would, with the great proportion of the increment leaving the country in the form of royalty payments to the foreign owner. Better, it was thought, for Brazilians to pay lower prices, leaving them with more money to spend on domestic products. (Of course, two can play the territoriality game: Congress can direct U.S. courts to impose liability on anyone who ships shrimp deveiner components to Brazil for assembly there, and the U.S. patent owner could obtain a judgment against an infringer in a U.S. court. But if the patent owner sought to enforce that judgment in Brazil it could expect a cold reception—if not outright laughter—from the Brazilian judge.)

No nation should better understand the economic viewpoint of intellectual asset importing countries than the United States. As a net importer for the first century of its existence, the United States flatly refused to protect books and other literary and artistic works coming from abroad. Even though American authors and publishers would have preferred not to compete with cheap American-made copies of English works, American printers objected that protection for English works would cut into their profits from copying these works royalty-free. Only in 1891, under pressure from American and British authors and publishers, did the United States first enter into treaties agreeing to protect works created by nationals of other countries.

Instead of challenging the territoriality principle, a country that is a net intellectual property exporter could enter into a treaty with a net importer, obligating it to extend strong protection to foreign intellectual assets. Why would a net importing country agree to a treaty that would result in higher prices for its citizens? In the mid-nineteenth century, France proposed to Belgium, which imported French-language works but denied them copyright protection, that the two countries enter into a bilateral treaty under which France would protect Belgian literary works if, and to the extent that, Belgium in return protected French works. French authors and publishers of course applauded the proposal because such a treaty would ensure them royalties from Belgian readers. But—and this is the striking lesson of the trade economics of intellectual property—Belgian authors and publishers supported the treaty too, for competition with cheap books coming from France made it hard for them to price their own French-language books profitably. The Belgian nation also had an interest in a level playing field with French imports, for, by reducing Belgian literary production, cheap imports also depressed a home-grown national culture.

Multilateral Treaties and the North-South Divide

Bilateral agreements of the sort entered into between France and Belgium suffered two deficiencies: they had a limited duration, and their principle of reciprocity—I'll protect your works to the same extent you protect mine—required sometimes unwieldy inquiries by the courts of one country into the practices of the other. In the case of copyright, dissatisfaction with these bilateral treaties ultimately led to the adoption in 1886 of the Berne Convention for the Protection of Literary and Artistic Works, a multilateral treaty with Belgium, France, Germany, and the United Kingdom, but not the United States, among the initial signatories. Unlike the short-term bilateral treaties, the Berne Convention had no termination date and, instead of reciprocity, its governing principle was *national treatment*. (France agreed to give nationals of other member countries at least the same protection it gave to French nationals.) To this, the Berne treaty added *minimum standards* to guard against backsliding into local protectionism: however poorly a country protected its own nationals, it had to meet prescribed minimum standards on the duration of copyright, types of subject matter protected, and rights granted to works from other Berne countries. The Berne Union today has 162 members, including China, which joined in 1992. (The United States, an international copyright pariah for over a century, until it began signing bilateral treaties in 1891, adhered to the Berne Convention only in 1989.)

Like the Berne Convention, the Paris Convention for the Protection of Industrial Property, adopted in 1883 as the multilateral convention for patents, trademarks, and unfair competition, follows the principle of national treatment. But unlike Berne, whose many minimum copyright standards have regularly been tightened over the years, the Paris Convention has never had more than a small handful of minimum standards. Indeed, a country could belong to the Paris Convention even though it neither granted patents to foreign nationals nor registered their trademarks (so long as it was similarly stinting in its treatment of its own nationals). This difference partly explains why the United States has had fewer occasions to extend its copyright standards extraterritorially than to extend its patent and trademark standards: the other countries of the Berne Union already apply high copyright standards as part of their Berne treaty obligations, while many of the other 170 countries of the Paris Union have historically applied—because the Paris Convention lets them apply—standards lower than those of U.S. law.

The benefits of protecting works from abroad will not always be as clear to a net intellectual asset importing country as it was to Belgium in the 1850s. Creating and publishing literature, music, and art required comparatively little capital expenditure—even less today with our digital capabilities—and a country like Belgium could be confident that, over time, protection for works coming from France would create a level playing field for Belgian writers and publishers to compete with their French counterparts. Pharmaceutical research and development, by contrast, requires huge capital and infrastructure costs, and for most developing economies in Asia, Africa, and Latin America the economic case for protecting pharmaceutical inventions from abroad is nonexistent. When Kenya compares the reality of cheap generic drugs with the speculative possibility of a thriving local research and development establishment, cheap drugs understandably win.

In the 1950s, following their political independence from European colonial powers, a great many of these developing countries fought to free themselves from the Berne and Paris conventions to which their colonial masters had committed them. Although membership in the conventions may have served the economic interests of the colonialists, the newly independent nations did not believe that it served their own, and it was opposition from these countries through the 1960s that undermined attempts by the industrialized countries to strengthen Berne and blocked efforts to introduce new minimum standards into the Paris Convention. Piracy flourished in the newly destabilized environment.

The industrialized countries responded with a carrot and a stick. The carrot came wrapped in the argument that only if the developing countries adopted strong intellectual property protection could they hope to attract the foreign direct investment essential to their economic development. Protection of foreign intellectual assets might increase domestic prices, but—or so the argument went—the social benefits of more rapid industrialization would more than offset the social cost of these increases. And although trade economists disagree on whether the overall benefits of strong intellectual property enforcement outweigh their costs for developing economies—there is evidence that the trade-off is less costly for copyright industries than for patent industries—effective intellectual property enforcement does appear to attract foreign direct investment in plants and in research and development if for no other reason than that it signals a business-friendly environment.

The stick to be wielded against countries that failed to adopt and enforce strict intellectual property protections was trade sanctions. The World Trade Organization's Agreement on Trade-Related Aspects of Intellectual Property Rights—TRIPs—adopted in April 1994 as part of an agreement amending the General Agreement on Tariffs and Trade, expressly incorporates the minimum standards of the Berne and Paris conventions and adds substantial minimum standards of its own, including standards for enforcement. A WTO member country whose nationals are injured by another member country's failure to comply with TRIPs standards can file a complaint with a WTO panel. If the panel finds a violation of TRIPs standards and the offending party still declines to comply, the successful party can impose economic sanctions against the offending member. This promise of sanctions separates the

TRIPs Agreement from all intellectual property agreements that preceded it, for although the Berne and Paris conventions authorize proceedings in the International Court of Justice, the prospects of relief there have always been sufficiently speculative that no member has ever filed a complaint.

For American intellectual asset owners, the result of the TRIPs Agreement has been a receding frontier of lawlessness and the emergence of comparatively stable markets that more or less honor and enforce intellectual property rights. The message for American businesses is that it is increasingly safe to market intellectual assets in these countries and, in the more promising of them, to invest in research and development there.

If the prospects for U.S. companies are upbeat, the prospects for the United States itself are not. The United States was a net intellectual property importer through the nineteenth century and, as such, resisted treaty obligations like the Berne Convention that required protection of foreign works. In the twentieth century, as a net intellectual property exporter for the first time, the United States took the lead in high-protection initiatives like the TRIPs Agreement that would ensure protection for American intellectual goods in less developed countries. But as investment and innovation migrate to other regions—most notably Asia—there is no assurance that the United States will continue as the world's leading intellectual asset exporter over the course of the twenty-first century, nor that American citizens will continue to benefit from high intellectual property standards in their own country.

Price Discrimination and Parallel Imports in Global Markets

Few marketing opportunities are more attractive than charging different prices for the same good in different markets. If the profit-maximizing price for a particular model of digital camera is $800 in Country A but $600 in Country B, the camera's manufacturer will usually want to differentiate prices in the two countries accordingly, and if the product is protected by a patent, copyright, or trademark in Country A, the manufacturer will try to use that country's law to bar the import of the lower-priced cameras from Country B. The key question in any case is whether and to what extent the laws of Country A will bar such "parallel imports," for without a bar it is difficult if not impossible for a company to maintain a global program of price discrimination.

Patent, copyright, and trademark laws in all countries provide that a protected good's first sale inside the country terminates the intellectual property owner's right to control resales of the good in that country. (This is called the "first sale" doctrine in the United States, the "exhaustion" doctrine elsewhere.) Countries differ, however, on the extraterritorial impact of the first sale of a patented or copyrighted good outside the country. Some countries—the United States is one—follow a rule of "national exhaustion" and hold that the first sale of a patented or copyrighted good outside the country will not terminate the intellectual property owner's right to control that good's resale inside the country. Other countries extend the exhaustion rule for patented and copyrighted goods globally, and hold that an intellectual property owner exhausts its right to control resale of the good in the country once it allows the good to be sold anywhere in the world. Thus, if Country A followed this rule, called "international exhaustion," the camera manufacturer would not be able to bar the resale in Country A of the $600 cameras it put on the market in Country B. Intellectual property owners sometimes try to circumvent international exhaustion by contractually imposing territorial limitations on their distributors. But contracts generally bind only those who make them, and a reseller from the distributor will rarely be constrained by such a territorial undertaking.

Trademark goods are different, and are governed by a rule of international exhaustion even in countries like the United States that apply the rule of national exhaustion to patented and copyrighted goods. The premise behind this difference is that, unlike patent and copyright, the object of trademark law is not to protect goods as such, but to safeguard consumers against confusion about the quality and origin of goods; so long as the imported and domestic goods are identical and come from the same manufacturer, limiting their resale would not serve consumer welfare. This explains why camera retailers in the United States will sometimes offer the identical model camera at two different prices: a U.S. price, which typically includes the manufacturer's warranty, and a gray market price, which comes with only a store warranty. Brand name companies can at least partially sidestep trademark law's international exhaustion rule by relying on the copyright in a product's label to bar parallel imports of the product itself.

The trade economics of a country's decision to adopt or reject a rule of national exhaustion are complex, and the lineup of countries on one side of the question or the other only roughly approximates the division between industrialized and developing economies. (For example, Japan and Canada generally follow a rule of international exhaustion, while Egypt and Paraguay follow national exhaustion.) Even so, when the question of parallel imports arose in the TRIPs negotiations, the United States argued for a global rule of national exhaustion, the developing countries favored a rule of international exhaustion, and the European Community sought a rule that would preserve its unique hybrid of regional exhaustion within the community but national exhaustion outside it. The TRIPs negotiators ultimately resolved the division by taking no position at all, and Article 6 of the agreement provides that "nothing in this Agreement shall be used to address the issue of the exhaustion of intellectual property rights."

Harmonizing and Diverging Tendencies in National Laws

Of all the countries in the world intellectual property community, the United States has been the most inward-looking, and its patent, copyright, trademark, and trade secret rules differ on the most fundamental points, not only from those in the countries of continental Europe, Latin America, and parts of Africa and Asia, but also from Britain and the Commonwealth countries with which it shares its legal tradition. However, globalization has changed U.S. business practices, and these changes have in turn drawn American law toward international norms. At the same time, globalization has pushed other countries toward adopting some of the less eccentric American intellectual property norms, particularly under the prodding of the TRIPs Agreement and the newer bilateral treaties between the United States and developing countries.

PATENTS. The U.S. Patent Act, alone among the patent laws of the world, awards a patent to the first person to invent the patentable subject matter; other countries award the patent to the first inventor who applies for it. This American emphasis on fairness (costly "interference" proceedings are sometimes required to determine which of two or more inventors made the invention first) contrasts with the emphasis on efficiency everywhere else (first-to-file systems leave no doubt as to who is entitled to the patent). Fairness—or at least inefficiency— characterizes other aspects of American patent law as well. Inventors in the United States can use, sell, and publish information disclosing their inventions for up to one year before applying for a patent; some other countries allow a more limited grace period, and still others, most notably in Europe, allow virtually no grace period at all. The U.S. Patent Act has historically postponed publication of patent applications until the patent is issued, enabling the inventor whose application is rejected by the Patent Office to continue to practice his invention as a trade secret. Other countries publish applications eighteen months after they are filed.

As a growing number of American companies adjust their patent management practices to the rules for obtaining patents abroad— filing as early as possible; taking care not to publish before filing; accepting early publication—domestic political pressures to retain these age-old rules have receded. A switch from first-to-invent to first-to-file has been on the patent reform agenda since at least 1966 and continues to be a feature of contemporary reform bills. (The principal opposition to the change comes from small companies that believe their relatively limited resources for preparing and filing patent applications will hamper them in a race to the Patent Office.) In 1999, Congress amended the Patent Act to establish a default rule that patent applications will be published eighteen months from filing unless the applicant requests earlier publication or no publication at all. As an incentive to early publication, the act provides that a patent owner can accrue reasonable royalties for infringements starting from the date of publication (rather than from the date the patent issued) if the infringer knew of the publication.

A second distinctive emphasis in U.S. patent law is its breadth of coverage. Not only has Congress historically cast the patent net widely—"any new and useful process, machine, manufacture, or composition of matter, or any new and useful improvement thereof "—but courts, led by the Supreme Court, have read the terms broadly, bringing such fields as software and biotechnology under patent protection before other countries did. Years after patent protection for software-related inventions became a U.S. norm, the European Parliament rejected a proposed directive that would have introduced software patents in Europe, and many countries have historically excluded patent protection for pharmaceutical products or processes, food products or processes, and therapeutic methods for treating humans or animals that are protectible in the United States.

The TRIPs Agreement has greatly widened the range of subject matter that WTO member countries must protect to include "any inventions, whether products or processes, in all fields of technology," a standard closer to the U.S. statute's encompassing formula than to the earlier national prescriptions. The change was particularly important to pharmaceutical firms, which previously saw some of their most valuable inventions copied freely in some of the world's richest markets. The "products or processes" clause ends the distinction that many countries once drew between unpatentable pharmaceutical and chemical products and the processes used in making them; the "all fields of technology" clause bars member countries from denying protection to inventions in such lucrative fields as foods and beverages.

U.S. patent law is also unique in the rigor of its exclusive rights, allowing compulsory licenses in only the narrowest circumstances. Other countries widely allow such licenses—and deny the patent owner injunctive relief—for any one or more of three reasons: the public interest, such as compelling reasons of public health; the patent owner's failure to exploit the patent within a prescribed period; and the patent owner's refusal to license the invention to another inventor who has improved upon it (one commonly imposed condition of such licenses is that the second patent owner must cross-license its improvement to the first patent owner). In practice, compulsory licenses in these countries are rarely enforced but instead provide the basis for negotiated licenses between patent owner and licensee—albeit, as would be expected, at royalty rates lower than could be obtained under threat of an injunction.

COPYRIGHT. Over most of its history, American copyright was tied to formalities such as registration and affixation of a copyright notice (the familiar "Copyright Ernest Hemingway"), and, since the twentieth century, compulsory licenses and other limitations have increasingly modified the law's exclusive rights. Other countries long ago dropped formalities as a condition to protection, and although they impose some limitations on exclusive rights, those limitations are nowhere as extensive as they are in the United States. The American tilt toward formalities and limited rights stems from the utilitarian tradition that underlies U.S. copyright law, while the inclination elsewhere toward rigorous, formality-free rights traces to the European precept that an author has a natural right to protection for the products of his mind; indeed, Europeans commonly refer to these rights not only as copyright, but as "author's right."

The competing emblems of U.S.-style utilitarianism and European-style natural rights are the American doctrine of fair use and the continental doctrine of moral right. Fair use is a wide-ranging doctrine that excuses otherwise infringing uses when transaction costs will stand in the way of a license between copyright owner and user; it was fair use that excused home videotaping in the *Sony* case and the decompilation of object code in the *Sega* case. Fair use is only faintly approximated in other countries where, unlike the United States, collecting societies abound to meliorate the problem of transaction costs. And where other countries embrace the doctrine of moral right to protect authors against distortions of their works and failures to credit their authorship, Congress and the courts have steadfastly rejected a categorical moral right in the United States.

Despite these doctrinal differences, the Berne Convention (and the TRIPs Agreement's incorporation of the Berne Convention's minimum standards into its own minimum standards) works to harmonize copyright law and practice across borders. In 1976, Congress altered the duration of copyright from fifty-six years to the Berne minimum of the author's life plus fifty years in anticipation of the United States' joining the Berne Union; in 1989, when the United States joined Berne, Congress made other conforming changes, including elimination of the notice formality; and in 1995, when the United States joined the World Trade Organization, Congress made further changes to comply with Berne and to avoid the imposition of WTO sanctions.

Doubtless the most powerful harmonizing force—and, not coincidentally, a force that is responsible for increasing levels of copyright protection worldwide—is that the community of copyright owners crosses national boundaries. When it comes to copyright, an American movie studio has far more in common with a French movie studio than it does with an American Web site that streams video over the Internet. A Nashville music publisher has more in common with a Berlin music publisher than it does with a Nashville restaurant that plays its music. It is this community of copyright owners that lobbies for protection around the world, and it is no surprise that the resulting national laws have so much in common. When American music publishers failed to stop Congress from allowing a restaurant of a certain size to perform their music free, they could be confident that fellow publishers in Europe would challenge the new exemption before a WTO dispute resolution panel on the ground that the exemption violated one or more of the minimum standards imposed by the Berne Convention. The WTO panel so ruled, giving the United States a choice between rescinding the exemption and paying compensation to the Europeans.

TRADEMARK. As in the United States, trademark ownership around the world originally turned on trademark use; a merchant could not reserve a brand for future use, and would enjoy rights only when he actually used the brand. The advantage of the use requirement was that it prevented companies from hoarding marks they had no intention to use. But the requirement also had several disadvantages: exposing the brand-name owner to the risk that an interloper would use its brand, and acquire priority, in corners of the country it had not yet entered, and also the risk that it would itself expand into a market already claimed by a competitor's earlier use. Centralized trademark registers in the United States and elsewhere meliorated some of these disadvantages by providing that a mark's registration would establish the brand owner's exclusive rights throughout the country, except in pockets of prior use by others. The difference between the United States and other countries today is that while the United States continues to condition a mark's registration on its prior use, most other countries have detached registration from use.

Just as the TRIPs Agreement prodded other countries to protect a wide range of patent subject matter, American-style, so it has made the encompassing U.S. approach to protectible trademarks a new international norm. All national trademark systems follow the principle that a brand should be registered if it signifies, or has come to signify, a single source. However, where American trademark law accepts as registrable everything from the shape of a package, to a handful of musical notes, to a fragrance applied to sewing thread, other countries have been slow to allow newer forms of marks on their registers. While all countries accept word marks for registration, some reject applications for such indicators of source as surnames, letters, numerals, signatures, portraits, and colors. Presumably, TRIPs will accelerate acceptance of these newer forms with its provision for trademark registration of "any sign, or any combination of signs, capable of distinguishing the goods or services" of one company from those of another.

Even as the TRIPs Agreement has begun to harmonize international trademark registration practice around a single, expanded conception of protectible marks, it has failed to stabilize—indeed it may have aggravated—another, and far more volatile, division over commercial marketing tools. The object of controversy is the so-called geographical indication—Cognac, Champagne, and Roquefort are examples—names that, like trademarks, indicate both the source and quality of goods but, unlike trademarks, indicate a region rather than a particular company as the source, as well as some aspect of product quality associated with the region. TRIPs requires member countries to protect geographic indications for all types of products, industrial as well as agricultural, against any use that "misleads the public as to the geographical origin of the good." In the case of wines and spirits, TRIPs establishes a higher minimum standard, requiring protection even against uses that don't mislead consumers as to source.

Not surprisingly, geographical indications have flourished as a legal concept in Europe, with its wealth of hugely valuable geographic associations, and have pitted these countries against such comparatively impoverished countries as the United States where marketers would like to sell their products as "Champagne style" or as "Roquefort type." The TRIPs provisions on geographical indications were, and continue to be, hard-fought. One area of controversy is how much elbow room TRIPs leaves for earlier customary uses of geographical indications. There is a question, for example, about the legitimacy of U.S. Alcohol and Tobacco Tax and Trade Bureau regulations permitting the use of names such as "Burgundy," "Claret," "Chablis," and "Champagne" if the bureau finds that the name is "semi-generic," the bottler discloses the product's true origin, and the wine is of the same general quality as the wine from the indicated region.

What if the same name—"Budweiser"—is used by one company as a brand and by another as a geographical indication? Litigation between America's Anheuser-Busch and Czech brewer Budêjovický Budvar has since the early 1900s brought the "Budweiser" brand, in one form or another, before the courts of no fewer than fifty countries. (The Czech brewer is named after its location in the southern Bohemian town of Ceské Budêjovice, or, as the town has been known by its German-speaking citizens for centuries, Budweis.)

The origin of the disputes between Anheuser-Busch and Budweiser Budvar traces back to the first sale of Budweiser beer in the United States in 1876 by an Anheuser-Busch predecessor, C. Conrad & Co., and to C. Conrad's 1886 registration in the U.S. Patent Office of a trademark consisting of the word "Budweiser" together with the company's name and monogram. In 1907, Anheuser-Busch registered the mark "Budweiser" standing alone, but in 1909 Burgher's Brewery, a Bohemian brewer with claims to the "Budweis" designation, challenged this registration on the ground that, because it was a geographical indication, it could not be registered as a trademark—particularly since the Anheuser-Busch beer did not originate in Budweis. An agreement between the two

companies, and a subsequent agreement with Budweiser Budvar, settled the dispute on terms that called for a payment by Anheuser-Busch
to the two Bohemian companies and also Anheuser-Busch's concession
of their right to use "Budweiser" on their packages, labels, and advertisements anywhere in the world, including the United States, to describe their beer as produced "at Budweis, in Bohemia." For their part,
the Bohemian brewers acknowledged the validity of Anheuser-Busch's
trademark and agreed not to oppose the American brewer's use of
"Budweiser" anywhere in the world, other than Europe, so long as the
company used no term, such as "original," that might connote production in Budweis.

In 1934 Budweiser Budvar registered "Budweiser" as a trademark,
rather than as a geographic indication, in Czechoslovakia, and with the
repeal of Prohibition began exporting "Budweiser Beer" to the United
States, obtaining a U.S. trademark registration in 1937. Anheuser-
Busch considered suing, but one of its lawyers, thinking that evidence
in the case could "seriously affect, if not destroy" the goodwill of the
Budweiser brand, advised against litigation. The companies ultimately
settled in 1939, with the Bohemian company ceding to Anheuser-
Busch the names "Budweiser," "Budweis," and "Bud" in North America in exchange for a payment. That agreement remains in force today,
and although Budweiser Budvar has since reintroduced its beer into
the United States, it is under a new brand, "Czechvar."

It was Anheuser-Busch's decision in the early 1980s to distribute the
brands "Budweiser" and "Bud" into foreign markets that precipitated
the current conflict between the American and Czech brewers. After
years of negotiations, the conflict moved to the courts, and by 2006
there were more than forty lawsuits and seventy administrative proceedings in patent and trademark offices around the world. Much of
the litigation involved the usual trademark issues—registration, use,
similarity, confusion—but the TRIPs provisions on geographical indications are also becoming part of the fray. With lawyer's understate-
ment, two commentators observed, "The lesson for trademark
owners—and for would-be owners selecting new marks—is to take due
account of the disadvantages of adopting a geographic name as the focus of a worldwide brand-identity campaign."

TRADE SECRETS. Before TRIPs, few countries enforced trade secret protection as robustly as the United States; most other nations generally relied on such broad rubrics as unfair competitive practices and the Paris Convention standards of "honest practices in industrial or commercial matters" to protect confidential information. Japan's unfair competition legislation, adopted in 1934, followed the model of German legislation, but omitted the crucial remedy of injunctive relief; traditions of lifetime employment, and the consequent bonds of loyalty between employees and their employers, it was thought, sufficed to ensure against information leakage. However, in the face of increased labor mobility, and pressures from the United States during the then-pending TRIPs discussions, Japan amended its Unfair Competition Prevention Act in 1990 to strengthen trade secret protection, including provision for injunctive relief.

Even in countries like the United States with strong trade secret laws, legal protection is no more than a safety net for failed industrial security measures. Indeed, the connection to security measures is so close that trade secret law expressly makes adoption of reasonable security measures a condition to the grant of legal protection. Thus, just as they do in countries with strong trade secret protection, companies that do business in countries where trade secret protection is weak—particularly in the developing world—rely on physical security measures, such as dividing operations among foreign facilities so that employees at no single facility know the full details of a secret process, to protect their confidential information. The eventual adoption in these countries of the TRIPs Agreement's rigorous standards for protection of "undisclosed information" is likely to mean no more than that companies doing business in these countries will relax their beefed-up physical security measures to the levels they employ in countries where trade secret law is already robust.

Intellectual Property Meets Trade Law

When in 1990 Fusion Systems CEO Donald M. Spero complained in the pages of the *Harvard Business Review* about his company's unhappy encounters with the Japanese patent system, he was echoing the frustrations of a great many American businesses—patent owners complaining that their most valuable drugs were being copied by generic drug producers in places like India; copyright owners be-moaning the piracy of software, CDs, and videocassettes; trademark owners concerned about counterfeiting—in attempting to exploit their intellectual assets under foreign rules. According to the World Health Organization, counterfeit drugs account for about 10 percent of drug sales worldwide, and 25 percent of sales in developing coun-tries, with the figure in some countries thought to be as high as 50 percent. The principle of territoriality entitles every country to deter-mine for itself whether and how it will extend intellectual property rights to foreign nationals. Although the great intellectual property treaties of the late nineteenth century—the Paris Convention for patents and trademarks, and the Berne Convention for copyrights—sought to subordinate the sovereign will of member countries to new international norms of protection, the displacement was never more than partial: minimum standards were incomplete and sanctions for noncompliance were illusory.

The first explicit step toward using trade sanctions to solve intellec-tual property law's international failings came in 1979 in the closing days of the Tokyo Round of the General Agreement on Tariffs and Trade. It took the form of an initiative from the European Community and the United States to obtain an "Agreement on Measures to Dis-courage the Importation of Counterfeit Goods." Behind this initiative and subsequent, more successful efforts to put intellectual property on the agenda of the ensuing Uruguay Round was the belief that the trade process could extract concessions on high intellectual property standards from countries otherwise disposed to resist them, and that the GATT dispute settlement process could inject rigor into interna-tional intellectual property enforcement.

By September 1982, the United States, the European Community, Japan, and Canada agreed on a draft commercial counterfeiting code, which the United States submitted to the GATT in October 1982. De-veloping countries, led by Brazil and India, challenged the proposal, but discussions nonetheless advanced, aided by diplomacy and no little arm-twisting. In September 1986, a special session of GATT members formally launched the Uruguay Round of the talks, with "Trade-Related

Aspects of Intellectual Property Rights" high on its agenda. By the time the TRIPs Agreement was signed at Marrakesh, Morocco, on April 15, 1994, its text incorporated the Paris and Berne conventions; added minimum standards of its own; specified extensive remedies, including measures to block infringing goods at national borders; and made concessions for developing and least developed country members that gave them an extra four years' and ten years' leeway, respectively, from the agreement's effective date to bring their intellectual property laws into compliance with all but a prescribed handful of TRIPs standards.

In the years since adoption of the TRIPs Agreement, WTO member countries, some more quickly than others, strengthened their intellectual property standards and enforcement tools to meet the agreement's minimum standards. Estimates by the World Bank of a sharp rise in the patent payments being made from the developing, intellectual asset importing economies of the South to the industrialized, intellectual asset exporting countries of the North, offer strong evidence of the impact of compliance with TRIPs standards. One such estimate shows the United States, Germany, Japan, France, the United Kingdom, and Switzerland receiving a net increase in patent payments of $40 billion each year.

Departures, large and small, from TRIPs norms persist in developed and less developed economies. The U.S. Trade Representative's 2006 review of intellectual property protection worldwide put forty-eight countries on a "watch list" for further monitoring, among them China and Russia ("top priorities," for weak protection and enforcement); Canada ("weak border measures continue to be a serious concern for IP owners"); and the European Union ("because of concerns over EU rules concerning geographical indications"). Counterfeiting of brandname products, including pharmaceuticals, and piracy of copyrighted works—principally CDs, DVDs, and CD-ROMs—receive particular attention, as do the unauthorized disclosure of test and other data submitted by drug companies seeking local approval for their products. Few countries are immune to complaints. For example, the European Commission's 2005 "Report on United States Barriers to Trade and Investment" charged, among other derelictions, that the United States failed to protect the moral rights of authors, as required by the Berne Convention; to protect EU appellations of origin and geographical indications for wine; and to protect famous brands of European perfumes from advertisements for low-price imitations.

Private businesses have no right to lodge complaints against violations of TRIPs standards; only nations can initiate proceedings. Nonetheless, private industry plays an important role in influencing government choice on which disputes to prosecute, and in the United States the administration's trade lawyers will use prosecutorial discretion to select among competing industry claims. "To be sure," a former general counsel in the Office of the U.S. Trade Representative observed, "private parties will be limited in the extent to which they can determine which cases to bring, on which TRIPs provisions to focus, and what aspects of TRIPs rules to seek to develop through the dispute settlement process. On the cases they select, however, the government's trade lawyers will collaborate closely with legal counsel for the private parties most directly affected by the foreign government practices being challenged."

Industrialized countries sold TRIPs to developing countries on two premises: that in return for strengthening their rules on the protection of intellectual goods they would receive trade benefits on other goods; and that the adoption of rigorous intellectual property rules would stimulate their own domestic innovation industries. The second premise was debatable at the time it was offered, and remains so today. Many countries—Japan, Taiwan, and Korea among them—developed robust innovation economies in the absence of strong intellectual property systems. Nor does the strengthening of existing intellectual property systems necessarily increase innovative activity. A careful study of the impact on hundreds of local companies of Japan's 1988 reforms expanding the scope of patents shows no evidence either of increased research and development spending or of innovative output, even though such increases would have been expected in an advanced industrialized economy. Indeed, the two years following the reform saw a relative decline in research and development spending.

It is also debatable whether foreign direct investment in a developing economy requires strong intellectual property rights. Certainly,

Asian countries, including China, where intellectual property protection has historically been weak, attracted substantial foreign investment even before they started down the path of intellectual property reform. As Keith Maskus, a leading expert on the economics of intellectual assets in trade has observed, there "are indications that strengthening [intellectual property rights] can be an effective incentive for inward [foreign direct investment]," but "it is only a component of a broader set of factors," including local market liberalization and deregulation and technology development policies.

Every country has an inflection point, before which its relative industrial development, market orientation, and educational levels dictate weak intellectual property laws and enforcement, and beyond which they call for strong laws and enforcement. A country will reach its inflection point—if it ever does—only in the natural economic order of events, and until then will resist external pressures, like TRIPs, to implement strong intellectual property laws. Albeit crudely, the TRIPs Agreement accommodated the fact that inflection points differ from country to country by postponing the required implementation of all but a handful of standards in developing countries for an extra four years, and in less developed countries for an extra ten years; the decision in November 2005 to postpone compliance in the least developed countries for another seven and one-half years, to July 1, 2013, reflects a growing appreciation of economic forces and political economy in the developing world.

The China Question

China is an example of what happens when industrial-strength intellectual property standards are introduced before their time. The country's first, halting steps toward international intellectual property relations took the form of bilateral commercial agreements with Great Britain, Japan, and the United States in 1902 and 1903. The treaties centered on trademarks—the 1903 treaty with the United States also covered patents—but in only the sketchiest terms, reflecting China's lack of a national trademark law. From this beginning, intellectual property law in China evolved slowly, sporadically, and with a clear bias against foreigners. According to China scholar William Alford, "although the Chinese had committed themselves in 1903 to provide patent protection for certain American inventions, more than two decades passed before foreigners received even the nominal protection first accorded Chinese nationals in 1912, which itself produced fewer than 1,000 patents over its first thirty years."

Even as China moved toward a market economy at the end of the century, enacting patent, copyright, and trademark laws, adhering to the Paris and Berne conventions, and in the mid-1990s revising its patent, trademark, and copyright laws to approach the standards being proposed for the TRIPs Agreement, this same pattern persisted, reflecting what intellectual property-trade expert Frederick M. Abbott has called a "passive-aggressive" strategy. The U.S. Trade Representative twice labeled China a priority target country for its deficient protection of U.S. intellectual assets, and China escaped the consequent trade sanctions by negotiating two successive Memoranda of Understanding with the United States, the first, in 1992, imposing several TRIPs-level standards on China, the second, in 1995, detailing at the most granular level the specific enforcement measures China would take. ("Retail units dealing with computer software must possess licenses to operate, and unlicensed retail peddlers of these products will be strictly banned.")

China became a member of the WTO on December 11, 2001, having once again revised its patent, copyright, and trademark legislation to comply with the WTO's TRIPs standards, and strengthened available legal remedies to enforce these rights. But sanctions on the books were one thing, and enforcement on the streets, in piracy mills, and even in the courts another. By 2006, U.S. intellectual asset companies were complaining of unabated losses of about $2.5 billion to copyright piracy and trademark losses from every conceivable product, from counterfeit auto parts to counterfeit running shoes, toys, and games. American pharmaceutical companies complained that they were losing 10 to 15 percent of their potential revenues in China to counterfeits.

A 2005 report of the U.S. Trade Representative said little more than what the USTR had been saying for years: China's efforts to amend its intellectual property laws were generally satisfactory, but enforcement "remained ineffective." The report invoked the tired bromide that "the

United States used high-level meetings to strongly urge China to take immediate and substantial steps to put it on the path toward compliance with its critical TRIPs Agreement obligation to make available effective enforcement mechanisms." By 2006 the USTR had elevated China to its "Priority Watch List" and announced that it would "step up consideration of its WTO dispute settlement options." For its part, China announced a "2006 Action Plan on IPR Protection," including "special crack down efforts." Finally, on April 10, 2007, the United States initiated WTO dispute settlement proceedings by requesting formal WTO consultations on China's failed protection of copyrights and trademarks, as well as consultations on the country's market barriers to distribution of legitimate DVDs, CDs, and books—barriers that effectively boost the market for pirated goods.

The problem with the WTO dispute settlement option in the case of a country's deficient enforcement efforts, such as in China, is that, unlike deficient legal rules, the failure cannot be measured against a crisp legal standard. Also, no complaint can go forward without costly and time-consuming fact-gathering by the USTR and the complaining companies, and onerous fact-finding by the WTO panel. There is also the cost of time: preliminary consultations between the parties, the WTO panel proceedings, and the decision-making itself, as well as subsequent appeals and a grace period to bring enforcement procedures into compliance, can consume as many as three to four years in the most straightforward case—and an enforcement complaint against China will not be a straightforward case. The proceedings initiated in April 2007 might not ultimately be resolved until 2011 or later, by which time, at its current rate of industrial development, China may be three or four years, or fewer, away from its intellectual property inflection point, and ready to begin enforcing strict intellectual property standards for its own benefit, without any need for advice or sanctions from outsiders.

Mapping Change in the International Arena

Evolving global compliance with TRIPs standards holds out three prospects to American companies that seek to exploit their intellectual assets abroad. First, because TRIPs generally embodies the high standards of U.S., European, and Japanese intellectual property laws, an American company can increasingly expect the same high level of protection abroad as it does at home. Second, because the new standards will not only be high, but roughly uniform, the company will encounter fewer legal surprises than in the past. Third, as the legal playing field between developed and developing economies levels off, intellectual property protection will disappear as a source of comparative advantage for developed countries, and companies will begin to weigh other comparative advantages in deciding where to exploit and develop their intellectual assets. One such comparative advantage will be the availability of highly trained but low-cost researchers. This is evident in decisions already made by such intellectual asset companies as AstraZeneca, GE, Hewlett-Packard, IBM, Intel, Microsoft, and dozens of others to locate research facilities in China.

Microsoft opened its Beijing research facility in 1998, and by 2005 two hundred researchers and one hundred developers were working there on new digital entertainment, networking, and search technologies, including such projects as an interface to enable users to communicate with computers through speech, gestures, and expressions. Contributions from the facility can be found in a wide range of Microsoft products marketed worldwide. For the long term, the contributions of Microsoft Research Asia may also lie in the network of collaborative relationships it fosters with academics, universities, research institutes, and government agencies. According to Microsoft, the organization supports an exchange program that sends its researchers to work with faculty and graduate students in Chinese universities; a joint research-funding program with China's National Science Foundation for long-term basic research in applied mathematics, computer science, and electrical engineering; programs for academic cooperation with Seoul National University and the Korean Institute of Science and Technology; and a framework for research partnerships with Japanese academics and universities.

Research and development spending is as useful an index of a nation's future innovative capacities as it is of an individual company's future performance. When Microsoft or another American multinational invests in research and development in China, the results will—it is hoped—benefit the company's shareholders and, to some extent, the American economy. But the seeds planted by Microsoft and the work-force that it trains will also directly benefit the Chinese economy. As late as 2002, foreign multinationals continued to invest more in re-search and development in the United States—$27.5 billion—than for-eign affiliates of U.S. multinationals invested abroad—$21.2 billion. But the comparative advantage of a motivated and well-trained work-force in countries like China, India, South Korea, and Taiwan may eventually tip the balance in the other direction, a prospect underlined by continuing declines in American training of scientists and engineers as compared to increases among Asian countries. One economist has projected that, at its current rate of growth, China, which as recently as 1975 produced almost no science and engineering doctorates, will by 2010 produce more than the United States.

Other numbers add detail to America's shrinking place in global research and development activities. Although the United States con-tinues to spend more on research and development than any other country—about 34 percent of the total—and together with Japan ac-counts for about 50 percent of the total, 2002 data reported by the National Science Foundation, covering the years 1998 and 2000–2003, on spending as a proportion of gross domestic product puts the United States sixth worldwide. (Israel led all countries, spending 4.9 percent of GDP on research and development, followed, in order, by Sweden, Finland, Japan, and Iceland.) U.S. spending as a proportion of GDP drops even more precipitously, to twenty-second place among coun-tries belonging to the Organisation for Economic Co-operation and Development, if defense-related research and development is ex-cluded from the total. Also, less developed countries are for the first time reporting higher research and development spending than OECD members from developed economies: in 2000, $13.6 billion was spent on research and development in Brazil, roughly half the amount spent in Britain, and India spent $20 billion, placing it sev-enth worldwide. Roughly $72 billion was spent on research and devel-opment in China in 2002, putting it third in worldwide expenditures that year.

Not surprisingly, patent statistics mirror trends in research and development spending. The National Science Foundation's *Science and Engineering Indicators 2006* shows that the share of U.S. patents granted to U.S. resident inventors declined modestly, from 56 percent in 1996 to 52 percent in 2003, reflecting increased inventive activity outside the country. By 2003, Taiwan and South Korea joined Japan, Germany, and France as the top five foreign recipients of U.S. patents. In 2005, the number of international patent applications filed from China rose 46.8 percent over the previous year, placing the country for the first time ahead of Australia, Canada, and Italy. Comparing patent grants to a country's population or its gross domestic product offers a possibly more precise index of the country's relative patent intensity or inventiveness. According to OECD figures for 2002, the United States was sixth in patents per million population (after Switzerland, Finland, Japan, Sweden, and Germany) and eighth in patents in relation to GDP (after Finland, Switzerland, Japan, Sweden, Germany, the Netherlands, and Israel).

Trademark figures indicate a similar shift in the national sources of branded business value. In the years 1990–2005, the proportion of U.S. trademark registrations granted to U.S. companies fluctuated between 80 and 90 percent. Over that period, Southeast Asian companies increased their share of the U.S. trademark registrations granted to foreign companies from about 14 percent to 20 percent, while the European share declined from over 60 percent to about 50 percent. *Business Week*'s annual Interbrand list of the world's one hundred most valuable brands showed sixty-one belonging to U.S. companies in 2001 but only fifty-one in 2006, while the number of European brands increased from thirty-one to thirty-seven and Asian brands from seven to eleven over the same period.

Data on global performance of copyright industries, though harder to find, indicate a very different trend, with estimated revenues from foreign sales by major U.S. copyright industries increasing, on average, 9.45 percent annually between 1991 and 2002. However, one copyright industry—book publishing—had a far lower export growth rate over the period and, indeed, declined in the ratio of exports to imports, from about 1.65 ($1,415.1 million exports against $855.1 million imports) at the beginning of the period, to 1.01 ($1,681.2 million exports against $1,661.2 million imports) at the end; the decline was continual, not episodic, and by 2003 had dipped into the negative range, with a .96 ratio. Much as research and development facilities are growing in the developing world, so are motion picture production in such countries as India and Nigeria. According to a widely cited PricewaterhouseCoopers report, India's motion picture industry, Bollywood, is growing faster than Hollywood, with revenues expected to more than double between 2005 and 2010; the same report predicts that the entire Indian entertainment industry will grow at a 21 percent compound annual rate through 2010.

Although U.S. receipts of royalties and fees generated from the exploitation abroad of all forms of intellectual property continue to grow (after a one-year decline in 2001), with an increase of 8.7 percent in 2002 and of nearly 9.2 percent in 2003, the gap between receipts from, and payments to, foreign sources began to shrink in the late 1990s. Where U.S. receipts were once four to five times greater than U.S. payments to foreign firms, the ratio of receipts to payments declined to about 3:1 in 1999 and to nearly 2:1 by 2002. The National Science Foundation's *Science and Engineering Indicators 2006* concludes, "These trends suggest both a growing internationalization of U.S. business and a growing reliance on intellectual property developed overseas."

These several trends point to a single fact: although the United States may not soon revert to its nineteenth-century status as a net importer of intellectual assets, the intellectual trade margins it enjoyed during the latter part of the twentieth century will probably continue to decline in the twenty-first century. Thomas Friedman's shrewd generalization that "the world is flat" applies as directly to the production of intellectual goods as it does to other goods and services. As, over time, the TRIPs Agreement's high standards become the norm for intellectual property protection worldwide, the United States will lose the comparative legal advantage it has long shared with Europe, and to attract investment in the American production of intellectual goods the nation will need to offer other points of advantage, such as the cost and skill of its resident workforce, a competitive battle that, on the present evidence, it is not certain to win on all fronts.

Whatever its implications may be for the American economy, this newly flat world offers significant investment opportunities for American and other intellectual asset companies, not only in recently developed economies like Singapore—which has become an important world center for stem cell research—but also in developing economies like China. Investment in still-developing countries will, to be sure, require particular attention to questions of intellectual property enforcement, and companies would be wise to observe a paraphrase of Tolstoy that Jin Haijun of Renmin University's School of Law offered at a conference at Stanford late in 2006: "Developed countries, to their intellectual property, are all alike; but every developing country is to intellectual property uneasy in its own way."

ACKNOWLEDGMENTS

A great many people helped with this book. My colleagues Michael Jacobs, at Morrison & Foerster LLP, and Mark Lemley, at Stanford Law School, read and commented on the entire manuscript. I am grateful to them for their suggestions, as I am to Fred Abbott, Joe Grundfest, Rose Hagan, Dan Ho, Fred von Lohmann, and Michael Risch for their comments on individual chapters, and to Bob Fletcher for an early conversation that helped to sharpen the book's focus. I am also indebted to Daniel Bookin, Walter Hanley, Oliver P. Howes Jr., Thomas J. Nolan, John Place, Cecil Quillen, Herbert F. Schwartz, and Hon. Rya W. Zobel for agreeing to interviews on events recounted in these pages; the sources identify their particular contributions.

Stanford Law School offers a wonderfully congenial environment for research and writing, and as so often in the past, I have relied heavily on the superb services of the Stanford Law Library staff—especially, Paul Lomio, Sonia Moss, Erika Wayne, Kate Wilko, and George Wilson. Lynne Anderson has my deepest gratitude for transcribing interviews and typing endless drafts of manuscript, all with her usual great care and good cheer. My thanks, too, to Mary Ann Rundell and Ginny Turner for timely assists with the manuscript.

Several generations of students—Kevin Bovard, Reuben Chen, Andrew Coan, Jesse Cuevas, Alexander Fursenko, Adam Goldman, Mark

Hancock, Jill Ho, Michael Meehan, Chris Montague-Breakwell, Josh Olson, Ji-Hyun Park, Jim Pastore, Jeya Paul, Aaron Thacker, Rachel Walsh, and Brian Wolfe—deserve warm thanks for searching sources, compiling facts, conducting interviews, and checking citations; the John M. Olin Program in Law and Economics at Stanford Law School, the George R. Roberts Program in Law, Business and Corporate Governance, and the Claire and Michael Brown Estate supported their work.

My agent, Wendy Strothman, was involved in this project from the start, and I am indebted to her, as I am to Adrienne Schultz at Penguin Portfolio, for their fine editorial guidance.

SOURCES

Judicial decisions referred to in the text are cited mainly by their location in the West Publishing Company's National Reporter System, available in county law libraries as well as in law school libraries and many law offices. Federal district court decisions are cited to the *Federal Supplement* (F. Supp. or F. Supp. 2d, depending on the date of decision), and circuit court opinions to the *Federal Reporter* (Fed., F.2d, or F.3d, depending on the date of decision). Supreme Court opinions are, where possible, cited to the official *United States Reports* (U.S.). References to federal legislation are to the United States Code (U.S.C).

Introduction

The figures on intangible assets as a proportion of firm value are from Peter J. King, as quoted in the frontispiece to Kevin G. Rivette and David Kline, *Rembrandts in the Attic* (2000) (76 percent), and Peter Wallison, "Accounting Lags Behind a Knowledge Economy," *Financial Times* (London), Mar. 8, 2004, p. 13 (80 percent). The estimates of copyright and patent industry contributions to gross domestic product are from Stephen Siwek, *Engines of Growth: Economic Contributions of the U.S. Intellectual Property Industries* 3 (2005).

Ted Turner's divestiture of MGM's tangible assets is described in Geraldine Fabrikant, "Turner to Sell MGM Assets," *New York Times,* June 7, 1986, Sec. 1, p. 35. The figure for the James Bond franchise is from Ronald Grover, "Is James Bond Worth $1 Billion?" *Business Week,* Sept. 20, 2004, p. 104. Ford's product placement in *Die Another Day* is described in Phil Patton, "The Spy Who Drove Me," *New York Times,* Nov. 10, 2002, Sec. 12, p. 1. Sam Walker, "George Foreman's Endorsement In Perpetuity Nets $137.5 Million," *Wall Street Journal,* Dec. 10,

1999, Sec. B, p. 9, describes the Salton deal with George Foreman. The Prozac result is reported in David Firn and David Pilling, "Pfizer Loses Viagra Patent Ruling: Court Decision May Open Way for Cheaper Rival Products," *Financial Times* (London), Nov. 9, 2000, p. 33. The ITC ruling in the Gemstar case is *In the Matter of Certain Set-Top Boxes and Components Thereof,* USITC Inv. No. 337-TA-454 (2002 WL 31556392), June 21, 2002, and the effect of the decision on the company's stock is reported in John Lippman, "Gemstar's Stock Declines 39% in Wake of ITC Patent Ruling," *Wall Street Journal,* June 25, 2002, Sec. B, p. 15. The stock market response to the Visx ruling is reported in Laura Johannes, "U.S. Says Japanese Firm Doesn't Infringe on Visx," *Wall Street Journal,* Dec. 8, 1999, Sec. B, p. 8.

Background on the *Polaroid Corp. v. Eastman Kodak Co.* litigation draws in part on interviews with Walter Hanley (New York City, August 27, 2003); Cecil Quillen (Washington, D.C., 2003); Herbert Schwartz (New York City, August 26, 2003); and Judge Rya Zobel (Boston, Mass., July 15, 2004), as well as on Alison Frankel, "Great Expectations: How Polaroid Won $900 Million in Its Patent Case Against Kodak— And Ended Up Looking Like the Loser," *American Lawyer,* Vol. 13, No. 2, p. 92 (1991). The liability opinion in *Polaroid Corp. v. Eastman Kodak Co.* is at 641 F.Supp. 828 (D. Mass. 1985) and the damage opinion is at 16 *United States Patents Quarterly Second Series* 1481 (D. Mass. 1990). Kodak's losses in the instant photography business and the damage award against it are from Judge Mazzone's decision in the damages phase. The range of analyst's estimates of the monetary award in *Polaroid Corp. v. Eastman Kodak Co.* is taken from Herbert Schwartz, *Polaroid Co. v. Eastman Kodak Co.: A Retrospective* 2 n.2 (unpublished, 1991).

1. The Intellectual Property Paradox

References to background sources on the *Polaroid v. Kodak* litigation appear in the sources for the introduction. The description of Land as "fierce" about patents is from Elkan Blout, "Polaroid: Dreams to Reality" *Daedalus,* Vol. 125, No. 2, pp. 39, 47 (1996). The "our very soul" remark by Land is from Victor K. McElheny, *Insisting on the Impossible: The Life of Edwin Land* 447 (1998). The early history of George Eastman's patenting activity is drawn from Reese V. Jenkins, "Technology and the Market: George Eastman and the Origins of Mass Amateur Photography," *Technology and Culture,* Vol. 16, No. 1 (1975). The figures on Polaroid and Kodak sales, profitability, and market share are from Glenn Merry and Norman Berg, "Polaroid-Kodak," *Harvard Business School Case No. 376-266,* Mar. 1, 1984. The figures on document production are from Helen O'Connor, "Polaroid v. Eastman Kodak," *American Lawyer,* Vol. 11, No. 2, p. 19 (1989); on depositions, from Herbert F. Schwartz, *Polaroid Co. v. Eastman Kodak Co.: A Retrospective* (unpublished, 1991); and on attorneys' fees, from the damages opinion.

The legal standard of "nonobviousness" is set forth at 35 U.S.C. §103. Francis Carr described his counseling work for Kodak in *Polaroid v. Kodak—A Reminiscence* (unpublished, 1991). The findings on patent invalidity appear in John R.

Allison and Mark A. Lemley, "Empirical Evidence on the Validity of Litigated Patents," 26 *American Intellectual Property Law Association Quarterly Journal* 185, 205–206 (1998). The Supreme Court requirement of a "synergistic effect" can be found in *Sakraida v. Ag Pro, Inc.*, 425 U.S. 273 (1976), rehearing denied, 426 U.S. 955 (1976). Judge Zobel's observations on declining to grant the stay of injunctive relief appears at *Polaroid Corp. v. Eastman Kodak Co.*, 641 F.Supp. 828, 875 (D. Mass. 1986). Herbert Schwartz's law review note on patent injunctions is "Injunctive Relief in Patent Infringement Suits," 112 *University of Pennsylvania Law Review* 1025 (1964).

Background on the trial is in part from Victor K. McElheny, *Insisting on the Impossible: The Life of Edwin Land* 441–446 (1998). The Carr observation on the Development Committee's suggestion is in his *Polaroid v. Kodak—A Reminiscence* 9 (unpublished, 1991). Background on the international litigation comes in part from Mark Olshaker, *The Instant Image: Edwin Land and the Polaroid Experience* 226 (1978). The question from Land's daughter is reported in Peter C. Wensberg, *Land's Polaroid: A Company and the Man Who Invented It* 83 (1987). The impact of 35mm photography, as well as the observation by Polaroid's vice president, are from Judge Mazzone's opinion, at 23.

Thomas Jefferson's observation on the nature of public goods is quoted from his letter to Issac McPherson, Aug. 13, 1813, reprinted in Merrill D. Peterson, ed., *Thomas Jefferson: Writings* 1286, 1291–1292 (1984). Polaroid's capital investment in R&D rather than facilities and equipment is described in Glenn Merry and Norman Berg, "Polaroid-Kodak," *Harvard Business School Case No. 376-266*, Mar. 1, 1984. The reference to Lenovo is in Glenn Rifkin and Jenna Smith, "Quickly Erasing 'I' and 'B' and 'M,'" *New York Times*, Apr. 12, 2006, Sec. C, p. 9. Figures on Kodak's market share and margins for film are from Peter Nulty, "Kodak Grabs for Growth Again," *Fortune*, May 16, 1994, p. 76. Coca-Cola has been the number one brand in the *Business Week*/Interbrand rankings for many years; the most recent ranking is in "The Best Global Brands," *Business Week*, Aug. 7, 2006, p. 60. The data on federal research and development funding is from National Science Foundation, "Federal Funds for Research and Development: Fiscal Year 2003–05," Vol. 53, Table 1 (Apr. 2006), available at www.nsf.gov/statistics/nsf 06313/tables.htm (last accessed Nov. 30, 2006).

Robert W. Kastenmeier and Michael J. Remington, "The Semiconductor Chip Protection Act of 1984: A Swamp or Firm Ground?" 70 *Minnesota Law Review* 417, 441–42 (1985), describes Kastenmeier's new legislative test. The attempt to prove aggregate public benefit was made by Stanley Gortikov at the hearings, "Record Rental Amendment of 1983," U.S. House of Representatives Bill 98-1027 (1985). The two cable television cases from the Supreme Court are *Teleprompter Corp. v. Columbia Broadcasting Systems, Inc.*, 415 U.S. 394 (1974) and *Fortnightly Corp. v. United Artists Television, Inc.*, 392 U.S. 390 (1968). The cable television provisions appear at 17 U.S.C. §111. The broad-based lobbying campaign by rental stores and their customers is described in James Lardner, *Fast*

Forward: Hollywood, the Japanese, and the Onslaught of the VCR 294–303 (1987).

The Frito-Lay example is from *Frito Co. v. Buckeye Foods, Inc.*, 130 *United States Patents Quarterly* 347 (Trademark Trial and Appeal Board 1961). The history leading to Kodak's abandonment of a color film development project when Polaroid released the SX-70 appears in Judge Zobel's liability opinion at *Polaroid Corp. v. Eastman Kodak Co.*, 641 F.Supp. 828, 831. The observations on licensing are from Dan McCurdy and Marshall Phelps, "Why Exclusion Is Not Profitable," *Managing Intellectual Property*, Nov. 2002, p. 58. Background on the licensing-supply relationship between Polaroid and Kodak is from Judge Zobel's opinion; Victor K. McElheny, *Insisting on the Impossible: The Life of Edwin Land* 351–355 (1998); and Francis T. Carr, *Polaroid v. Kodak—A Reminiscence* 7 (1991) (unpublished). The "splendid collaboration" quote is from Elkan Blout, "Polaroid: Dreams to Reality," *Daedalus*, Vol. 125, No. 2, p. 44–46 (1996). The McCune testimony is reported in "Polaroid Chief Says Firm Tried to Build Own Niche," *Los Angeles Times*, May 3, 1989, Sec. 4, p. 13.

Lear, Inc. v. Adkins is reported at 395 U.S. 653 (1969). The 1-Click patent case, *Amazon.com, Inc. v. BarnesandNoble.com, Inc.*, is reported at 239 F.3d 1343 (Fed. Cir. 2001). Honeywell's autofocus patent victories are described in Arthur S. Hayes, "Minolta to Pay $127.5 Million to Honeywell," *Wall Street Journal*, Mar. 4, 1992, Sec. B, p. 7; "Three More Japanese Firms Settle in Camera Patent Case," *Wall Street Journal*, Dec. 29, 1992, Sec. A, p. 3; and Randy Meyers, "Fighting Words: Growing Ranks of Litigants are Putting Price Tags on Ideas," *CFO Magazine*, Mar. 1, 1998, available at www.cfo.com/Article?article=1529. The antipatent movement in nineteenth-century Europe is described in Fritz Machlup and Edith Penrose, "The Patent Controversy in the Nineteenth Century," *Journal of Economic History*, Vol. 10, No. 1 (1950). The antipatent experience in the United States is recounted in William B. Ball, ed., *Dynamics of the Patent System* 56 (1960).

Xerox's encounters with intellectual property during this period are recounted in Charles J. Goetz and Warren F. Schwartz, "Industry Structure Investigations: Xerox's Multiple Patents and Competition," in Kenneth W. Clarkson and Timothy J. Morris, eds., *The Federal Trade Commission Since 1970* (1981); Michael A. Hiltzik, *Dealers of Lightning: Xerox PARC and the Dawn of the Computer Age* 335–45, 395–98 (1999); and Douglas K. Smith and Robert C. Alexander, *Fumbling the Future: How Xerox Invented, Then Ignored, the First Personal Computer* 117–20 (1988). The consent order in the antitrust proceedings involving Xerox's photocopy patents is reported at *In the Matter of Xerox Corporation*, 86 *Federal Trade Commission* 364 (1975). *Kodak v. Sony* is described in Rachel Zimmerman and James Bandler, "Kodak Sues Sony in Patent Dispute—Digital-Camera Rivals Spar Over Intellectual Property In Hot Photography Sector," *Wall Street Journal*, Mar. 10, 2004, Sec. B, p. 4.

The example of managed copying of a popular economics text is taken from *McGraw-Hill, Inc. v. Worth Publishers, Inc.*, 335 F. Supp. 415 (S.D.N.Y. 1971). The

Chanel copycat fragrance case is *Smith v. Chanel, Inc.,* 402 F.2d 562 (9th Cir. 1968), and the Tom Waits case is *Waits v. Frito-Lay, Inc.,* 978 F.2d 1093 (9th Cir. 1992), certiorari denied, 506 U.S. 1080 (1993). Licensing industry data appear in The Beanstalk Group, "Licensing Industry Facts," at www.beanstalk.com/basics/ facts.html, and EPM Communications, Inc., "The Licensing Letter," at www.epm com.com/html/licensing.html#1 (last accessed Feb. 16, 2007). Coca-Cola's successful strategy in protecting its bottle shape is discussed in Julius R. Lunsford Jr., "The Protection of Packages and Containers," 56 *Trademark Reporter* 567 (1966).

The number of start-up companies founded by people applying ideas first developed in previous jobs is reported in Amar V. Bhide, *The Origin and Evolution of New Businesses* (2000). The inevitable disclosure rule was applied in *Pepsico, Inc. v. Redmond,* 54 F.3d 1262 (7th Cir. 1995). The Van Graafeiland quote and background on the lawsuit by Kodak against 3M are from Mike Mills, "Testing the Limits on Trade Secrets," *Washington Post,* Dec. 9, 1997, Sec. C, p. 1, and on Kodak's purchase of Imation, Claudia H. Deutsch, "Kodak Buying Medical Imaging Operation," *New York Times,* Aug. 4, 1998, Sec. D, p. 8.

The $29.5 million judgment in *MercExchange L.L.C. v. eBay, Inc.* is reported at 275 F. Supp.2d 695 (E.D. Va. 2003). The agreement between Warner Bros. and BitTorrent is reported in Julie Bosman and Tom Zeller Jr., "Warner Bros. to Sell Movies Using the Software of Pirates," *New York Times,* May 9, 2006, Sec. C, p. 3, and in Ellen Lee, "BitTorrent Goes Legal in Warner Film Deal," *San Francisco Chronicle,* May 10, 2006, Sec. C, p. 1.

Johnson & Johnson's patent results in the United States, Germany, and the Netherlands are described in James Bandler and Lara Johannes, "Johnson & Johnson Loses German Patent Case," *Wall Street Journal,* May 16, 2001, Sec. B, p. 4. Donald M. Spero's observations appear in "Patent Protection or Piracy—A CEO Views Japan," *Harvard Business Review,* Vol. 68, No. 5, p. 58 (1990).

A list of the current members of the World Trade Organization and signatories to the Agreement on Trade-Related Aspects of Intellectual Property Rights (TRIPs) can be found at www.wto.org/english/thewto_e/whatis_e/tif_e/org6_ e.htm.

2. Patents

Emery Simon, the Business Software Alliance lawyer, is quoted in Neil E. Graham, "eBay Roundtable Spotlights Long-Standing Rift Between High-Tech, Big Pharma Sectors," *BNA Patent, Trademark & Copyright Journal,* Vol. 71, No. 1760, p. 491 (2006). The litigation data are drawn from Erik Larson, "Industry Groups Alarmed By Sharp Rise In Patent Litigation," *IP Law360,* Aug. 1, 2005. The September 2005 Intellectual Property Organization survey reference is from "U.S. Executives Eye Jump in IP Litigation Costs Amid Weak Patent Quality," *IP Law360,* Sept. 13, 2005. Patent grant data are available at www.uspto.gov/web/ offices/ac/ido/oeip/taf/us_stat.htm (last visited Feb. 16, 2006).

The assertion that patents can extend to "everything under the sun" was made in the committee reports accompanying the 1952 Patent Act, Senate Report Number 82-1979 (1952) and House of Representatives Report No. 82-1923 (1952). The Telephone Cases, deciding the validity of Alexander Graham Bell's basic telephone patents, are reported in *Dolbear v. American Bell Telephone Co.*, 126 U.S. 1, 567–570 (1888). The Federal Trade Commission Report is *To Promote Innovation: The Proper Balance of Competition and Patent Law and Policy* (2003). The National Research Council Report is Stephen A. Merrill, Richard C. Levin, and Mark B. Myers, eds., *A Patent System for the 21st Century* (2004).

Background on the early history of patents is in Paul A. David, "Intellectual Property Institutions and the Panda's Thumb," in Mitchel B. Wallerstein, Mary Ellen Mogee, and Roberta A. Schoen, eds., *Global Dimension of Intellectual Property Rights* 19–64 (1993); Adam Mossoff, "Rethinking the Development of Patents: An Intellectual History 1550–1800," 52 *Hastings Law Journal* 1255 (2001); and Oren Bracha, "The Commodification of Patents 1600–1836: How Patents Became Rights and Why We Should Care," 38 *Loyola of Los Angeles Law Review* 177 (2004). Nineteenth-century arguments for and against patents are taken from Fritz Machlup and Edith Penrose, "The Patent Controversy in the Nineteenth Century," *Journal of Economic History*, Vol. 10, No. 1 (1950).

The work of the Temporary National Economic Committee is described in George E. Folk, *Patents and Industrial Progress: A Summary, Analysis, and Evaluation of the Record on Patents of the Temporary National Economic Committee* (1942). The statistics on patent validity are drawn from P. J. Federico, "Adjudicated Patents, 1948–54," 38 *Journal of the Patent Office Society* 233, 244 (1956). The Supreme Court established the "flash of creative genius" test in *Cuno Engineering Corp. v. Automatic Devices Corp.*, 314 U.S. 84, 91 (1942). Justice Jackson's comment on the stringency of the Court's standard is in *Jungersen v. Ostby & Barton Co.*, 335 U.S. 560, 572 (1949).

The "Nine No-Nos" were authoritatively criticized in Abbott B. Lipsky Jr. in "Current Antitrust Division Views on Patent Licensing Practices," 50 *Antitrust Law Journal* 515, 517 (1982). The Supreme Court cases are *Diamond v. Chakrabarty*, 447 U.S. 303 (1980) (live, man-made organisms), and *Diamond v. Diehr*, 450 U.S. 175 (1981) (patents for computer programs).

Visicalc's history and the quote from Robert Frankston are from Marc S. Friedman, "Long Term Strategic IP Planning—Avoiding A Trap for the Unwary! (Part II)," *Metropolitan Corporate Counsel*, Vol. 10, No. 10, p. 10 (2002); William M. Bulkeley, "Inventors of PC Spreadsheet to Unveil New Version for Pen-Based Computers," *Wall Street Journal*, Jan. 27, 1992, Sec. B, p. 8. On the impact of Patent Office personnel deficiencies, see Harold L. Johnson Jr., "Computer Program Patentability—The CCPA Refuses to Follow the Lead of the Supreme Court in *Parker v. Flook*," 58 *North Carolina Law Review* 319 (1980).

The Supreme Court's first software patent case was *Gottschalk v. Benson*, 409 U.S. 63, 70–72 (1972). The case rejecting a claim for a computer's calculation of alarm limits signaling abnormalities in the catalytic conversion process is *Parker v. Flook,* 437 U.S. 584, 594 (1978). *Diamond v. Diehr,* 450 U.S. 175 (1981), opened the door to software patentability. The 1994 Federal Circuit software decisions are *In re Alappat,* 33 F.3d 1526 (Fed. Cir. 1994); *In re Schrader,* 22 F.3d 290 (Fed. Cir. 1994); and *In re Warmerdam,* 33 F.3d 1354 (Fed. Cir. 1994). The Patent Office's retreat from its antisoftware position was first announced in *In re Beauregard,* 53 F.3d 1583 (Fed. Cir. 1995). *State Street Bank & Trust Co. v. Signature Financial Group, Inc.,* is at 149 F.3d 1368 (Fed. Cir. 1998). Background on financial instrument patents is from Paul E. Schaafsma, "A Gathering Storm in the Financial Industry," 9 *Stanford Journal of Law, Business & Finance* 176 (2004). Richard S. Gruner's article is "Everything Old Is New Again: Obviousness Limitations on Patenting Computer Updates of Old Designs," 9 *Boston University Journal of Science & Technology Law* 209 (2003).

The Supreme Court's early decision denying a patent for a mixture of bacteria is *Funk Brothers Seed Co. v. Kalo Inoculant Co.,* 333 U.S. 127, 130 (1948). *Diamond v. Chakrabarty* is at 447 U.S. 303, 309–310 (1980). The decision on plant varieties is *Ex Parte Hibberd,* 227 *United States Patents Quarterly* 443 (1985), and for polyploid oysters, *Ex Parte Allen,* 2 *United States Patents Quarterly Second Series* 1425 (1987). The Oncomouse patent, issued in 1988, is U.S. Patent Number 4,736,866. The history of the Oncomouse patent in the European Patent Office is retold in "Harvard Patent on Genetically Altered Mouse Upheld," *Oncology Business Week,* Aug. 1, 2004, p. 47, and the rejection of the Oncomouse patent by the Canadian Supreme Court is *Harvard College v. Canada (Commissioner of Patents),* reported in [2002] 4 *Supreme Court Reports* 45 (Supreme Court of Canada 2002).

Background on the Cohen-Boyer patents, and the history of Genentech and university patent practices, is drawn from Sally Smith Hughes, "Making Dollars Out of DNA: The First Major Patent in Biotechnology and the Commercialization of Molecular Biology, 1974–1980," *Isis,* Vol. 92, Iss. 3, pp. 541–575 (2001). Genentech's stock price increase upon its initial public offering is reported at www.gene.com/gene/about/corporate/history/timeline/index.jsp (last accessed Oct. 12, 2006). The Bayh-Dole Act is codified at 35 U.S.C. §§ 200–212, and background on Bayh-Dole is from Scott D. Locke, "Patent Litigation Over Federally Funded Inventions and the Consequences of Failing to Comply with Bayh-Dole," 8 *Virginia Journal of Law & Technology* 3 (2003); and Rebecca S. Eisenberg, "Public Research and Private Development: Patents and Technology Transfer in Government-Sponsored Research," 82 *Virginia Law Review* 1663 (1996). Data on university technology licensing deals are in Association of University Technology Managers, Ashley J Stevens, ed., *AUTM U.S. Licensing Survey: FY 2004,* p. 26. The story behind DuPont's licensing of the Oncomouse is in Sasha Blaug, Colleen Chien, and Michael J. Shuster, "Managing Innovation: University-Industry Partnerships and the Licensing of the Harvard Mouse," *Nature Biotechnology,* Vol. 22, No. 6, pp. 761–63 (2004), and Eliot Marshall, "DuPont Ups Ante on Use of Harvard's OncoMouse," *Science,* May 17, 2002, p. 1212.

Patent grant data are reported in Adam B. Jaffe and Josh Lerner, *Innovation and Its Discontents* 11–12 (2004). Patent statistics reports compiled by the PTO are available at www.uspto.gov/go/taf/reports.htm (last accessed Nov. 9, 2006). The reference to patent thickets is in Carl Shapiro, "Navigating the Patent Thicket," in Adam B. Jaffe, Josh Lerner, and Scott Stern, eds., *Innovation Policy and the Economy* 119–150 (2000). Description of the early-twentieth-century commercial radio industry and formation of the Radio Corporation of America is from Peter Grindley and David J. Teece, "Managing Intellectual Capital: Licensing and Cross-Licensing in Semiconductors and Electronics," *California Management Review*, Vol. 39, No. 8 (1997). Background on the Lemelson story is from Susan Hansen, "Breaking the Bar Code," *IP Law & Business*, Vol. 4, No. 3 (2004); Nicholas Varchaver, "The Patent King," *Fortune*, May 14, 2001, p. 202 (quoting Lemelson's former lawyer); and Robert G. Sterne, Michael Q. Lee, Patrick E. Garrett, Michael V. Messinger, and Donald R. Banowit, "The U.S. Patent Landscape for Electronics Companies," *Computer & Internet Lawyer*, Vol. 22, No. 9., p. 1 (2005). The Federal Circuit decision is *Symbol Technology, Inc. v. Lemelson Medical, Education & Research Foundation*, 422 F.3d 1378 (2005), as amended by 429 F.3d 1051 (2006).

The "policy levers" reference is to Dan Burk and Mark A. Lemley, "Policy Levers in Patent Law," 89 *Virginia Law Review* 1575 (2003). The patent extension provision of the Hatch-Waxman Act of 1984 is codified at 35 U.S.C. §156. The limited prior user right with respect to business method patents is codified at 35 U.S.C. §273. The opinions in *MercExchange L.L.C. v. eBay, Inc.* are: the Eastern District of Virginia opinion ruling on post-trial motions and setting damages, 275 F.Supp. 2d 695 (2003); the Federal Circuit opinion citing the "general rule" of permanent injunctions against patent infringement, 401 F.3d 1323, 1339 (2005); the Supreme Court's decision is 126 S. Ct. 1837, 1839 (2006). The Supreme Court oral arguments, from which quotes are drawn, are available at www.supremecourtus.gov/oral_arguments/argument_transcripts/05-130.pdf (last accessed Oct. 13, 2006). The illustrative case of a court withholding a permanent injunction in a real property case is *Boomer v. Atlantic Cement Co.*, 257 North Eastern Reporter, Second Series (Court of Appeals of New York 1970).

Background on the Research in Motion-NTP dispute is from Catherine Yang, "The BlackBerry Widow's Tale," *Business Week*, Dec. 19, 2005, p. 33; Mark Heinzl and Amol Sharma, "Insistent Message: Facing Shutdown Threat, Maker of Black-Berry Digs in for Battle," *Wall Street Journal*, Feb. 24, 2006, Sec. A, p. 1; and Ian Austen, "BlackBerry Maker Reaches Deal in Patent Dispute," *New York Times*, Mar. 3, 2006.

The April 2007 Supreme Court decision is *KSR International v. Teleflex, Inc.* 127 *Supreme Court Reporter* 1727. Patent reform bills introduced in the House and Senate from 2004 to 2006 include House of Representatives Bill 5299, 108th Congress, 2d Session (2004); the Patent Reform Act of 2005, House of Representatives Bill 2795, 109th Congress, 1st Session (2005); and the Patent Reform Act of 2006, Senate Bill 3818, 109th Congress, 2d Session (2006).

3. Copyrights

The Google "moon shot" reference is from Jeffrey Toobin, "Google's Moon Shot," *New Yorker,* Feb. 5, 2007, p. 30. Background on the Google case is from Jonathan Band, "The Google Library Project: Both Sides of the Story," *Plagiary: Cross-Disciplinary Studies in Plagiarism, Fabrication and Falsification,* Vol. 1, p. 17 (2006). I served as consultant to counsel for the publishers in their lawsuit against Google. Estimates on the size of the U.S. copyright industry are from Stephen E. Siwek, *Copyright Industries in the U.S. Economy 2004,* a report prepared for the International Intellectual Property Alliance, available at www.iipa.com/pdf/2004_SIWEK_FULL.pdf. The average window between theatrical and home video release of movies is reported in Laura M. Holson, "With Popcorn, DVD's and TiVo, Moviegoers Are Staying Home," *New York Times,* May 27, 2005, Sec. A, p. 1; Philip Marchand, "Say Goodbye to Celluloid," *Toronto Star,* June 24, 2006, Sec. H, p. 14. Soderbergh's "simultaneous release" observation is reported in Xeni Jardin, "Thinking Outside the Box Office," *Wired,* Dec. 2005, p. 257.

Examples of price discrimination in the movie industry are from Michael J. Meurer, "Copyright Law and Price Discrimination," 23 *Cardozo Law Review* 55 (2001). Paramount's failed attempted at price discrimination is described at Julie Holland Mortimer, "Price Discrimination in Copyright Law: Evidence from the Introduction of DVDs," *Harvard Institute of Economic Research Discussion Paper #2055* (Dec. 2004), available at post.economics.harvard.edu/hier/2004papers/HIER2055.pdf (last accessed Dec. 15, 2006). Background on the movie studios' attempt to amend the first sale doctrine appears in James Lardner, *Fast Forward: Hollywood, the Japanese, and the Onslaught of the VCR* 207, 235, 293–302 (1987). Blockbuster's negotiated solution to video rentals with the movie studios is described in Sumner Redstone, *A Passion to Win* 290–291 (2001). The 1993 decision that a copyright contract did not convey home video rights is *Subafilms Ltd. v. MGM-Pathé Communications Co.* 24 F.3d 1088 (9th Cir. 1994). On these cases generally, see Paul Goldstein, *Goldstein on Copyright* §5.3.3. (2007).

The early history of copyright is from Paul Goldstein, *Copyright's Highway: From Gutenberg to the Celestial Jukebox* 29–45 (rev. ed., 2003). Photographs came into copyright on Mar. 3, 1865, 13 Stat. 540; sound recordings on Oct. 15, 1971, 85 Stat. 391; computer programs on Dec. 12, 1980, Public Law Number 96-517.

The story of the major studios' release of films to television is drawn from Kerry Segrave, *Movies at Home: How Hollywood Came to Television* 4, 30, 101, 106 (1999). The Boyd and Disney stories are from Christopher Anderson, *Hollywood TV: The Studio System in the Fifties* 33, 56–57 (1994). The early history of cable TV is from the report by the Sloan Commission on Cable Communications, *On the Cable: The Television of Abundance* 23–34 (1971). The 1931 Supreme Court decision is *Buck v. Jewell-LaSalle Realty Co.,* 283 U.S. 191 (1931). The *Fortnightly* decision is *Fortnightly Corp. v. United Artists Television, Inc.,* 392 U.S. 390 (1968). The *Teleprompter* decision is *Teleprompter Corp. v. Columbia Broadcasting*

System, Inc., 415 U.S. 394 (1974). The 1976 Copyright Act is Public Law Number 94-553, and was enacted on Oct. 19, 1976. The "shook Hollywood" observation is from Gerald Phillips, "Five Cases that Shook Hollywood," *Los Angeles Lawyer,* May 2002, pp. 35–42. The discussion of cable in the Supreme Court draws in part on B. Scott Silverman, "CATV and Copyright Liability: Teleprompter Corp. v. CBS Inc., and the Consensus Agreement," 25 *Hastings Law Journal* 1507 (1974). The transaction costs explanation is from the House Report on the 1976 Copyright Act, *House of Representatives Report Number 94-1476,* Public Law Number 94-533, enacted Sept. 3, 1976, p. 89.

The *Maxwell's* case is *Columbia Pictures Industries, Inc. v. Redd Horne, Inc.,* 749 F.2d 154 (3d Cir. 1984); the *Aveco* case is *Columbia Pictures Industries, Inc. v. Aveco, Inc.,* 800 F.2d 59 (3d Cir. 1986); the Ninth Circuit decision is *Columbia Pictures Industries, Inc. v. Professional Real Estate Investors, Inc.,* 866 F.2d 278 (9th Cir. 1989), and the *On Command* case is *On Command Video Corp. v. Columbia Pictures Industries,* 777 F.Supp. 787 (N.D. Cal. 1991). I worked with counsel for the motion picture studios in the *On Command* case.

The lower court decision in the photocopying case is *Williams & Wilkins Co. v. U.S.,* 487 F.2d 1345, 1362 (U.S. Court of Claims 1973), affirmed by an equally divided Court, 420 U.S. 376 (1975). Background on the *Betamax* case is from James Lardner, *Fast Forward* (1987). The district court decision is *Universal City Studios, Inc. v. Sony Corp. of America,* 480 F. Supp. 429 (C.D. Cal. 1979); the circuit court decision is 659 F.2d 963 (9th Cir. 1981); and the Supreme Court decision 464 U.S. 417 (1984). I consulted with counsel for Universal in this case. Discussion of the interplay between the MPAA's efforts in the courts and in Congress is drawn from Paul Goldstein, *Copyright's Highway* 121 (rev. ed., 2003).

Data on the rapid increase in VCR ownership in America during the *Betamax* case are from Andrew Pollack, "Fight Over Home Videotaping," *New York Times,* July 6, 1983, Sec. D, p. 1; the U.S. Department of Commerce, *1991 U.S. Industrial Outlook,* pp. 32–35, available at 1991 WLNR 3255003. Information on the early history of the video rental industry is from Video Software Dealers' Association, "A History of Home Video," available at www.idealink.org/Resources.phx/vsda/pressroom/history-of-industry.htx (last accessed July 11, 2006). Statistics on TiVo use in 2006 are from David Kiley, "Learning to Love the Dreaded TiVo," *Business Week*, Apr. 17, 2006, p. 88; predictions are from the Carmel Group Study, *Digital Video Recorders: Time in a Magical Box* (2003), as quoted in "Interactive Quarterly," *Adweek,* Sept. 20, 2004. David O. Selznick's product placement proposal is discussed in *Hollywood TV* 48–51 (1994). The Nielsen product placement measuring service is reported in Wayne Friedman, "'Idol,' Coke Top Placement Tallies," *Television Week,* Sept. 6, 2004, p. 6.

The article on competitive success in information technologies is Charles R. Morris and Charles H. Ferguson, "How Architecture Wins Technology Wars," *Harvard Business Review,* Vol. 71, No. 2, p. 87 (1993). Background on IBM's System/360, and on interoperability issues generally, is from Jonathan Band and

Masanobu Katoh, *Interfaces on Trial: Intellectual Property and Interoperability in the Global Software Industry* 18–25 (1995). The landmark U.S. Supreme Court idea-expression decision is *Baker v. Selden,* 101 U.S. 99 (1879). The two Supreme Court decisions that cast a shadow over the patentability of computer programs are *Gottschalk v. Benson,* 409 U.S. 63 (1972), and *Parker v. Flook,* 437 U.S. 584 (1978). Discussion of the difficulties in protecting computer programs under patent and trade secret law draws on Duncan M. Davidson, "Protecting Computer Software: A Comprehensive Analysis," *Arizona State Law Journal* 611 (1983), and Richard I. Miller "The CONTU Software Protection Survey," 18 *Jurimetrics Journal* 354 (1978). The Berne Hearings can be found in *The Berne Convention, Hearings Before the Subcommittee on Patents, Copyrights, and Trademarks of the Committee on the Judiciary on S. 1301, S. 1971* 100–801 (1988). The 1980 legislation granting copyright to computer programs is Public Law Number 96-517, enacted Dec. 12, 1980. The Apple Computer lawsuit is *Apple Computer, Inc. v. Franklin Computer Corp.,* 545 F.Supp. 812 (D.Penn. 1982), reversed by 714 F.2d 1240 (3d Cir. 1983). The Whelan decision is reported as *Whelan Associates, Inc. v. Jaslow Dental Laboratory, Inc.,* 797 F.2d 1222 (3d Cir. 1986).

The Supreme Court decision is *Feist Publications Inc. v. Rural Telephone Service Co., Inc.,* 499 U.S. 340 (1991). *Computer Associates International, Inc. v. Altai, Inc.* is reported at 982 F.2d 693 (2d Cir. 1992). The discussion of the EC software directive draws on Bridget Czarnota and Robert J. Hart, *Legal Protection of Computer Programs in Europe* (1991). The Directive is the *Council Directive of 14 May 1991 on the Legal Protection of Computer Programs* 91/250/EEC. The Sega case is *Sega Enterprises Ltd. v. Accolade, Inc.,* 785 F.Supp. 1392 (N.D. Cal. 1992), reversed in part by 977 F.2d 1510 (9th Cir. 1992). I wrote the amicus brief filed by the American Committee for Interoperable Systems in support of Accolade. The Breyer article is Stephen Breyer, "The Uneasy Case for Copyright," 84 *Harvard Law Review* 281 (1970). The 2 Live Crew case is *Campbell v. Acuff-Rose Music, Inc.* 510 U.S. 569 (1994). The quote from Register of Copyrights Peters is taken from Marybeth Peters, "Copyright Enters the Public Domain," 51 *Journal of the Copyright Society* 701, 723 (2004).

4. Trademarks

The Economides quote is from Nicholas Economides, "The Economics of Trademarks," 78 *Trademark Reporter* 523, 527 (1988). The legislative observations on the 1995 dilution amendments are from *House of Representatives Report Number 104-374* (1995). Background on the Disney trademark dispute is from Greg Miller, "Disney Pegs Cost of Logo Ruling at $40 Million," *Los Angeles Times,* Nov. 16, 1999, Sec. C, p. 1, and "Disney and Goto.com Settle Logo Suit," *New York Times,* May 26, 2000, Sec. C, p. 1; The judicial opinion is *Goto.com, Inc. v. Walt Disney Co.,* 202 F.3d 1199, 1208 (9th Cir. 2000). Background on the NBC trademark dispute is at "Nebraska Agency and NBC Settle Dispute on Logotype," *New*

York Times, Mar. 6, 1976, p. 38; "Nebraska Educational TV Sues NBC Over Use of the N Symbol," *New York Times,* Feb. 19, 1976, p. 52; "NBC's New Logo," *Business Week,* Jan. 12, 1976, p. 36; and "Broadcasting: Bye Bye Birdie," *Newsweek,* Jan. 12, 1976, p. 62. The Hilfiger appellate decision is *International Star Class Yacht Racing Ass'n v. Tommy Hilfiger, U.S.A., Inc.,* 80 F. 3d 749 (2d Cir. 1996); the district court ruling on remand is at 959 F.Supp. 623 (S.D. N.Y. 1997), affirmed, 146 F.3d 66. The Lemon Tree case is *SCM Corp. v. Langis Foods Ltd.,* 539 F.2d 196 (D.C. Cir. 1976), and the "intent-to-use" amendments are Public Law 100-667, enacted Nov. 16, 1988. The Humble case is *Exxon Corp. v. Humble Exploration Co., Inc.,* 695 F.2d 96, 103-04 (5th Cir. 1983).

McDonald's' enforcement of the "Mc" prefix against McTeddy is reported in *McDonald's Corp. v. McBagel's, Inc.,* 649 F.Supp. 1268 (S.D. N.Y. 1986); against McDental, *McDonald's Corp. v. Druck & Gerner, DDS., P.C.,* 814 F.Supp. 1127 (N.D. N.Y. 1993); and against McClaim, *McDonald's Corp. v. McClain,* 37 *United States Patents Quarterly Second Series* 1274 (1995). The McFish and McBeans litigation is discussed in Theodore C. Max, ed., "International Review of Trademark Jurisprudence," 84 *Trademark Reporter* 799, 815, 839 (1994); MacDog, in Reese Taylor and Lanning G. Bryer, eds., "Seventh Annual International Review of Trademark Jurisprudence," 90 *Trademark Reporter* 213, 349 (2000). Other cases involving the Mc prefix are from "Danish Hotdog Salesman McAllen triumphs over McDonald's," Agence France-Presse, Dec. 4, 1996; "Big Trouble in Little McChina," *Brand Strategy,* Feb. 1, 2002, p. 6; "Market Overview: Singapore," *Managing Intellectual Property,* Apr. 1, 2005, No. 148, p. SSS322 (MacTea, MacChocolate, and MacNoodles). The McSleep case is *Quality Inns International, Inc. v. McDonald's Corp.,* 695 F.Supp. 198 (D. Md. 1988). The Yastrow quote is from Bruce Rubenstein, "Knockoffs Are Generic for McDonald's General Counsel," *Corporate Legal Times,* Mar. 1994, p. 13. The reference to the "Big Mac Index" is from "McAtlas Shrugged," *Foreign Policy,* May 1, 2001, p. 26.

The Dawn Donuts case is *Dawn Donuts Co. v. Hart's Food Stores, Inc.,* 267 F.2d 358 (2d Cir. 1959). The First Interstate case is *First Interstate Bancorp. v. Stenquist,* 16 *United States Patents Quarterly Second Series* 1704 (N.D. Cal. 1990). Famous marks obtained federal protection under Public Law Number 104-98, enacted Jan. 16, 1996. The 3M tape dispenser case is reported at 92 *United States Patents Quarterly* 76 (1952). Background on the Coca-Cola bottle registration is from Julius Lunsford, "The Protection of Packages and Containers" 56 *Trademark Reporter* 567 (1966). The NBC chimes are registration number 0916522; Mickey Mouse, registration number 2704887; Bugs Bunny, registration number 1872300; GE's "We Bring Good Things to Life," registration number 2771951. The Owens Corning case is *In re Owens-Corning Fiberglass Corporation,* 774 F.2d 1116; the Levi Strauss pocket tab case is 165 *United States Patents Quarterly* 348 (1970); Fotomat is service mark registration number 911388; the flower-scented yarn case is 17 *United States Patents Quarterly Second Series* 1238 (1991). The Tour 18 case is *Pebble Beach Co. v. Tour 18 I, Ltd.,* 942 F.Supp. 1513

(S.D. Tex. 1996). The farm equipment case is *Deere & Co., Inc. v. Farmhand, Inc.,* 560 F.Supp. 85 (S.D. Iowa 1982), affirmed, 721 F.2d 253 (8th Cir. 1983).

The 1922 observation about the Thermos trademark is in *American Thermos Bottle Co. v. W.T. Grant Co.,* 279 F. 151 (D. Mass. 1922). The Aladdin litigation is *American Thermos Products Co. v. Aladdin Industries, Inc.,* 207 F.Supp. 9 (D. Conn. 1962), affirmed, 321 F.2d 577 (2d Cir. 1963). The discussion of the use of descriptive terms alongside trademark terms by Jell-O and Coca-Cola is from a Nov. 20, 2004, telephone interview with Oliver P. Howes Jr.

The Kleenex, Rolodex, Weight Watchers, and Realtor advertisements are in the March 1999 issue of *Writer's Digest.* The rankings of top world brands are from Dean Foust, "The Best Global Brands," *Business Week,* Aug. 7, 2006, p. 44. The Borden decision is *Borden Ice Cream Co. v. Borden's Condensed Milk Co.,* 201 F. 510 (7th Cir. 1912); the Tiffany decision, *Tiffany & Co. v. Tiffany Productions,* 264 *New York Supplement* 459 (N.Y. Sup. Ct. 1932), affirmed, 188 *North Eastern Reporter* 30 (N.Y. 1933); the Rolls-Royce decision, *Wall v. Rolls-Royce of America,* 4 F.2d 333 (3rd Cir. 1925); the Dunhill decision, *Alfred Dunhill of London v. Dunhill Shirt Shop,* 3 F.Supp 487 (S.D. N.Y. 1929).

The "Crest" observation is from Larry Light, "Brand Loyalty Management: The Basis for Enduring Profitable Growth," *Direct Marketing,* Vol. 59, No. 11, p. 36 (1997). Discussion of the Rolls-Royce-Austin connection is drawn from John M. Murphy, *Brand Strategy* 112–13 (1990). The first Massachusetts antidilution statute is General Law 110 §7(A) (May 2, 1947), currently codified at Massachusetts General Law Annotated 110 (B) §12. The 1995 federal antidilution statute is codified at 15 U.S.C. §§ 1125(C). The list of famous marks is from Thomas McCarthy, *Trademarks and Unfair Competition,* Vol. 4 §24.92 1–2 (4th ed., 1996). The "Polo" litigation is *Westchester Media Co. L.P. v. PRL USA Holdings, Inc.,* 103 F.Supp.2d 935 (S.D. Tex. 1999), reversed, 214 F.3d 658 (5th Cir. 2000).

The 1991 Apple litigation is *Apple Corps Ltd. v. Apple Computer Inc.,* [1991] 3 Common Market Law Reports 49, Court of Appeal (Civil Division, U.K.). Discussion of the litigation is drawn from Ron Wolf, "Apple Computer Meets the Beatles in London Courtroom," *Toronto Star,* Nov. 5, 1990, Sec. C, p. 4; Ken Siegmann, "Apple Settles Lawsuit with Beatles Company," *San Francisco Chronicle,* Oct. 12, 1991, Sec. B, p. 1; and Richard Brandt and Mark Maremont, "Let It Be? Not on Your Life," *Business Week,* Aug. 5, 1991, p. 31. The 2004 Apple case is *Apple Corps Ltd v. Apple Computers Inc.,* [2004] England and Wales High Court 768 (Chancery Division), 2004 WL 960848, and [2006] England and Wales High Court 996 (Chancery Division). The description of the February 2007 settlement is drawn from Don Clark and Ethan Smith, "Apple, Beatles Make Some Peace," *Wall Street Journal,* Feb. 6, 2007, p. A7.

The Grotrian-Steinweg case is *Grotrian, Helfferich, Schulz, Th. Steinweg Nachf. v. Steinway and Sons,* 523 F.2d 1342 (2d Cir. 1975); the Pegasus case is *Mobil Oil Corp. v. Pegasus Petroleum Corp.,* in 818 F.2d 254 (2d Cir. 1987). The Fish-Fri case is *Zatarains, Inc. v. Oak Grove Smokehouse, Inc.,* 698 F.2d 786 (5th

Cir. 1983); the Bob's Volkswagen Repair case is *Volkswagenwerk Aktienge-sellschaft v. Church,* 411 F.2d 350 (9th Cir. 1969); the Coty case is *Prestonettes, Inc., v. Coty,* 264 U.S. 359 (1924); the smell-alike case is *Smith v. Chanel, Inc.,* 402 F.2d 562 (9th Cir. 1968); the *New Kids* case is *New Kids on the Block v. News America Pub., Inc.,* 971 F.2d 302 (9th Cir. 1992).

The $71.2 billion merchandising industry revenue is reported in *Licensing Letter Business Survey,* available at www.epmcom.com/html/newsroom.html? inc=2006010501. The NHL case is *Boston Professional Hockey Ass'n, Inc. v. Dallas Cap & Emblem Mfg., Inc.,* 510 F.2d 1004 (5th Cir. 1975). The Vanna White case is *White v. Samsung Electronics America, Inc.,* 971 F.2d 1395 (9th Cir. 1992); the Waits case is *Waits v. Frito-Lay, Inc.,* 978 F.2d 1093 (9th Cir. 1992); the Carson case, *Carson v. Here's Johnny Portable Toilets, Inc.,* 698 F.2d 831 (6th Cir. 1983); the human cannonball case, *Zacchini v. Scripps-Howard Broadcasting Co.,* 433 U.S. 562 (1977); and the race car case, *Motschenbacher v. R. J. Reynolds Tobacco Co.,* 498 F.2d 821 (9th Cir. 1974). The Elvis Presley transaction is reported in Nathan Koppel, "Blond Ambitions: A Battle Erupts over the Right to Market Marilyn," *Wall Street Journal,* Apr. 10, 2006, Sec. A, p. 1.

The observation by Veblen is from Thorstein Veblen, *The Theory of the Leisure Class* 115–16 (Great Minds ed., 1998), and those by Klein are from Naomi Klein, *No Logo: Taking Aim at the Brand Bullies* 5, 8, 24 (2000).

5. Trade Secrets

The historical background of trade secret law in America draws on Robert G. Bone, "A New Look at Trade Secret Law: Doctrine in Search of Justification," 86 *California Law Review* 241, 251–260 (1998). The Peabody case is *Peabody v. Norfolk,* 98 Mass. 452, 457-8 (Supreme Judicial Court of Massachusetts 1868). The description of security risks is from ASIS International, *Trends in Proprietary Information Loss* 2, 8 (Sept. 2002), available at www.asisonline.org/newsroom/ surveys/spi2.pdf (last accessed Feb. 22, 2007); the description of security measures is from Victoria A. Cundiff, "How to Conduct Exit Interviews: An Intellectual Property Law Perspective," 1166 *Practicing Law Institute Corporate Law and Practice Course Handbook Series* 155 (2000); Arthur J. Schwab and David J. Porter, *Guarding the Crown Jewels: A Guide to Protecting Your Trade Secrets* (2002); and Eric J. Wallach, ed., *Corporate Raiding, Retention & Restructuring* (2002). The founding dates of semiconductor start-ups are from www.shockley transistor.com; www.britannica.com/eb/article-214871 (subscription required); www.national.com/company/pressroom/history.html; and intel.com/museum/ corporatetimeline/index.htm (last accessed Sept. 9, 2006). The DuPont case is *E.I. duPont deNemours & Co. v. Christopher,* 431 F.2d 1012, 1016–17 (5th Cir. 1970).

Background on the Hitachi and Mitsubishi sting is from Louise Keyhoe, "How High-Technology Spies Work in Silicon Valley," *Financial Times* (London), July 6,

1982, p. 12; Stuart Auerbach, "Sting Tapes Stir Anger at Hearing," *Washington Post*, June 28, 1982, Sec. D, p. 8; reports of foreign espionage in the 1990s, including the Air France bugging story, are from "Air France Denies Spying on Travelers," *International Herald Tribune,* Sept. 14, 1991, and Chris Carr, Jack Morton, and Jerry Furniss, "The Economic Espionage Act: Bear Trap or Mouse-trap?" 8 *Texas Intellectual Property Law Journal* 159 (2000). Data on prosecution under the Economic Espionage Act are from www.usdoj.gov/criminal/cyber crime/eeapub.htm (last modified Feb. 1, 2006). The trial court ruling in the Bristol-Myers Squibb case is *U.S. v. Hsu,* 982 F. Supp. 1022, 1025 (E.D. Pa. 1997), reversed, 155 F.3d 189, 198 n.15 (3d Cir. 1998). The study of litigation costs is Yuval Feldman, "Experimental Approach to the Study of Normative Failures: Divulging of Trade Secrets by Silicon Valley Employees," 2003 *University of Illinois Journal of Law, Technology, and Policy* 105, 118 (2003).

The description of the Cadence-Avant! trade secret dispute is drawn from interviews with Daniel Bookin on April 8, 2004, and Thomas J. Nolan on February 4, 2004, and from D. M. Osborne, "Technical Difficulties," *American Lawyer,* Vol. XX, No. 1, p. 45 (1998); Jon Littman, "Justice for All?," *Electronic Business*, Vol. 25, No. 9, p. 58 (1999) (including the stock price drop following the raid); Dean Takahashi, "Showdown in the Valley," *Upside,* Vol. 9, No. 7, p. 78 (1997); Peter Burrows, "Does Crime Pay?" *Business Week,* September 3, 2001; "A Nest of Software Spies?" *Business Week,* May 19, 1997; David Diamond, "Raging Bulls: Trade-Secret Battle between Cadence Design Systems and Avant," *PC Week,* Oct. 21, 1996; and John W. Glynn Jr., Pratap Mukherjee, and Peter Chen, "Cadence v. Avant!" *Case E-61A, Stanford Graduate School of Business* (1999).

Information on Avant!'s countersuit is from Craig Matsumoto, "Avant! Files Countersuit Against Cadence," *Electronic Engineering Times,* Jan. 22, 1996; on share trading volume on the day before the raid is from Jon Swartz, "Avant Moves to Dismiss DA in Suit; Fight with Rival Cadence Heats Up," *San Francisco Chronicle,* June 10, 1997, Sec. C, p. 3. The stock price drop following the filing of the criminal complaint is from Jon Swartz, "Felony Charges Halve Avant's Stock," *San Francisco Chronicle,* Apr. 16, 1997, Sec. D, p. 3. Judge Whyte's stay of the civil proceedings, "9th Cir. Hears Argument in Cadence's Appeal; Judge Whyte Stays Civil Case," is reported in *Andrews Computer & Online Litigation Reporter,* Sept. 2, 1997. The restitution order against Avant! is reported in "Avant! Ordered to Pay $190 Million in Restitution for Trade Secret Theft," *Andrews Computer & Online Litigation Reporter*, July 31, 2001. The quote from Finkelstein is from Shannon Lafferty, "Avant Guard," *Fulton County Daily Report,* June 1, 2001.

The Avant!-Synopsys merger is reported in "Synopsys Agrees to Acquire Avant," *Los Angeles Times,* Dec. 4, 2001, and the civil settlement terms are outlined in Cadence Press Release, "Cadence v. Avant! Litigation Settled," Nov. 13, 2002, available at www.cadence.com/company/newsroom/press_releases/pr .aspx?xml=111302_Avant (last accessed Feb. 22, 2007). The Synopsys insurance policy is reported in "Late News," *Business Insurance,* Nov. 18, 2002, p. 1, and the quote from Synopsys's legal counsel is from Shannon Lafferty, "A Calculated Risk," *Recorder*, Dec. 10, 2001. Synopsys's amended 10-K for the 2002 fiscal year is available at sec.gov/Archives/edgar/data/883241/000116606303000006/amend snps-fy02_10k3.txt (last accessed Feb. 22, 2007), and the company's proxy statement in connection with the merger is at sec.gov/Archives/edgar/data/883241/000095012302004643/y60272dfdef14a.txt (last accessed Feb. 22, 2007).

The discussion of post-employment covenants draws on Katherine V. W. Stone, "Knowledge at Work: Disputes Over the Ownership of Human Capital in the Changing Workplace," 34 *Connecticut Law Review* 721, 741–44 (2002), and John Siegal, "Protecting Corporate IP Assets: Enforcing Restrictive Covenants in the Employment Context," 816 *Practicing Law Institute; Patents, Copyrights, Trademarks, and Literary Property Course Handbook Series* 33, 56–60 (2004). California's statutory bar against covenants not to compete is *California Business & Professions Code* §16600; North Dakota's is at *North Dakota Century Code* §9-08-06.

The Saxenian study is AnnaLee Saxenian, *Regional Advantage: Culture and Competition in Silicon Valley and Route 128* 32 (1994). Turnover rates are drawn from Saxenian, p. 34, and Alan Hyde, *Working in Silicon Valley: Economic and Legal Analysis of a High-Velocity Labor Market* xi (2003). The Gilson article is Ronald J. Gilson, "The Legal Infrastructure of High Technology Industrial Districts: Silicon Valley, Route 128, and Covenants Not to Compete," 74 *New York University Law Review* 575, 578 (1999). Employment tenure perspectives draw on Katharine V. W. Stone, "The New Psychological Contract: Implications of the Changing Workplace for Labor and Employment Law," 48 *UCLA Law Review* 519, 544–49 (2001); Richard Sennett, *The Corrosion of Character: The Personal Consequences of Work in the New Capitalism* 22 (1998); Rosabeth Moss Kanter, *Rosabeth Moss Kanter on the Frontiers of Management* (1997); and Annette D. Bernhardt, Martina Morris, Mark S. Handcock, and Marc A. Scott, *Divergent Paths: Economic Mobility in the New American Labor Market* 64–87 (2001).

The history of the back-and-forth between the Texas Legislature and the Texas Supreme Court is summarized in Katharine V. W. Stone, "The New Psychological Contract," 28 *UCLA Law Review* 519, 582–83 (2001), and Jeffrey W. Tayon, "Covenants Not to Compete in Texas: Shifting Sands from Hill to Light," 3 *Texas Intellectual Property Law Journal* 143 (1995). The Texas Supreme Court cases that triggered the original statute include *Hill v. Mobile Auto Trim, Inc.*, 725 *South Western Reporter, Second Series* 168 (Supreme Court of Texas 1987), and *DeSantis v. Wackenhut Corp.*, 31 *Texas Supreme Court Journal* 616 (Supreme Court of Texas 1988) (superseded following the passage of the statute by 793 *South Western Reporter, Second Series* 670 (Supreme Court of Texas 1990). The Texas Supreme Court decision declining to apply the statute to at-will employees is *Martin v. Credit Protection Ass'n, Inc.*, 793 *South Western Reporter, Second Series* 667 (Supreme Court of Texas 1990); and the decision declining to apply the amended statute in the case of an at-will employee is *Light v. Centel Cellular Co. of Texas*, 883 *South Western Reporter, Second Series* 642, 643–644 (Supreme Court of Texas 1994).

Business method patents are discussed in chapter 2. Background on General Motors' 1996 lawsuit against Volkswagen is from Robert L. Simison and Rebecca Blumenstein, "GM's New Lawsuit Against VW Aims to Keep Lopez Battle Alive," *Wall Street Journal*, Mar. 11, 1996, Sec. B, p. 5; and "Federal Judge Denies VW's Bid to Dismiss Allegations by GM," *Wall Street Journal*, Dec. 3, 1996, Sec. B, p. 8. The Supreme Court case establishing the misappropriation doctrine is *International News Service v. Associated Press*, 248 U.S. 215 (1918); the Dow Jones case is *Board of Trade of the City of Chicago v. Dow Jones & Co., Inc.*, 456 *North Eastern Reporter, Second Series* 84 (Supreme Court of Illinois 1983). The district court decision in the PepsiCo case, is *PepsiCo, Inc. v. Redmond*, 1996 WL 3965 (N.D. Ill. 1996), and the appellate opinion is *PepsiCo, Inc. v. Redmond*, 54 F.3d 1262 (7th Cir. 1995). The case ordering an injunction contingent on monthly payments by the former employer is *Emery Industries, Inc. v. Cottier*, 202 *United States Patents Quarterly* 829 (S.D. Ohio 1978). The description of the Nortel settlement is from Ian Austen, "World Business Briefing Americas: Canada: Nortel Settles Dispute Over Chief," *New York Times*, Nov. 2, 2005, Sec. C, p. 17.

6. Intellectual Assets on the Internet

The eBay case is *eBay, Inc. v. MercExchange LLC*, 126 S. Ct. 1837 (2006). The 2004 auction of thirty-nine basic Internet patents is reported in John Markoff, "Auction of Internet Commerce Patents Draws Concern," *New York Times*, Nov. 16, 2005, Sec. C, p. 4, and the Electronic Frontier Foundation's 2004 poll is reported in Teresa Riordan, "A Patent Owner Claims to Be Owed Royalties on Much of the Internet's Media Content," *New York Times*, Aug. 16, 2004, Sec. C, p. 6. The Amazon case is *Amazon.com, Inc. v. BarnesandNoble.com, Inc.*, 73 F.Supp.2d 1228 (W.D. Wash. 1999), vacated, 239 F.3d 1343 (Fed. Cir. 2001). IBM's patent infringement lawsuit against Amazon is reported in Harry Maurer, ed., "Old Tech vs. New," *Business Week*, Nov. 6, 2006, p. 32.

Background on the *Eolas* case is drawn from "Jury Awards $520.6 Million Against Microsoft for Infringement of Web Browser Patent," *BNA Patent, Trademark & Copyright Journal*, Vol. 66, No. 1634, p. 452 (2006); the case is *Eolas Technologies Inc. v. Microsoft Corp.*, 399 F.3d 1325 (Fed Cir. 2005). The World Wide Web Consortium's request for reexamination of the Eolas patent is described in Steve Lohr, "Web Group Backs Microsoft in Patent Suit," *New York Times*, Oct. 19, 2003, Sec. C, p. 6. Discussion of the World Wide Web Consortium's actions is drawn from Kurt Kleiner, "Calling All Geeks," *New Scientist*, May 15, 1999, p. 10, and of reexamination of Amazon's 1-click patent, from "Amazon's 'One-Click' Patent Will Be Reexamined by Agency," *BNA Patent, Trademark & Copyright Journal*, Vol. 72, No. 1771, p. 81 (2006). Beth Noveck's goal to get "1,000 eyeballs" is drawn from Eric Yeager, "PTO Holds Meeting for Launch of Peer Pilot Project to Aid Patent Examination," *BNA Patent, Trademark & Copyright Journal*, Vol. 72, No. 1770, p. 55 (2006).

Statistics on CD sales in the early 2000s are from "RIAA 2005 Year-End Statistics," available at www.RIAA.com/news/newsletter/pdf/2005yrEndStats.pdf (last accessed Dec. 15, 2006). Ed Felten's "speed bump" reference is from Patricia O'Connell, ed., "A 'Speed Bump' vs. Music Copying," *Business Week Online*, Jan. 9, 2002, available at www.businessweek.com/bwdaily/dnflash/jan2002/nf2002019_ 7170.htm (last accessed on Dec. 15, 2006). Discussion of the RIAA lawsuits is drawn from Amy Harmon, "New Parent to Child Chat: Do You Download Music?" *New York Times*, Sept. 10, 2003, Sec. A, p. 1; Adam Liptak, "The Music Industry Reveals Its Carrots and Sticks," *New York Times*, Sept. 14, 2003, Sec. 4, p. 5; Nick Wingfield and Ethan Smith, "The High Cost of Sharing—Record Industry Files Suits Against 261 Music Uploaders; Move May Alienate Customers," *Wall Street Journal*, Sept. 9, 2003, Sec. B, p. 1; and *Internet Project and Comscore Media Metrix Data Memo*, "The Impact of Recording Industry Suits Against Music File Swappers," Jan. 2004, available at www.pewinternet.org/pdfs/PIP_File_Swapping_ Memo_0104.pdf (last accessed Dec. 15, 2006).

Description of the Napster and Grokster cases is drawn from Paul Goldstein, *Copyright's Highway*, 165–69 (rev. ed., 2003). The cases are *A&M Records, Inc. v. Napster, Inc.*, 284 F.3d 1091 (9th Cir. 2002), and *Metro-Goldwyn-Mayer Studios, Inc. v. Grokster Ltd.*, 545 U.S. 913 (2005). The "Induce Act" is the *Inducing Infringement of Copyrights Act of 2004*, 108 S. 2560. The quote from the Grokster opinion is at *Metro-Goldwyn-Mayer Studios, Inc. v. Grokster Ltd.*, 125 S.Ct. 2767. Discussion of the Bertelsmann-Napster relationship draws in part on Matt Richtel, "If Bertelsmann Wed Napster, It Could Sue Itself and More," *New York Times*, Apr. 22, 2002, Sec. C, p. 5. Warner Bros.' use of BitTorrent as a legal distribution channel is reported in Ellen Lee, "BitTorrent Goes Legal in Warner Film Deal," *San Francisco Chronicle*, May 10, 2006, Sec. C, p. 1, and Julie Bosman and Tom Zeller Jr., "Warner Bros. to Sell Movies Using the Software of Pirates," *New York Times*, May 9, 2006, Sec. C, p. 3. The quote from Kevin Tsujihara is in the Bosman and Zeller article.

The copyright safe harbors for Internet service providers are codified at 17 U.S.C. §512, and the legislative history for the safe harbors is at *Senate Report Number 105-190*, p. 48 (1998); *House of Representatives Report Number 105-551*, part 2, p. 57 (1998). The discussion of Yahoo!'s efforts to come within the safe harbors is drawn from an interview with John Place on October 4, 2004. The discussion of Universal's lawsuit against MySpace draws on Greg Sandoval, "Universal Sues MySpace for Copyright Violations," CNET News.com, Nov. 17, 2006, available at news.com.com/2100-1030_3-6136829.html (last accessed Feb. 22, 2007); and Jeff Leeds, "Universal Music Sues MySpace for Copyright Infringement," *New York Times*, Nov. 18, 2006, Sec. C, p. 3.

Sales figures for domain names in 2005 are from Jon Swartz, "Sellers of Internet Addresses Surf for—and Get—Some Big Payoffs," *USA Today*, Apr. 14, 2006, p. A1. Discussion of Dennis Toeppen's cybersquatting activities draws in part on Peter H. Lewis, "The Internet's Gatekeeper May Cash In on Its Role," *New York*

Times, Sept. 12, 1996, Sec. A, p. 1. The Panavision case is *Panavision International v. Toeppen,* 141 F.3d 1316, 1327 (9th Cir. 1998). The Anticybersquatting Consumer Protection Act is Public Law l06-113. The Uniform Domain Name Dispute Resolution Policy is at www.icann.org/udrp.

Discussion of the Delta.com domain dispute draws in part from Peter Wayner, "Compressed Data; What's in a Web Name? Sometimes, Mistaken Identity," *New York Times,* Sept. 21, 1998, Sec. C, p. 3; Nancy Fonti, "Delta Carves Out E-unit, Buys Delta.com Address," *Atlanta Journal-Constitution,* Sept. 1, 2000, p. 1F; "No Winner In Delta.com Deal," Elliott.org, Sept. 5, 2000, available at www.elliott.org/interactive/2000/delta.htm (last accessed Feb. 22, 2007); "The Pain of the Delta Domain," Elliott.org, May 14, 1998, available at www.elliott.org/inter active/1998/delta.htm (last accessed Feb. 22, 2007). The West Coast Video case is *Brookfield Communications, Inc. v. West Coast Entertainment Corp.,* 174 F.3d 1036, 1062 (9th Cir. 1999); and the *Playboy* case is *Playboy Enterprises, Inc. v. Netscape Communications Corp.,* 354 F.3d 1020, 1035 (9th Cir. 2004). The discussion of trademark dilution on the Internet draws in part on Jennifer E. Rothman, "Initial Interest Confusion: Standing at the Crossroads of Trademark Law," 27 *Cardozo Law Review* 105 (2005), and Jaqueline D. Lipton, "Beyond Cybersquatting: Taking Domain Name Disputes Past Trademark Policy," 40 *Wake Forest Law Review* 1361 (2005).

The use of wired communities of volunteers for feedback on products is reported in Robert D. Hof, "The Power of U.S. Mass Collaboration on the Internet Is Shaking Up Business," *Business Week,* June 20, 2005, p. 74. A copy of the GNU General Public License can be found online at www.gnu.org/copyleft/gpl.html, and the story of the adoption of the GPL for Linux is from Linus Torvalds and David Diamond, *Just for Fun: The Story of an Accidental Revolutionary* 94–96 (2001). The viral nature of the GPL license is explained in Victoria Murphy, "Open Season," *Forbes,* Apr. 19, 2004, p. 88. The discussion of IBM's 2005 donation of patents to open source projects draws on Steve Hamm, "One Way to Hammer at Windows," *Business Week,* Jan. 24, 2005, p. 36, and of the Linux trademark draws on Andrew Colley, "Torvalds Asked to Step Into Linux Trademark Fight," CNET News.com, Aug. 11, 2004, available at news.com.com/Torvalds+asked +to+step+into+Linux+trademark+fight/2100-7344_3-5305663.html (last accessed Feb. 22, 2007). The information on Wikipedia is from http://en.wikipedia.org/wiki/ Wikipedia:About (last accessed Feb. 16, 2007).

Background on the SCO lawsuit against IBM draws on Stephen Shankland, "SCO Warns of IBM Lawsuit Risks," CNET News.com, Mar. 31, 2003, available at news.com.com/SCO+warns+of+IBM+lawsuit+risks/2100-1007_3-994811.html (last accessed Feb. 22, 2007); Steve Lohr, "R.I.P.: The Counterculture Aura of Linux," *New York Times,* May 25, 2004, Sec. C, p. 11; Steve Lohr, "An Effort to Help Free-Software Developers Avoid Suits," *New York Times,* Feb. 1, 2005, Sec. C, p. 8; Spencer E. Ante and Steve Hamm, "A Linux Nemesis on the Rocks; SCO's Lawsuit Is Floundering—and Now the Company Faces Regulators' Scrutiny,"

Business Week, Mar. 14, 2005, p. 80; and Laurie J. Flynn and Steve Lohr, "2 Giants in a Deal Over Linux," *New York Times,* Nov. 3, 2006, Sec. C, p. 1. Judge Kimball's comments are at *SCO Group v. I.B.M., Memorandum Decision and Order,* Feb. 9, 2005, reported in 2005 *Corporate Law Decisions* P28957. The order dismissing 187 of SCO's claims is "Order Granting in Part IBM's Motion to Limit SCO's Claims," June 28, 2006, case no. 2:03cv00294 DAK, www.groklaw.net/pdf/IBM-718.pdf or for a fee at the Federal District Court of Utah Web site, www.utd.uscourts.gov/documents/ibm_hist.html. The quote discussing the order is from Andrew Orlowski, "Judge Guts SCO Claims," TheRegister.com, June 30, 2006, available at www.theregister.com/2006/06/30/sco_ibm_claims (last accessed Feb. 22, 2007). The quote of SCO's chairman is from John Markoff, "Copyright Lawsuit Is Turnabout for SCO," *New York Times,* Oct. 13, 2003, Sec. C, p. 2.

7. Intellectual Assets in International Markets

Background on Canada's amicus brief on behalf of RIM is from Ian Austen, "In Suit, BlackBerry Maker Pleads Canadian," *New York Times,* Jan. 24, 2005, Sec. C, p. 4. The 1972 Supreme Court territoriality case is *Deepsouth Packing Co. v. Laitram Corp.,* 406 U.S. 518 (1982); the statute overturning it is 35 U.S.C. § 271(f). The discussion of bilateral copyright treaties preceding the Berne Convention is from Paul Goldstein, *International Copyright: Principles, Law and Practice* §2.1 (2001) and Stephen P. Ladas, *The International Protection of Literary and Artistic Property* (1938). Description of the conflicts of the 1950s is from Paul Goldstein, *Copyright's Highway: From Gutenberg to the Celestial Jukebox* 153–55 (rev. ed., 2003).

International Association for the Protection of Intellectual Property, Proceedings of 38th Congress, "Report on Question 156: International Exhaustion of Industrial Property Rights" (2001), surveys the variety of exhaustion rules around the world. Frederick Abbott, "First Report (Final) to the Committee on International Trade Law of the International Law Association on the Subject of Parallel Importation," 1 *Journal of International Economic Law* 607 (1998), locates the parallel import issue in the context of the TRIPs discussions, as does Jeff Atik and Hans Henrik Lidgard, "Embracing Price Discrimination: TRIPs and the Suppression of Parallel Trade in Pharmaceuticals," 27 *U. Pa. J. Int'l Econ. L.* 1043 (2006).

The switch to a first-to-file system was proposed by the President's Commission on the Patent System in *To Promote the Progress of Useful Arts in an Age of Exploding Technology* (1966), and the eighteen-month publication rule appears at 35 U.S.C. §122(b). Discussion of the comparative scope of patentable subject matter draws on Joseph Straus, "Implications of the TRIPs Agreement in the Field of Patent Law," in Friedrich-Karl Beier and Gerhard Schricker eds., *From GATT to TRIPs: The Agreement on Trade-Related Aspects of Intellectual Property* 160 (1996).

The Sony case is *Sony Corp. of America v. Universal City Studios, Inc.,* 464 U.S. 417 (1984), and the Sega case is *Sega Enterprises Ltd. v. Accolade, Inc.,* 977

F.2d 1510 (9th Cir. 1992). The WTO ruling on the U.S. restaurant exemption is United States—Section 110(5) of the U.S. Copyright Act, Report of the Panel, WTO, WT/DS160/R, June 15, 2000.

The agreements between Anheuser-Busch and the Bohemian breweries, and the history of the dispute, are reproduced at *Anheuser-Busch, Inc. v. Budejovicky Budvar N.P.*, [1984] *Fleet Street Reports* 413 (U.K. Supreme Court of Judicature—Court of Appeals 1984); *Anheuser-Busch v. Budejovicky Budvar, N.P.*, [2002] *Federal Court of Australia* 390, ¶¶ 37–54 (2002). The decision not to sue to protect the goodwill of the Budweiser brand is discussed in Peter Hernon and Terry Ganey, *Under the Influence: The Unauthorized Story of the Anheuser-Busch Dynasty* 38 (1991). The description of the recent litigation between the two companies draws in part on Robert M. Kunstadt and Gregor Buhler, " 'Bud' Battle Illustrates Peril of Geographic Marks," *National Law Journal*, May 18, 1998, p. C3. The description of Japanese trade secret practice draws on Holly E. Svetz, "Japan's New Trade Secret Law: We Asked for It—Now What Have We Got?" 26 *George Washington Journal of International Law and Economics* 413 (1992).

Donald M. Spero's article is "Patent Protection or Piracy—A CEO Views Japan," *Harvard Business Review*, Vol. 68, No. 5, p. 58 (1990). The statistics on counterfeit drugs are drawn from WHO, *Counterfeit Medicines Fact Sheet*, available at www.who.int/mediacentre/factsheets/fs275/en (last accessed Feb. 22, 2007). The discussion of the history of the TRIPs Agreement draws on Paul Goldstein, *International Copyright: Principles, Law and Practice* §2.3.2.1 (2001). The estimate of the combined $40 billion net annual increase in patent payments received from developing economies is reported in J. Michael Finger, *The Doha Agenda and Development: A View from the Uruguay Round* 13–19, 25 (2002); and the underlying data are at World Bank, *Global Economic Prospects and the Developing Countries 2002* Ch. 5, Table 5.1 (2001). The U.S. Trade Representative's *2006 Special 301 Report* is available at www.ustr.gov/assets/Document_Library/Reports_Publications/2006/2006_Special_301_Review/asset_upload_file473_9336.pdf (last accessed Dec. 17, 2006). The European Commission's fifteenth annual "Report on United States Barriers to Trade and Investment" (1999) is available at ec.europa.eu/comm/external_relations/us/trade_barriers_report_99/usrbt99.pdf (last accessed Dec. 20, 2006); the 2005 report is available at trade.ec.europa.eu/doclib/docs/2006/march/tradoc_127632.pdf (last accessed Dec. 17, 2006). The observations of a former USTR general counsel are from Judith H. Bello, "Some Practical Observations About WTO Settlement of Intellectual Property Disputes," 37 *Virginia Journal of International Law* 357, 361 (1997).

The study of the impact of Japan's 1988 patent reforms is Mariko Sakakibara and Lee Branstetter, "Do Stronger Patents Induce More Innovation? Evidence from the 1988 Japanese Patent Reforms," *RAND Journal of Economics*, Vol. 23, No. 1, pp. 77, 88 (2001). The discussion of the impact of intellectual property protection on foreign direct investment draws on Keith E. Maskus, "Lessons from

Studying the International Economics of Intellectual Property Rights," 53 *Vanderbilt Law Review* 2219 (2000), and that of developing country response to heightened intellectual property standards on Keith E. Maskus and Jerome H. Reichman, "The Globalization of Private Knowledge Goods and the Privatization of Global Public Goods," 7 *Journal of International Economic Law* 279 (2004). The Alford quote is from William P. Alford, *To Steal a Book Is an Elegant Offense: Intellectual Property Law in Chinese Civilization* 41–42 (1995), and the "passive-aggressive" reference and estimated U.S. revenue losses due to counterfeits in post-WTO China are from Frederick M. Abbott, "China in the WTO 2006: 'Law and Its Limitation in the Context of TRIPS,'" in Petros C. Mavroidis, ed., *WTO Law and Developing Countries* (2007). The second Memorandum of Understanding between the United States and China is reported in "China–United States: Agreement Regarding Intellectual Property Rights," 34 *International Legal Materials* 881, 895 (1995). The 2004 report of the U.S. Trade Representative is the *2004 Report to Congress on China's WTO Compliance*, available at www.ustr.gov/assets/Document_Library/Reports_Publications/2004/asset_upload_file281_6986.pdf (last accessed Feb. 22, 2007).

Information on the Microsoft Research Asia laboratory in Beijing is drawn from research.microsoft.com/aboutmsr/labs/asia/default.aspx (last accessed Dec. 17, 2006). The 2002 data comparing investment by foreign multinationals in the United States and by U.S. multinationals abroad is from the National Science Foundation, *Science and Engineering Indicators 2006* 4–6 (2006). Data on science and engineering doctorates awarded to U.S. citizens from 1983 to 2003 are from *Science and Engineering Indicators* Appendix Table 2-32, and those awarded by selected Asian countries during the same period are from Appendix Table 2-43; those awarded by country (2002 or most recent year available) are in Appendix Table 2-40. The projection respecting Chinese science and engineering doctorates is from Richard B. Freeman, "Does Globalization of the Scientific/Engineering Workforce Threaten U.S. Economic Leadership?," NBER Working Paper No. 11457, p. 6, available at www.nber.org/papers/w11457 (last accessed Feb. 22, 2007). Research and development expenditure as a proportion of GDP is reported in *Science and Engineering Indicators 2006* 4-44. U.S. ranking in research and development spending as a proportion of GDP after the exclusion of defense-related expenditures is drawn from OECD, *Main Science and Technology Indicators,* Vol. 2006, No. 1, p. 15. Information on U.S. patent grants by country is from *Science and Engineering Indicators 2006* at 6-28, 6-29, and Appendix Table 6-12; data on PCT international patent applications are drawn from WIPO, *WIPO Patent Report 2006* 22, available at www.wipo.int/ipstats/en/statistics/patents/pdf/patent_report_2006.pdf (last accessed Dec. 17, 2006); for patents granted in relation to population and GDP see OECD, *Compendium of Patent Statistics 2005,* 14, available at www.oecd.org/dataoecd/60/24/8208325.pdf (last accessed Dec. 17, 2006). Trademark figures are compiled from the USPTO annual reports and workload tables published between 1993 and 2005, available generally at www.uspto.gov/web/offices/com/annual (last accessed Jan. 9, 2007). *Business Week's* 2001 and 2006 Interbrand lists are available at bwnt.businessweek.com/brand/2001 and bwnt.businessweek.com/brand/2006, respectively (last accessed Feb. 22, 2007). Estimated revenues from foreign sales by major U.S. copyright industries are from Stephen E. Siwek, *Copyright Industries in the U.S. Economy: The 2004 Report* 10 (2004), and book publishing data from Albert Greco, "The Changing Market for U.S. Book Exports and Imports," in *The Bowker Annual Library and Book Trade Almanac 2004* 514 (49th ed., 2004). The PricewaterhouseCoopers report on the Indian entertainment industry is FICCI and PricewaterhouseCoopers, *The Indian Entertainment and Media Industry: Unravelling the Potential* 12, available at www.pwc.com/extweb/pwcpublications.nsf/docid/BE 7E56C3FF8E90A6CA257185006A3275/$file/Frames.pdf (last accessed Feb. 22, 2007). The trend in U.S. receipts and payments of royalties and fees in connection with intellectual property is noted in *Science and Engineering Indicators 2006* 6-23.

INDEX